THE EXPANDING ART OF COMICS

THE EXPANDING ART OF COMICS
Ten Modern Masterpieces

THIERRY GROENSTEEN
Translated by ANN MILLER

University Press of Mississippi / Jackson

www.upress.state.ms.us

The University Press of Mississippi is a member of the Association of American University Presses.

Cet ouvrage est publié avec l'aide du Centre National du Livre.
This book is published with the help of the Centre National du Livre.

Cet ouvrage, publié dans le cadre d'un programme d'aide à la publication, bénéficie du soutien de la Mission Culturelle et Universitaire Française aux Etats Unis, service de l'ambassade de France aux EU.
This work, published as part of a program of aid for publication, received support from the Mission Culturelle et Universitaire Française aux Etats Unis, a department of the French Embassy in the United States.

Originally published in 2015 by Les Impressions Nouvelles as *Un Art en expansion: Dix chefs-d'œuvre de la bande dessinée moderne*

Copyright © 2015 by Les Impressions Nouvelles
This edition of *The Expanding Art of Comics* is published by arrangement with Les Impressions Nouvelles.
Translation and foreword copyright © 2017 by University Press of Mississippi
All rights reserved

First printing 2017
∞

Library of Congress Cataloging-in-Publication Data

Names: Groensteen, Thierry, author. | Miller, Ann, 1949 September 1– translator.
Title: The expanding art of comics : ten modern masterpieces / Thierry Groensteen ; translated by Ann Miller.
Other titles: Art en expansion: dix chefs-d'œuvre de la bande dessinée moderne. English
Description: Jackson : University Press of Mississippi, 2017. | Includes bibliographical references and index. |
Identifiers: LCCN 2017018214 (print) | LCCN 2017033650 (ebook) | ISBN 9781496813701 (epub single) | ISBN 9781496813718 (epub institutional) | ISBN 9781496813725 (pdf single) | ISBN 9781496813732 (pdf institutional) | ISBN 9781496808028 (hardback)
Subjects: LCSH: Comic books, strips, etc.—History and criticism. | Graphic novels—History and criticism. | BISAC: LITERARY CRITICISM / Comics & Graphic Novels. | SOCIAL SCIENCE / Popular Culture.
Classification: LCC PN6710 (ebook) | LCC PN6710 .G75613 2017 (print) | DDC 741.5/9—dc23
LC record available at https://lccn.loc.gov/2017018214

British Library Cataloging-in-Publication Data available

CONTENTS

Translator's Foreword   VII

Introduction   3

HUGO PRATT, *Ballad of the Salt Sea*   7

MŒBIUS, *Airtight Garage*   26

ALAN MOORE and DAVE GIBBONS, *Watchmen*   48

DAVID B., *Epileptic*   73

ALISON BECHDEL, *Fun Home*   97

DOMINIQUE GOBLET, *Pretending Is Lying*   111

SHAUN TAN, *The Arrival*   126

CRAIG THOMPSON, *Habibi*   145

CHRIS WARE, *Building Stories*   163

JENS HARDER, *The Grand Narrative: Alpha, Beta*   190

Notes   209

Sources   223

Index   224

TRANSLATOR'S FOREWORD

The relatively small proportion of Thierry Groensteen's writing on comics that is so far available in English consists of groundbreaking theoretical work, notably *The System of Comics*,[1] concerned with layout and the articulation of panels, and its follow-up, *Comics and Narration*,[2] which explores the complexity of intersecting narrative instances in comics, verbal and visual, and includes sections on subjectivity and rhythm. The frameworks that Groensteen sets out in these books are exemplified with reference to a wide range of comics, some well-known, some less so. Individual texts are necessarily dealt with in a relatively brief and fragmented way, since their purpose is to illustrate a particular theoretical point. Nonetheless, one of the pleasures for readers of *The System of Comics* and *Comics and Narration* has been the deepening of our appreciation of the chosen comics extracts, as a result of our greater awareness of their formal and narrative operations. *The Expanding Art* now offers the opportunity to enjoy far more extended readings of ten key comics, covering a period from the 1960s to 2015 and originating from a number of different countries, in which Groensteen draws upon the theoretical principles set out in his own work and in that of other comics scholars.

Groensteen is not alone in producing critical analyses of well-known comic books: as the study of the medium has gained academic respectability, the secondary literature around a canon of primary texts has begun to occupy an increasing amount of space on library shelves and students' reading lists. However, his approach differs from that of much scholarship in English, which has tended to adopt a cultural studies perspective, viewing comics through, for example, a postcolonial or gender-based lens, with a selective focus on relevant formal qualities. Groensteen's readings are, in contrast, more formal, although by no means exclusively so, since they are informed by the work of philosophers, psychoanalysts, and sociologists. It is nonetheless likely to be his insights into the resources and potential of the medium that will make us want to return to these ten key primary texts, each one chosen for its innovatory contribution to the comics medium, and to read them alongside him. I summarize below some of the issues that he explores in each chapter.

HUGO PRATT, *BALLAD OF THE SALT SEA* (1967–1969)

In his first chapter, Groensteen sets out to account for the epic qualities of Hugo Pratt's ballad, tracing its literary sources in the nineteenth-century adventure novel, and its iconographic sources from American cinema of the 1930s, '40s, and '50s and from the Italian comics artist Franco Caprioli. In a comic book that has no single hero but is instead a "choral narrative," Groensteen's analysis of text and image demonstrates the interaction of character and plot, and the role of silent panels and close-ups in intensifying emotional impact. His discussion of Pratt's graphic line focuses on its economy of means for evoking places and people, and the facility with which realism can dissolve into symbolism.

MŒBIUS, *AIRTIGHT GARAGE* (1979)

Groensteen begins this chapter by showing how Mœbius's radically offbeat and enduringly cult comic disrupts and reinvents the conventions of the serial story, including the Western serial of which the artist (or rather his alter ego Jean Giraud) was a noted exponent. In his analysis of Mœbius's improvisational strategies, Groensteen tracks the dense network of verbal and visual motifs that provide exemplification of his notion of "braiding," infranarrative series that set up chains of semantic and formal relations. He then supplies further readings of this multilayered work, first tracing the metanarrative allusions to the operations of the medium of comics itself, and then discerning coded references to the artist's unconscious.

ALAN MOORE AND DAVE GIBBONS, *WATCHMEN* (1987)

Groensteen discusses *Watchmen*'s deconstruction of one of the foundational genres of the medium, the superhero comic, through Moore and Gibbons's critique of its mythology of masculinity, along with their exploration of the logical, political, and psychological implications that ensue from the possession of superpowers. He examines each of the six main characters in relation to Charles Hatfield's postulation of tensions played out within the genre: individualism versus altruism, vigilantism versus obedience to the law, and self-effacement versus flamboyance.[3] He then shows how *Watchmen* is also noteworthy for the complexity that it achieves in the representation of time and offers a detailed analysis of the recurring instances of symmetry and the circle that give the comic book its thematic resonance.

DAVID B., *EPILEPTIC* (1996–2003)

Groensteen begins by examining the progression of the covers of the six volumes of the original French edition, and he notes David's B.'s insistent and repeated portrayal of the face (sometimes deconstructed or obliterated) as a rhetorical device, an expression of the violence of the artist's feelings toward his brother. He goes on to analyze David B.'s use of "concept images" to represent an inner life that invades the external reality of the autobiographical protagonist. He also closely investigates the development in David B.'s drawing style over the seven-year period of the publication of the work, and demonstrates how it may be read not simply as a family history, but as the story of David B.'s own development as an artist.

ALISON BECHDEL, *FUN HOME* (2006)

Groensteen argues that here too there is a second narrative of artistic development accompanying the main narrative, in this case an investigation into the personality and the death of the artist's father. He points to Bechdel's unusual focus on the physicality of bodies, to the atypical structure of the book as spiral and recursive rather than linear, and to the exceptional dominance of texts: those in textboxes that convey an intrusive narrative voice, and those within the images in the form of books or book extracts through which the reader is invited to interpret the events and characters. He finally looks at the complexity of the autobiographical stamp on the images, and their tense relationship with their (often photographic) sources.

DOMINIQUE GOBLET, *PRETENDING IS LYING* (2007)

Where Bechdel's autobiographical account was text-heavy, Goblet, a visual artist who has worked across several media, dispenses with the role of the verbal narrator, or "reciter," in Groensteen's term. In the absence of a voiceover, the subjectivity of the autobiographical character is conveyed in considerable depth, Groensteen suggests, through poetic techniques that include an allusive, elliptical narration, striking variations in graphic style and the recurring metaphor of a haunting, elusive presence. At the same time, he points out, the text within the diegesis is very conspicuous: remarkably, a television commentary on a racetrack accident serves to narrate the climactic domestic drama, onomatopoeias provide an atmospheric soundtrack, and the materiality of the lettering conveys the tonality of voices.

SHAUN TAN, *THE ARRIVAL* (2006)

Tan's album abandons text altogether and tells its migration story entirely through images, thereby taking up its place in a lineage of silent comics that Groensteen enumerates. He goes on to show how this silence lends a dreamlike, unreal atmosphere to Tan's portrayal of a fantastic city, and forces the reader to be highly active, seeking out clues to meaning. The absence of language is, he argues, thematized within the work, as migrants rely on images to communicate with each other. The "poetic realism" of Tan's style is enhanced, Groensteen suggests, by a graphic style that evokes old photographs and by variations in page layout that set up rhythms and increase the intensity of the reading experience.

CRAIG THOMPSON, *HABIBI* (2011)

Groensteen analyzes Thompson's book as a graphic tour de force, in which the graceful shapes of Arabic calligraphy find visual rhymes in motifs that permeate the book, notably those connected with water, a key thematic element. He emphasizes Thompson's concern to create beauty in a medium that has often been associated with caricature and the grotesque, by drawing on a timeless mythologized version of the East that recalls Orientalist painting. Contemporary urban settings are not excluded, however, and Groensteen argues that the book can be read as a politically committed portrayal of depredations visited on the environment (metaphorically paralleled by the repeated violence inflicted on the female protagonist). Above all, he claims, it is an exercise in the art of storytelling.

CHRIS WARE, *BUILDING STORIES* (2012)

The requirement upon the reader to physically manipulate the fourteen separate elements of this work leads to greater participation, Groensteen argues, also noting that fragmentation, although rarely this extreme, is an intrinsic quality of the comics medium. He goes on to analyze Ware's achievement in giving access to the subjectivity of a female protagonist, through the recording of details of her everyday life and through panels that attempt to reach some psychological truth by portraying her naked or in close-ups. Images representing snapshots are also used to evoke personal, sometimes painful, memories. Groensteen finally analyzes the page layout, finding an alternation between a linear arrangement, used for "objective" sequences with no narrative voiceover, and a more deconstructed layout used for sequences recounted in the first person.

JENS HARDER, *THE GRAND NARRATIVE: ALPHA, BETA* (2009, 2014)

This monumental encyclopedia of the prehuman era, prehistory, and ancient history is a compendium of images from extremely diverse sources, both high- and mass-cultural. Groensteen notes the stylistic uniformity imposed upon them by Harder's systematic redrawing and analyzes his substitution of a principle of montage for that of breakdown. The gap between panels cannot be bridged by surmising what has intervened in a causal chain, as in traditional comics breakdown: the reader must instead interpret the meaning of the transition, whether based upon formal analogy or variations on a theme. The focus in *Alpha* on the mutation of forms (an enactment of the basic mutational principle of comics) gives way in *Beta*, he argues, to a more radical collapse of time frames and startling spatial juxtapositions.

IN THESE TEN CHAPTERS, Groensteen offers, then, a master class in comics analysis, always making his method and theoretical presuppositions clear. Students of comics will not only enrich their understanding of ten important comics, but are likely to be better equipped to approach other comics texts and produce their own readings, and, it is to be hoped, to develop their own theoretical frameworks by building on Groensteen's work.

I would like to thank the English translators and publishers of two of the comics originally written in French for so readily giving me access to their work: Sophie Yanow and Gabriel Winslow (for *Pretending Is Lying*), and Nora Goldberg and Tony Bennett (for *Alpha*), and I am very grateful to colleagues from the Comics Scholars List who generously came to my help when I needed to track down published English translations of *Ballad of the Salt Sea* and *Airtight Garage*: Maaheen Ahmed, Pedro Moura, Joachim Trinkwitz, Barbara Uhlig, and Waldomiro Vergueiro. I would also like to acknowledge the contribution made by Malcolm Hope, who reviewed every chapter in this book and whose many useful suggestions I have incorporated.

THE EXPANDING ART OF COMICS

INTRODUCTION

Once dismissed as escapist literature for children and disparaged by the cultural establishment, the comics medium has matured, as have attitudes toward it. Its standing has greatly improved, to the extent that it is now regarded as a form of literature in its own right. It has diversified by moving into new areas (history, personal life, science, philosophy, sometimes poetry) and by taking on new forms (diary, reportage, essay). It has attracted a new readership and has broken free from the traditional French-style album, still standard for the commercial genre- and series-based sector of production, by adopting multiple formats and embracing lengthy works, often designated as "graphic novels."[1] These developments are well documented.[2] The aim of the present book is to offer a different perspective on important evolutions in comics since the nineteen sixties, by focusing on ten key works and carrying out close (re)readings. It covers over half a century of comics production, sampling a single work from the sixties (*Ballad of the Salt Sea* by Hugo Pratt), seventies (*Airtight Garage* by Mœbius), eighties (*Watchmen* by Alan Moore and Dave Gibbons), and nineties (*Epileptic* by David B.) and then dwelling at greater length on more recent decades, represented by *Fun Home* by Alison Bechdel, *Pretending Is Lying* by Dominique Goblet, *The Arrival* by Shaun Tan, *Habibi* by Craig Thompson, *Building Stories* by Chris Ware, and finally the first two books in Jens Harder's still unfinished *Grand Narrative*, *Alpha . . . directions* and *Beta . . . civilizations*.

These ten titles, it need hardly be said, are arbitrarily chosen, given that dozens of other comics could equally well have featured on the list. But there is a rationale behind the selection: each of these books has created an opening, achieved a breakthrough, offered a new narrative model, or taken up an emerging tendency and perfected it. To be brief, and to oversimplify, Pratt introduced novelistic scope into the adventure comic; Mœbius blew narrative codes apart with a display of inventive pyrotechnics; Moore and Gibbons showed that genre narratives could accommodate psychological depth and raise serious political, social, and metaphysical questions; David B. originated a new visual rhetoric, with images that were at once conceptual and decorative; Bechdel took comics onto a terrain that allowed for the questioning of gendered identity; Goblet developed a visual artist's approach to the medium; Tan, by dispensing with the text, produced a humanist fable with universal application; Thompson conjured up an Orientalist tale in which Western graphic narration is nourished by Arabic calligraphy and Islamic art; Ware produced an interactive book-art object as well as an arresting portrayal of a woman; and Harder explored new ways of creating visual parallels and involving the reader in the process of making meaning. The ten works are all enthralling, and wholly unalike.

The selection is international, with Belgian, French, British, German, Italian, American, and Australian authors. No manga were included, because the point was to show how a tradition evolves, calls itself into question and becomes enriched. The addition of a Japanese example would therefore have necessitated further contextualization. On publication, each of the books that will be discussed here was hailed as a resounding success. Most became (or are in the process of becoming) classics of the "ninth art." And classics are, par excellence, works that should be revisited. But as time passes, their shock effect wears off; their innovations get imitated, quoted, and parodied, or in other words, trivialized. That is why it is important to recapture the impact with which these works, each in its own way, broke with what had gone before.

The notion of progress in relation to art is a frequent theme of philosophical essays. Comics is no more perfectible than any other form of artistic expression; no one will "do better" than McCay, Herriman, Hergé, or Franquin. That assertion does not prevent us from situating the medium in a historical context, and from noting that almost all the works that we are going to examine here would have been inconceivable twenty, thirty, or fifty years ago, because the conditions of their production did not yet exist. The evolution of the comics medium since the sixties has been characterized by a gradual and persistent expansion of the range of possibilities at its disposal. Of course, all media bring forth a stream of artistic achievements that were previously unthinkable, particularly since modernity has deemed novelty to be the sole criterion of creativity. But this is even more applicable in the field that concerns us, comics, on account of its particular history: in Europe, it was long sequestered within the covers of children's magazines, straitjacketed by publishing regulations, ignored by the media and other institutions that could have legitimized it, and stigmatized as intrinsically mediocre and infantile, if not pernicious. This was not a context in which it could fulfill its potential on an equal footing with other areas of creative production whose artistic credentials were better established. The barriers had to be broken down one by one. Of all the factors that enabled this evolution to take place, the most crucial were undoubtedly the rehabilitation efforts undertaken by fan organizations, the courage of a few farsighted publishers, the gradual abolition of censorship, the emergence of a body of specialized critics, the rise of an alternative comics scene, the increased international circulation of comic books, and finally the setting up of degree courses that enabled future comics authors and artists to engage with other disciplines and acquire a thorough artistic background.

Credit should be given first to the artists themselves, however, who *dared* to innovate, who broke taboos, and who ventured, at their own risk, onto unexplored terrain. If the creative freedom enjoyed by comics artists has never been greater, that is because each pioneering work becomes a potential new model, which means that it authorizes those who follow after it to do likewise.

We can use Hugo Pratt as an example, since we begin the book with him. When asked about the alternation of sequences with dialogue and long silent sections in his album *Peplum*,[3] the artist Blutch responded directly: "It's a revival of Hugo Pratt. In *Fort Wheeling*, there's a scene where Chris Kenton is being pursued by Indians.[4] He runs for pages and pages, with hardly a word spoken. You read that and you think 'Aha, so it is possible.'"[5] With *The Ballad of the Salt Sea*, Pratt dared to produce a story that was over 160 pages long, enabling him to imbue it with a breadth of fictional imagination denied to conventional comics. Without him, Eisner, and a few other pioneers, how could anyone have foreseen that one day there would appear a comic book of 672 pages, the exact length of Craig Thompson's *Habibi*?

If the concept of progress is inappropriate to account for these evolutions, comics still seems to be an *expanding art*. Not only because the works that it generates are increasing in size, but also because it is an art that has gradually become self-aware and conscious of its considerable potential, and one that unceasingly opens up new expressive terrain.

Given that it is a mixed art form, at the intersection of the verbal and the visual, it has taken two opposing pathways toward recognition. Comics has battered down the doors of galleries, museums, and the art market; but at the same time it has been consecrated—in spite of a few pockets of resistance—by the literary milieu. Novelists take inspiration from it; the terms "graphic novel" and "graphic literature" have gained currency; the formats of comics and books have become more alike; adaptations of the literary canon have proliferated; more and more space is given over to comics in forums for critical analysis and recommendation (such as broadcast media, written media, libraries, and universities).

This acceptance of comics as literature is perhaps more visible than its acceptance as visual art, because it is in literary networks that there is the highest output of commentary. A glance at what is typically being written gives the impression that, for many of today's critics, the quality of a comic is a function of its literariness. I take issue with this idea, and I hope to succeed in showing that in comics appreciation, all parameters are equally important. An art of drawing as much as narrating, a graphic as well as a literary art, comics draws its strength from the collective, concerted, intelligent deployment of all its resources.

The ten books that we are going to reread together will not enable us to produce a complete catalogue of these resources and of all the ways in which they can be brought into play. These books will, however, suffice to show how comics can serve the most disparate ambitions, run the whole gamut of human emotions, and comply with the most exacting aesthetic demands. This handful of masterpieces will speak on behalf of the ninth art in its entirety.

HUGO PRATT
Ballad of the Salt Sea (1967–1969)

BACKGROUND

Born in Rimini, Hugo Pratt (1927–1995) began working as a comics artist in 1945 but, until the *Ballad*, he spent most of his career in Argentina, where he lived from 1949 to 1962. There, he collaborated in particular with the greatest scriptwriter of his generation, Hector Oesterheld. He picked up the conventions of adventure comics by trying his hand at different genres: the war story (*Ernie Pike*), the Western (*Sergeant Kirk*, *Wheeling*), and the Jungle Story (*Ann of the Jungle*).

On his return to Italy, he worked for children's magazines, particularly the *Corriere dei Piccoli*.

In the city of Genoa where he was living at that time, Pratt made the acquaintance of Florenzo Ivaldi, a millionaire property investor who was interested in comics. Together, they founded a magazine called *Sgt. Kirk* (in which they republished the adventures of the eponymous character). A historian and cinema critic, Claudio Bertieri, was appointed editor.

Sgt. Kirk had a print run of 3000 and looked more luxurious than any comics magazine hitherto. Pratt drew several covers, in watercolors, which were striking in their composition. His groundbreaking contribution to the magazine was the *Ballad*, pre-published from July 1967 (when the author had just turned forty) to February 1969, from numbers 1 through 20 (although it was missing from numbers 2, 3, and 16). It was also in *Sgt. Kirk* that Pratt inaugurated another of his important series, *The Scorpions of the Desert*.[1]

In France, readers were able to read a serialized version of the *Ballad* in the daily newspaper *France Soir*, between July 3, 1973, and January 16, 1974. Part of it (fifty-one pages) was also published in the theoretical journal *Phénix* (1974), numbers 38 through 41.

The album was published by Casterman at the end of 1975, and in January of the following year it was awarded the prize for the best album at the third annual Angoulême comics festival (a panel from *Corto Maltese* had already been used two years earlier as a visual on the poster advertising the first festival).

But even before this belated discovery by the French public of the great opening story, the character Corto Maltese had appeared in *Pif Gadget*, beginning in 1969, for a series of about twenty-one stories of twenty pages each. He reappeared in *(À Suivre)* [To be continued] in 1980 and, later, in a more ephemeral magazine named after him, *Corto*. Through adventures that took him to Venice, Ireland, Africa, Russia, South America, and the Far East, he stamped his mark on modern comics as one of its mythical heroes.

PLOT

The story unfolds in Melanesia (a group of Pacific islands north-northeast of Australia) between November 1913 and January 1915.

Captains Corto and Rasputin are running contraband between the West Indies and Brazil. They work for a boss whose real identity is a mystery, even to them, and who calls himself "the Monk." The base from which the Monk and his gang conduct operations is the island of Escondida.

When the adventure opens, Corto Maltese has been abandoned on the high seas by his crew, who have rebelled against their captain. The pirate Rasputin arrives in the nick of time to save him, having already rescued two young people, a girl named Pandora and her cousin Cain. While Rasputin is attacking a Dutch merchant ship, Corto guards the two young prisoners on another catamaran. A fierce storm scatters them onto the shores of New Guinea, where they fall into the hands of Senik Papuans.[2] After escaping, Corto and his two young hostages find Rasputin on board a German submarine. They return to Escondida.

Cain and Pandora prove to be valuable captives, since they belong to a very wealthy family of British ship owners living in Australia, who will certainly be prepared to pay a heavy ransom. Throughout the story, Corto seeks to save the lives of the two young people. The Monk is overcome with emotion in the presence of the girl, although no one understands why.

However, Britain has declared war on Germany. The Monk supports the Germans, whose ships and submarines he refuels, working hand in hand with Lieutenant Slütter in particular.

The island is riven by various struggles for power and influence, driven both by the lure of gold (the Monk is believed to have amassed a hoard of treasure, of which everyone wants the largest share) and the pro-independence stirrings of the native inhabitants, who dream of a Great Melanesian Fatherland.

In a rash moment, the Monk pushes Corto off a cliff and leaves him for dead. He then quits the island, which he hands over to the control of Rasputin, on board Slütter's submarine. Cain profits from the situation to arrange Pandora's escape, aided by Tarao, an experienced Maori navigator. Meanwhile, Cranio, the Fijian trusted by the Monk, sinks a Japanese destroyer.

When the Monk returns, he realizes that Pandora's escape is a threat to the island's security, and he decides to abandon it permanently. In fact, a New Zealand detachment (wearing British uniforms) soon takes possession of Escondida. Cain and Pandora are reunited with their uncle Rinald Groovesnore. Thanks to their favorable testimony, all charges against Corto are dropped, and he in turn, by recourse to blackmail, manages to save Rasputin. Both are granted safe conduct. Slütter is condemned to death by firing squad. He leaves a letter that reveals to Corto the true identity of the Monk: he is none other than Thomas Groovesnore, the father of Pandora and the uncle of Cain.

SINCE THE ROMANTIC PERIOD, the term "ballad" has been applied to a narrative poem divided into stanzas whose subject matter is a legend or a historical episode. Hugo Pratt uses this generic term, uncommon in comics, for its literary and poetic connotations. His narrative contains an allusion to Samuel T. Coleridge and his famous work *The Rime of the Ancient Mariner*, which Cain is reading in a translation called "La Ballata del vecchio marinaio" (3:7).

By adopting the generic term "ballad," Pratt perhaps aspired to be a poetic descendent of Coleridge. Corto Maltese could be presented as a mariner who was still young, in contrast with the captain from the famous poem, who was advanced in years. The latter, cursed for killing an albatross, had seen all his crew die; Corto is in a very perilous situation when we first meet him, abandoned by his crew in the middle of the ocean after his crew has mutinied (following a quarrel over a woman). The ancient mariner had seen a ghost ship approach, with Death on board; Corto sees instead the catamaran commanded by Rasputin, who saves his life.[3] An improbable but timely apparition.

Rasputin undeniably has a ghostly dimension, with his jet-black beard, his unkempt hair, his hollow cheeks, and his wild stare. Furthermore, both the coincidence of name and physical resemblance make him a "double" of the famous Russian mystic, faith healer, and influential figure (1869–1916) who has often been demonized (in fact Raspoutnyi means "debauched"). The nature of the link between the historical person and his fictional avatar remains mysterious. The "real" Rasputin still had three years left to live on the day when the story recounted in the *Ballad* begins.

His graphic "double" may occasionally play the role of savior, but he holds human life cheap in general, and we quickly realize that he is used to dealing out death (he coldly slaughters the crew of a Dutch collier). Corto immediately calls him a "butcher" (1:13).

Pratt's story is partly legend and partly historical episode, and Rasputin, with his ambiguous connotations, is emblematic of this mixing of genres. The Venetian master story-teller has always been adept at maintaining ambivalence, deliberately fostering uncertainty as to the fictional or nonfictional status of his work. In this, he felt close to Jorge Luis Borges: "Borges and I use the same technique: an inextricable mixture of truth and mystification, real people and fictional characters."[4] And when he told his own life story, he also liked to blur the boundaries, to entangle the true and the false.

Corto, Rasputin, the Monk, Slütter, Pandora, Cain, Tarao—*Ballad of the Salt Sea* is a story without heroes, a story that intertwines the destinies of multiple characters, in what we would now call a "choral narrative."

The cover of the French edition, which features only Corto Maltese, is misleading and commercially motivated.[5] Casterman wanted to promote a character popularized by *Pif Gadget*, whose adventures had already appeared in five hardback albums since 1973. In the first number of *Sgt. Kirk*, the opening page was more faithful to the spirit of the work: it included most of the protagonists with the two young people, Cain and Pandora, in central position. Corto was less prominent.

On reading the book, it is hard to deny that Corto is the most salient character: we are quickly attracted to this sailor with an aura of mystery, whose nonchalance and humanity give him a natural charisma. For Pratt, though, the main character is Pandora,[6] the only female figure, the fixed point (she is a prisoner) who acts as a magnet for all the men around her. None of them is immune to her charms (if Escondida is a "treasure island," she is the treasure). A relationship of mutual seduction exists between her and Corto, even if both struggle not to give in to their inclinations.

The number of panels in which a character appears is not an exact gauge of his or her importance, but it is nonetheless a fairly reliable pointer. I have counted 335 images in which Corto appears without Pandora (alone or with other companions; these images become more numerous as the story goes on), 173 images in which Pandora appears without Corto, and 59 images in which they feature together.

The concept of a story without heroes was a bold one, and completely new in 1967, in the context of a comics medium that was subject to the iron laws of genre, series, and recurring heroes whose adventures could go on for decades. An album by Dany and Van Hamme, specifically called *Story without Heroes*, appeared ten years later, after prepublication in *Tintin* weekly magazine.[7] This

The title page as it appeared in *Sgt. Kirk*, not used in the French edition

story, whose protagonists are the survivors of a plane crash in the Amazonian jungle, made a big impression when it came out, and was thought very daring.

As if to depersonalize his fiction, Pratt attributes the opening words to the ocean itself: "I am the Pacific Ocean and I am the largest. This has been my name for a long time now, but it is not always true that I am pacific. I get angry sometimes, then everyone is in for a good thrashing" (1:3). Incidentally, this incipit introduces the theme of peace, which will soon be shattered by the outbreak of World War I. The "thrashing" promised to "everyone" presages the massacres and the destruction and seems to apportion equal blame to the future belligerents.

It can be said of the ocean and of the island of Escondida that they almost become characters in their own right. We know that Pratt took inspiration from the narrative art of the giants of the adventure novel (Jack London, James Fenimore Cooper, Rudyard Kipling, and Henry Rider Haggard) and particularly from Conrad, Melville, and Stevenson, the masters of the seafaring novel (even if none of them worked exclusively within this genre). Of Stevenson, Pratt said that he had shown him "that you could give adventure a poetic dimension."

The novel by the Irishman Henry de Vere Stacpoole *The Blue Lagoon* (1908, adapted for cinema several times) was a more direct source for the *Ballad*; Pratt found in it "this vision of a small island, atolls, the immensity of the Pacific, as well as the idea of smugglers, modern pirates."[8] And we should not forget that the heroes of the novel are two children of opposite sex.

The *Ballad* also has visual sources. From American cinema, first of all:[9] *Mutiny on the Bounty* (Frank Lloyd, 1935), *His Majesty O'Keefe* (Byron Haskin, 1953)—physically, Corto Maltese is modeled on the young Burt Lancaster—and *Wake of the Red Witch* (Edward Ludwig, 1948), which is the origin of the idea for the "crucifixion" of Corto on a raft. And then from comics. The determining influence is that of Franco Caprioli (1912–1974), the great Italian artist—almost completely unknown in France—whose comics had two favorite subjects: the sea and the "primitive" world. One of his most notable works was set on an island in the South Seas (*L'Isola Giovedi*, 1940).

Pratt defined himself as "a compiler and a *metteur en scène*," adding, "I have never hidden my sources nor those that have helped me."[10]

It begins with the ocean. The original place, the open space that seems to have no boundaries. The scenes that take place on the water (navigation) or in the water (swimming) take up about sixty pages and bring into play a large number of different vessels: catamaran, raft, cargo boat, motor launch, dugout canoe, submarine, torpedo boat, schooner, destroyer, and ketch.

Next comes the island. The archetypal place, mythologized by texts like *Robinson Crusoe*, *Treasure Island*, and *The Mysterious Island* and more recently by the television series *Lost*.

Hugo Pratt was fifteen when his father gave him an English edition of *Treasure Island* and said to him: "Now go and look for your own island." These were, if we believe Pratt's account, the last words his father spoke to him.[11]

"There exists somewhere, between Tonga and the Cook Islands, an umbilicus of the planet, out of which emerges the spirit of the seafaring hero Corto and his Venetian author Pratt. This oceanic navel is the foundational island, Escondida, the Polynesian island shrouded in taboo and inhabited by spirits. It is the refuge of Oro, the son of Tangaroa, the creator of man."[12] This lyrical presentation rightfully includes Escondida among the most beautiful islands, those given to us by Defoe, Verne, and Stevenson.

The legacy of Stevenson notably takes the form of the creation of a map. "The geographical map that most excited me when I was a child," recounts Pratt, "was the one from *Treasure Island* drawn by Stevenson himself. Imaginary maps are the most fun."[13] The Hetzel edition of *The Mysterious Island* included an engraving of the map made by the castaways on the island that they named "Lincoln." And we should not forget the "chart room" referred to at the beginning of *Moby Dick*. The map of Escondida, drawn to a scale of one to fifty thousand, indicating the artillery positions and the remains of two ships sunken off the coast, takes up the flyleaves at the beginning of the *Ballad*.[14] (Two other maps of the islands and archipelagos are included in the course of the story, on pages 1:5 and 3:3.)

The name of Escondida is pronounced for the first time by Pandora, on page 1:16. She calls it "the hidden island." And indeed, it remains hidden from us for quite some time, because we have to wait until page 3:11 before the characters with whom we embarked on this adventure reach the Monk's hideaway. And Corto leaves the island—now in the hands of the army—on the final page.

The island is a closed-off world, open only to the sea, a microcosm of the rest of the world: British (from Australia), Maltese, Germans, Japanese, and New Zealanders all land on it, mingling with the Melanesian indigenous people. The island is affected by the events that are shaking the world, but it is far away from old Europe, the main theater of operations. So although Pratt uses history as a backdrop, he chooses an oblique, decentered perspective, where the echoes of the war are muted.

Corto Maltese traverses the *Ballad* while revealing little of himself. Who is he? Where does he come from? What is his story? His ambition? Pratt gives very little away in answer to these questions.

He could not know, when he drew Corto tied to a makeshift raft with his arms outstretched in the form of a cross, that this powerful image would mark the beginning of the career of one of the most famous comics heroes of the modern era. This vision still seems astonishing. It would surely be mistaken to see in it an allusion to some Christlike nature of the character, which nothing in the book substantiates (apart from the fact that Corto, admittedly, "rises again" twice over, on pages 2:16 and 5:28, after he has been left for dead). Pratt claims that he was inspired by a Polynesian practice, applied particularly as a punishment for rape. At all events, the contrast could not be greater between this perilous situation and the opening images of many later stories, which show an idle and contemplative Corto, lounging nonchalantly in an armchair. The crucifixion victim that we meet at the beginning of the *Ballad* seems unlikely to survive. He is, from the outset, someone who has returned from the dead, a miraculous survivor. A character who has had time to take stock of his life, and who has no doubt cleansed himself of his past and cast it off, whatever it may have been.

Concerning the name of the character who would become his most emblematic hero, Pratt later explained "Corto Maltese sounded right, because Malta was on the point of gaining its independence, and he needed to be a character who was free."[15] When asked about the success of his creation, the author put forward this view: "He came along just at the right time. A year before the 1968 crisis, I invented this libertarian character engaged in the search for a new political virginity. Corto Maltese fitted with the sensibility of young people at that period."[16]

Regarding the circumstances under which Corto became a pirate, an explanation has been proposed by Juan Antonio de Blas, based on two conversations with Pratt. It requires us to go back to 1910: having shown solidarity with John Reed,[17] who was accused of causing the death of a cabin boy, Corto was, alleges de Blas, blacklisted by captains and forced to turn to piracy.[18] The biography written by the historian Michel Pierre—in which it is established that Corto was born on July 10, 1887, to a British sailor and a Spanish gypsy who worked as a prostitute in Gibraltar—does not confirm this version. It simply states that the Maltese "got on the wrong side of the law" at the beginning of 1913, and that he "was not a very good pirate. Piracy suited him because he liked the freedom, the chance to discover new places and meet new people, but not all the killing and spilling of blood. A little smuggling and a spot of arms trafficking were enough to keep him happy. What he enjoyed was hopping from island to island among the archipelagos."[19]

Of all the albums that Pratt drew after the *Ballad*, only one is situated chronologically before the Escondida episode: *The Youth of Corto Maltese* (1981) takes place in 1904–5, during the Sino-Japanese War.[20] Corto's path crosses that of Jack London, and Rasputin is already on the scene, although he has not yet turned to piracy.

There can surely be no better consecration for an imaginary character than to see his or her existence "accredited" by a biography that fills in the gaps in

Between Corto and his archenemy Rasputin, a tense and ambivalent relationship

the fiction. Few comics heroes have had this privilege. Apart from Corto, the most obvious example is Blueberry, whose entire life was recounted by Jean-Michel Charlier in a lengthy preface to another ballad, the 1974 album *Ballad for a Coffin*.[21]

There are two competing approaches available to anyone who wishes to unravel the narrative skein of the *Ballad*.

The first, the classic method, consists of enumerating its main themes, that is to say Pandora's emergence from childhood to womanhood, World War I and the various kinds of trafficking that it generates, the organization headed by the Monk and the enigma around the true identity of this mysterious figure, and, finally, the independence struggle of the indigenous peoples of the islands (a theme that is evoked but not developed in detail).

A second approach would be to study the one-to-one relationships that the characters have with each other, and how these evolve as the plot progresses. If we choose Corto as the pivotal character, we can then consider in turn his relationships with Rasputin, Pandora, the Monk, Slütter, and Tarao.

Rasputin is the eternal archenemy, the dark and malevolent double. Corto successively calls him a "damn fool" (1:7), a "butcher" (1:13), a "scorpion" (1:25) and "stark, staring mad" (3:6). He knows very well, and has known for a long time, where he stands with Rasputin.[22] On several occasions, each of them threatens to kill the other. Rasputin, treated as a pariah, would like to find in

Corto's farewell to Pandora: an unfulfilled romance

Corto a true friend, but, even if they "have certain things in common" (1:10), they are worlds apart, and, twice over, Corto refuses the offer of friendship (3:6 and 7:17). Even though he saves Rasputin from the death sentence hanging over him, this is to avenge Slütter rather than out of pity or friendship.

Pandora is initially wary of Corto, whom she associates with Rasputin. She tries nonetheless, for tactical reasons, to make him her friend, even whispering flirtatiously "I'm feeling a bit lonely" (1:24), but the sailor is not taken in by this ruse. Ten pages further on, she is franker in her choice of words: "I don't trust you and I don't like your company" (2:9). She goes so far as to shoot him, unconcerned as to whether she has killed him or not. Her feelings gradually change, first because Corto twice saves her from drowning and then because both Cranio and Slütter defend him, and sing his praises in front of her. From page 2:24, Cain can read her mind, and asks her: "Are you letting our handsome sailor with the earrings get to you?" The first time Corto calls Pandora "my little romantic petal" (2:10), he is being ironical. But he will address her as a "romantic petal" four more times (3:8, 3:16, 4:1, 7:20), becoming gradually more tender and sincere. While Cain remains hostile to Corto for a long time, to the point of shooting at his car, Pandora makes the sailor promise not to hurt her cousin.

The penultimate page of the *Ballad* is devoted to Corto's goodbyes. In a touching scene, which seals the end of a relationship that has remained platonic and confirms the strength of his feelings, he tells her: "I'd like to see you again always ... and everywhere ..." (7:21).

A text that is not included in the French edition,[23] but which was featured in the opening issue of *Sgt. Kirk* (see below) informed the reader that in his old age Corto had gone to live with Pandora, whose children regarded him as an uncle.

In the book jointly written by Pratt and Michel Pierre,[24] the authors attribute three letters to Pandora, supposedly written in January 1916, April 1917, and November 1918. The final one mentions that Cain has met up with Corto on the Flanders battlefield. And Pandora writes: "I became aware of a small scar at the memory of this name. It was a girl's scar, and the woman that I am now reopened it as a wound."

It is also worth noting that in the story called "Vaudeville between Zuydcoote and Bray-Dunes," which is included in the 1980 album *Celtic Tales*,[25] Corto runs into Cain, who tells him: "Pandora is getting married this year.... She was in love with you ... I think," and these words plunge the Maltese into profound nostalgia.

The Monk is a character who is constantly talked about, from the beginning of the story. His nom de guerre is pronounced five times in the course of pages 1:7 to 1:9, always with fear, deference, and respect. Anticipation builds up around him, but he does not make an appearance until 4:4, halfway through the album. And the reader cannot see his facial features, which are permanently hidden by the shadow of his large hood. Corto is the protégé and friend of the Monk, who nonetheless calls him to account for the loss of his schooner and crew. He concludes: "You are incapable of commanding, you are too individualistic and undisciplined. You are a subversive!" (4:6). However, a few pages further on, the mysterious gang leader declares that he is "a hundred per cent sure" of Corto (4:19). Pandora is the cause of the confrontation between the two men, in which the Monk gains the upper hand (just as, in another scene [6:5], he physically overcomes Rasputin). Not knowing that the Monk is the girl's father, Corto misinterprets the interest that the hooded man takes in her, and cannot suppress his laughter. The Monk believes that he has killed Corto, "the only friend [he] had" (4:20), and when the Maltese reappears, he is happy and relieved. It is Corto who convinces his "employer" of the imminence of the danger and the need to leave the island.

Lieutenant Christian Slütter, an officer of the Imperial German Navy, takes on the same protective role in relation to the young Groovesnores that Corto had sworn to perform (3:3). In fact, the two characters seem close to each other. Slütter merits, just as much as Corto, the title of "gentleman of fortune" (a designation that we owe to Robert Louis Stevenson, and one that has been routinely applied to Pratt's hero[26]) on account of his courage, his sense of honor and his chivalrous temperament. Moreover, the two men have a mutual liking for each other, which they express on two occasions (4:7 and 6:11) and even their rivalry over Pandora does not undermine the respect between them. But Slütter is a tragic figure. When he realizes that Germany is going to lose the war, he feels that he is "caught up in this affair, and it isn't going to be easy to get out again . . ." (6:9).

Corto tends Slütter's wounds and saves his life after the Monk has shot him (6:21), but he can do nothing to save him from a death sentence for "treason, piracy, murder, sabotage and espionage" (7:7).

Another man who earns Corto's esteem is the Fijian Cranio, Rasputin's boatswain, an educated man who went to school "with white men" (4:26) and worked for a lawyer. The gigantic wave that threatens to engulf him and Corto (1:27) seems to have symbolic resonance, for after the tsunami, Cranio evokes the destruction of the old world, that of his Polynesian ancestors. He expresses a view that Corto describes as "nationalist" (4:8). Speaking to Pandora, Cranio describes Corto as "a free spirit" who "has no homeland" and "knows many things" (4:26). But it is another indigenous islander, Sbrindolin, who speaks these words to Corto: "You tried to be one of us, and you almost managed it" (7:18). Corto bonds naturally with Cranio the Fijian, Tarao the Maori and Sbrindolin, just as he will in later adventures, with Cush the Danakil or

Changhaï Li the Chinese woman. He makes no distinction among the peoples of the Earth.

Cain, Pandora's cousin, is another interesting character. Courageous, hot-tempered, and impulsive, this boy who is not yet out of his teens wants to take up his place as a man. The events that he lives through are something of a rite of passage for him. He mistrusts everyone except Tarao, and only accepts Corto as an ally after lengthy resistance. Significantly, although perhaps unconsciously, Pratt sometimes draws his face like that of a child, sometimes like that of a man.

Speaking of Corto in general, and not his specific role in the *Ballad*, Pratt said: "Corto is just a pretext. He's there to introduce the reader, a sort of Virgil guiding Dante. He recounts things. He introduces characters to one another. He doesn't usually act, only occasionally. He helps the reader to get to know the characters. [...] He's just an intermediary."[27]

In the *Ballad*, it is indeed Corto who creates links among people. But, although he seems fatalistic, even indolent, by nature, he is certainly not passive: he takes initiatives and risks, saves others, and endangers his own life.

Ballad of the Salt Sea is not without faults. There is a certain flippancy in the treatment of violence and in the trigger-happy characters. From a more technical point of view, there are a few redundant scenes and some rather confused passages; ultimately, the plot is fairly thin, does not deliver what it promises (lacking any intrinsic interest, it is outweighed by the forcefulness of the characters), and makes several concessions to the usual adventure story clichés.

The first appearance of the Monk: a careful mise-en-scène

Dominique Petitfaux pointed out to Pratt that the discovery of the family relationship between Pandora and the Monk recalls nineteenth-century popular novels.[28] In fact, everything about the Monk seems to relate to popular literature, which teems with powerful, terror-inspiring characters whose real identity is shrouded in mystery, such as Edmond Dantès and Captain Nemo, along with a plethora of criminal masterminds or masked avengers.

The character of the Monk seems, for example, to be quite close to that of an adventure comics hero like the Phantom (Lee Falk and Ray Moore, 1936). This masked avenger was reputed to be immortal, just as the Monk is believed to be immortal by the local people, and his true identity was kept secret. However, the Phantom fought against pirates, whereas the Monk is a pirate. Even so, the motif of the disfigured character who is forced to hide his face is a cliché. The Monk has suffered serious burns to his face in a fire. That makes him a "colleague" of the Phantom of the Opera and of Doctor Doom (in *The Fantastic Four*).

The Monk, moreover, does not quite seem to live up to his own legend. Cain describes him as "a strange character who reigns over everything between the Gilbert Islands and the Leeward Islands. The sailors of three countries haven't managed to discover his island hideaway. Very few people have seen him" (1:16). This legend grew up around him before the period covered in the *Ballad*. In this album, he seems unable to control his emotions or to create harmony among his henchmen. As a leader, the main initiative that he takes consists of capitulating, by abandoning his hideout and disbanding his organization, at least in the form that it has taken up to that point. The fascination that the character exerts, therefore, arises exclusively out of the mystery of his identity. The patch of black color that devours his face and stands in for it is an audacious move by Pratt, an inspired graphic choice: it is impossible not to peer inquisitively into this pit of darkness.

Throughout the *Ballad*, the reader's interest is sustained by a series of questions that build dramatic tension: what is to be the fate of the young Groovesnores? Will the war work to the advantage of the pirates or will it prove fatal to them? Is Corto really dead? The Monk serves mainly as an object of curiosity: we want his identity to be revealed.

The *Ballad* transcends the limitations of popular literature (or paraliterature, as it used to be known) in two ways: through the complexity of the other characters and through the refusal to take up an ideologically polarized position.

Furthermore, it summons up a wider literary heritage. It is possible to identify references and allusions, some discreet and some more marked, to Bougainville's *A Voyage Around the World* (1:4), to *Robinson Crusoe* (2:5), to *Moby Dick* (2:25) (Tarao's face recalls that of the harpooneer Queequeg), to

Coleridge (3:7), to the poets Rilke and Shelley (7:14), and to Euripides (7:19). Pratt declared the importance of "making use of whatever is relevant in every cultural domain, and not being confined within just one."[29] But this degree of cultural eclecticism and fusion between popular literature and highbrow literature was completely unprecedented in comics at the time when he was writing.

I have alluded above to a text published in *Sgt. Kirk* 1, along with the first nine pages of the *Ballad*, and missing from most of the album versions.[30] This was a letter, dated June 1965 and attributed to one Obregan Carrenza, who presents himself as the nephew of Cain Groovesnore. Carrenza testifies to the editor of the magazine that he has handed over to "Mr Pratt" his uncle's manuscripts, Slütter's ship's log, and two nautical charts, out of which, he claims, Pratt composed the *Ballad*. The purpose of this apocryphal letter was to confer a certain weight of authenticity upon the fiction. This is also a distancing device common in literature—especially at the time when the novel was a controversial genre—by means of which the author affects to delegate to others the responsibility for what he or she is recounting. Cervantes, for example, pretended that *Don Quixote* was based on archival documents and an Arabic manuscript.

Pratt thought of comics as a form of literature and he was one of the first people, from the early 1980s, to refer to "drawn literature"—a term that has since been adopted in the discourse of some critics—thereby echoing, consciously or not, Rodolphe Töpffer's term "engraved literature."

This literary orientation did not in any way prevent him from according a rightful place to the image, and to drawing. Silent panels, with no dialogue, were still extremely rare in comics, which at that time offered no respite, no bouts of inactivity, no silence, perhaps because authors feared that with no text to retain readers' attention, they would glide too rapidly over the images.[31]

The abundance of silent panels is therefore all the more striking in certain sequences of the *Ballad*, such as the famous page that features the Monk's first appearance. It is made up of seven panels, and includes only the words "My dear friends, good day!" (4:4), addressed as much to the reader as to the characters who have gathered for the occasion. In Pratt's work, there are three main categories of silent image. There are images entirely devoted to unalloyed action: fights and exchanges of gunshot; contemplative images, often large-format, where the emphasis is on the background and the horizon (panels in which seagulls fly past, often punctuated by the outlines of a few palm trees, have indeed become emblematic of Pratt's art); and finally, close-ups of faces. The Monk is the main beneficiary of these, which may seem paradoxical, given that his face is invisible and, by definition, expressionless. The frequent silence of the Monk is proof that at these moments he is in the grip of a deep emotion. This silence intensifies the indecipherability of his appearance, imbuing the images with an enigmatic quality that invites readers to project their own feelings onto them.

A recurring element of Pratt's poetics is the silence that often accompanies the first encounter between characters. They size each other up wordlessly, giving nothing away at first.

In 1967, Pratt's style had not yet attained the stripped-back quality that would later become his trademark, when he would move toward a kind of "clear line with black patches." However, the most successful images in the *Ballad* are often those that prefigure this drawing-as-writing. In general, his pen stroke is still thin and restless; it seems to catch on the paper; we can almost hear the scratch of the nib. Even if Pratt has an innate sense of effective composition, not all his images are easily readable. For he has only two values to play with, black and white, and he uses them, sometimes in equal proportions, indiscriminately, as much for foregrounds as for backgrounds. When there are a large number of speech balloons, they often spill over into the gutters, or even the adjacent panels, which tends to disrupt the spatial structure of the page. Pratt's "touch" is evident above all in the placing of pools of black, with a brush. A few heavy verticals or horizontals are all he needs to evoke architectural forms: a few thick strokes can suggest a garment. Certain images with blurred outlines (such as the first panel on page 4:8) recall overexposed photographs. Certain others (particularly on pages 2:3 and 3:18–19) correspond to what Jean Arrouye has called "blind images." All that can be seen is a rhythmic pattern of ink traces, in which representational drawing seems to break down. These panels, "spaces of perplexity and reverie," that create a "syncopated effect, a break in continuity where the legibility of the panel is obscured" are described by Arrouye as "places where reality dissolves," like a "symbolic condensation of [Pratt's] world of deserts and seascapes where history and geography die away and are re-imagined as heightened, exotic mythologies."[32]

In spite of a few weaknesses and the casual way in which it seems to have been conceived, the *Ballad* holds the reader's interest, and time has not diminished its charm. Pratt proves to be a born storyteller, with every right to lay claim to the status of "son of Milton Caniff and Alexandre Dumas," as he had described himself to Petitfaux. Nonetheless, over the half century that has followed the initial publication of this story, a number of its innovations have become standard procedures. We need to remember that it was far from usual, in comics, to situate an adventure story in such a precise historical context; to give equal importance to half a dozen characters; to give a central role to a female character; to depict heroes who are acted upon as much as acting, are morally ambivalent, and avoid the extremes of Manichaeism; to have massive

In this shipwreck scene, Pratt pushes figuration to the limits of abstraction

recourse to literary references and silent panels; and, finally, to combine adventure with poetry.

(In Pratt's subsequent work, a dual evolution is noticeable, both toward a greater concern for documentary veracity, and toward a more and more marked interest in the esoteric and the oneiric—Rubis refers to the "primacy of *fantasia*."[33] Masonic symbols, Celtic legends, Jewish mysticism, the mysteries of Venice, the myth of lost continents [Atlantis, Mu]: all of these elements, which will become ever more important in the adventures of Corto Maltese, are missing from the *Ballad*.)

In addition to all the liberties taken by Pratt that enabled comics to take a leap forward by freeing the medium from the conventions that were restraining it, it was, of course, by its length and its scope that the *Ballad* was spectacularly innovative. With its 163 pages (165 including the map of Escondida), it developed its plot over the equivalent of almost four standard-length albums (the forty-four-page hardback format was the publishing norm in France). Comics could now aspire to an unprecedented breadth of fictional imagination,[34] the story could be digressive, multi-layered, sometimes contemplative, and its characters could be beset by doubt and undergo reversals of fortune. Pratt had no intention of calling his book a "novel" nor of dividing it into chapters like a work of literature. But it was nonetheless one of the first graphic novels.

During this same period, the second half of the 1960s, the publisher Éric Losfeld brought out, with no prepublication in magazines, several substantial comics albums by authors such as Crepax, Peellaert, Cuvelier, and Druillet. These too can be considered as precursors of the graphic novel, but none of them achieved the prominence of the *Ballad*, or marked the history of the medium so definitively.

For this album was the model on which Casterman based the monthly magazine *(À suivre)*, launched in 1978. Its editor, Didier Platteau, summarized the concept of the magazine in these terms: "A monthly magazine in black and white enabling the publication of stories chapter by chapter, in the style of *Ballad of the Salt Sea*, which could be regarded as the prototype of what we were aiming to do."[35]

The collection of "Romans (À suivre)" [Novels (to be continued)], which would include work by Comès, Tardi and Forest, Muñoz and Sampayo, F'Murr, Schuiten and Peeters, and many others, would be crucial in changing the perceptions of the French readership as to what a comic book could be.

The *Ballad* had epitomized the "breakthrough of comics into literature" that would become the slogan of *(À suivre)*.

MŒBIUS
Airtight Garage (1979)

BACKGROUND

In 1976, Mœbius (the penname of Jean Giraud, 1938–2012) drew two "nonsensical" pages "for no particular reason," to amuse himself, with no intention of publishing them or continuing them. The conventions of comics creation were so deeply rooted in him that the artist who had produced *The Deviation*[1] could not help giving these loose sheets a title, *The Airtight Garage of Jerry Cornelius* [*Le Garage hermétique de Jerry Cornelius*] (a title so weird that it seemed to rule out any further episodes," he later said). And he even added a subtitle: "1st episode: dangerous overhaul." In short, he was playing with narrative conventions with no intention of constructing a narrative.

Jean-Pierre Dionnet, the editor-in-chief of *Métal hurlant* (Heavy metal), the magazine that Mœbius had co-founded, decided to publish the two pages in issue 6. Mœbius's joke had now turned into a trap for him. Forced to invent a follow-up, he improvised, launched into a serial story and, beginning in the third episode, brought in a character who had turned up a few times in short sketches, wearing a pointed helmet or a solar topee: "Major Grubert."

Mœbius set himself the challenge of providing at least two pages of this improbable saga for each issue of *Métal*. The plot got thicker as it went along, more characters were introduced, and, above all, the story extended far beyond the limits of a normal comics adventure: the ending did not arrive until 1979, on the ninety-eighth page. The album version, which included all the adventures of Grubert (short stories as well as *Garage*) was published under the title *Major fatal*.

Along with *Arzach*, which immediately preceded it, *Airtight Garage* brought previously unimagined perspectives to graphic narration, and had a huge impact on younger artists, who began to see Mœbius as the standard-bearer for a "new comic art."

Moreover, the author must have gone on being haunted by the story world that he had constructed, given that he returned to it over ten years later. First of all by allowing himself to be compromised by a publishing (or rather marketing) venture, a lamentable five-volume cycle, *Airtight Garage: The Elsewhere Prince* (1990–92) scripted by Jean-Marc Lofficier and poorly drawn by American artists Shanower and Bingham;[2] then, more seriously, by drawing, between 1991 and 1994, an album called *The Man from the Ciguri*, presented as "volume 2" of *Major fatal*.[3] And finally, by composing part three, *The Depressed Hunter*, published in 2008.[4] And in *The Aedena Cycle*,[5] Grubert returns under the name "Master Burg."

PLOT

Reducing *Airtight Garage* to its plot can only trivialize a work that defies such simplification, and which deliberately transgresses all the rules of narration. We will nonetheless endeavor to summarize its twists and turns, since that is the pattern that we have adopted in this book. This exercise will at least serve to demonstrate that the plot is not unintelligible.

Major Grubert, human in appearance but possessing the gift of immortality, has created a world using only the power of his dreams. It is a spherical universe (called "The Garage") in the shape of an asteroid, the inside of which is an inhabited microcosm, structured into three levels. The story begins when an engineer called Barnier runs away after damaging a cable box because he is fearful of the wrath of his boss, Lewis Carnelian.

Grubert, who is orbiting the "Garage" in a spaceship, the Ciguri, accompanied by his fiancée Malvina and a large crew, learns that Carnelian has infiltrated the asteroid and is threatening to capture it on behalf of the Nagual, an omnipotent being from whom Grubert had once stolen some secret powers.

After first sending his spy, Samuel Mohad, the Major beams down to the asteroid in person in order to confront Carnelian, who has already taken control of the second and third levels. Then Malvina sends in one of the ship's officers, Lark Dalxtrey, to rescue the Major.

In the "Singing Caverns," Barnier has met an ally in the person of the mysterious Archer, who has come to help him escape in a submarine. A gatekeeper called Graad enables Grubert to access the first level. He runs into Carnelian there, but the two adversaries have to forget their differences in order to take on common enemies, first the "president" of the city of Armjourth (the capital of the asteroid), then the "Bakalite master of the intermediate zone" and finally Sper Gossi, "master of the first level." Carnelian is killed and Grubert survives only by escaping from the asteroid. By going through a door, he moves from the disorderly world of dreams to the orderly world of reality, and ends up in the Paris metro, on the platform of Opéra station.

READING *AIRTIGHT GARAGE* TODAY, as a complete text, is necessarily a very different experience from discovering it, month after month, fragment by fragment, in the pages of a magazine. Hindsight enables us to judge that thirty-five years of creation and experimentation in comics have not diminished the radical impact of the story, which is still a miracle of freedom, inventiveness, and irreverence, as well as richness and, who knows, secret coherence.

Many of his admirers see this atypical and disconcerting work as the quintessential Mœbius. At the point when its readers discovered it, *Garage* seemed like a sort of manifesto for a new comics, a comics that would be liberated from all the implicit rules that governed the industry, a call for freedom of inspiration, for the emancipation of the artist's pencil.

Over the preceding twelve years, under his real name Jean Giraud, Mœbius had built up a solid reputation as a virtuoso realist draftsman by regularly turning out episodes of a Western series that soon took on mythical status, the adventures of Lieutenant Blueberry. Jean-Michel Charlier's dense and fast-paced scripts had driven his artistic skill up to the highest level, but the form was restricting: a genre-based comic, with constant plot reversals and often wordy dialogues. However, as from the episode entitled *Chihuahua Pearl*, published in album format in 1973, Charlier himself had introduced some elasticity into the standard Franco-Belgian comics format by inaugurating a narrative cycle that would extend over many more albums, so that each book simply constituted a new chapter in an ongoing plot that was forever "to be continued . . ." From then on, the epic of Lieutenant Blueberry began to embody the very essence of the adventure serial.

By sustaining the artistic adventure of *Garage* for three years, Mœbius likewise played with the conventions of the serial, or flouted them. He took care to keep the script open-ended and to maintain a strict commitment to improvisation. "*Garage* is the perfect example of a comic with no predetermined script. Every time I was tempted to strengthen the storyline and some narrative goal started to take shape, I scuppered the whole thing and wandered off again."[6]

It was also in 1973 that readers of *Pilote* were able to discover a short seven-page story called *The Deviation*. Although it was signed Gir, it was the starting point—and a masterful one—of Mœbius's oeuvre.[7] Even its title was programmatic, heralding all the stories to come that were offbeat, deconstructed, branching, and going off into skids, controlled or otherwise. Three years later, Major Grubert, with *Garage*, stood out as the key figure of the new imaginative universe whose every nook and cranny Mœbius undertook to explore.

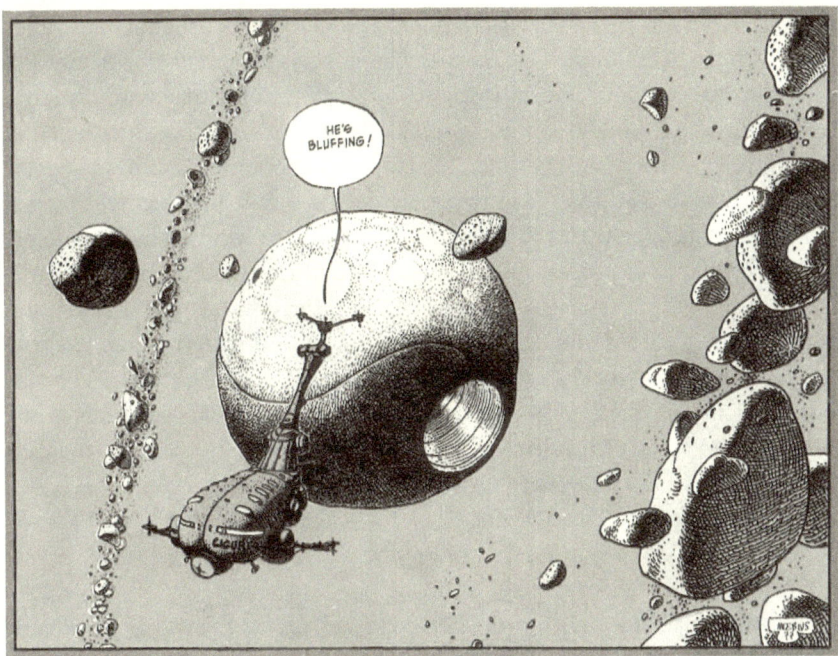
Aboard the Ciguri, the Major circles around his creation like a demiurge

In 1975, while he was immersed in the production of *Arzach*, as a response to readers who were disconcerted by it, Mœbius wrote these oft-quoted lines in the editorial to *Métal hurlant* 4: "There is no reason why a story has to be like a house with a door through which to enter, windows through which to look out at the trees, and a chimney for the smoke—it is easy to imagine a story in the shape of an elephant, a cornfield or the flame of a match."

The break with convention that was already apparent in *The Deviation* and *Arzach* is more thoroughgoing and more profound in *Airtight Garage*. It seems at first to be less transgressive—Mœbius does not put himself in the comics frame as he does in *The Deviation*, he does not spurn text as he does in *Arzach*, and the starting point seems to pertain to an acceptably identifiable genre, which happens to be one about which he is passionate, science fiction—but with each episode it becomes ever freer and more revolutionary in its form.

Among many others, the future comics critic and scriptwriter Thierry Smolderen was literally hypnotized by it: "I was crazy about Mœbius. I learned *Airtight Garage* by heart as each episode came out."[8] In 1983, his essay "The Major's stolen notebooks or the adventures of Hergé and Mœbius, serial writers" was published in Brussels by Schlirf-Book.[9] By analyzing a cluster of uncanny similarities, he uncovered a mystical and mysterious link between

Airtight Garage and Hergé's *Cigars of the Pharaoh* (in its original black-and-white version).[10] As far as I am aware, Mœbius has never confirmed nor denied that he was consciously inspired by *Cigars*. Coincidence and unconscious echoes cannot, of course, be excluded. We may also consider whether the points of convergence between the two works should be attributed to certain immutable laws that govern the adventure serial told through images, when it is at its purest. This theoretical issue is not really raised by Smolderen.

The world of *Garage*, as I have said, is divided into three levels, which the Major traverses successively. Smolderen has clearly shown that these levels each have a very different look. The first is wild and barely inhabited. The second presents a world that is technologically advanced, but not hyper-industrialized. It contains vestiges of ancient civilizations (like pyramids in the desert). The capital of this level is the city of Armjouth, the "pearl of the tundra." Finally, the third level presents a mechanical universe.

According to Smolderen, the three levels of *Garage* correspond to three developmental stages of the human brain: the reptilian stage, the higher mammal stage, and the ultimate stage of evolution.

But this tripartite division of the world created by the Major also lends itself to a psychoanalytic interpretation, given that the ternary structure characterizes Freud's first topography (in which he distinguished the unconscious, the preconscious, and the conscious) as well as the second (the id, the ego, and the superego), and finally the Lacanian triad of the Real, the Symbolic, and the Imaginary. The "levels" of *Garage* could, then, be taken as representing parts of the psyche, and the Major as confronting no other enemy than his own delirium, resulting from the conflict between his dreams and the mechanisms that censor their expression. (Freudian connotations are more explicit in *The Man from the Ciguri*, which invokes the notion of infantile trauma, stages a double killing of the father, and makes extravagant use of distortions in spelling that could be read as Freudian slips.)

It is nonetheless advisable to be wary of ready-made keys and of interpretative grids superimposed onto a work that was never premeditated: an open work par excellence, in which readers can find whatever they bring to it. The product of improvisation over a three-year period, *Garage* is a labyrinthine narrative that has, quite obviously, absorbed so many outside influences, personal experiences, and contradictory drives that its manifest content is full of clues that can be interpreted in manifold ways.

Mœbius is, of course, not the first comics scriptwriter to have jettisoned the programmatic script and chosen improvisation as a working method:

> Improvisation was far more widespread in former days, when comics was mainly a press-based medium and readers were less insistent on

well-structured plots. The casualness of the comics artist who turns out a serial story on a week-to-week basis is striking in, for example, the adventures of Zig and Puce, delivered in installments to *Dimanche-Illustré* [Illustrated Sunday supplement] by Alain Saint-Ogan with little idea where his inspiration would take him next. The story goes at a cracking pace, is chock-full of stereotypes, and the narrative thread linking the pages is often fairly tenuous.[11]

But among comics artists, it is the inventor of *Désert B*[12] who has transformed improvisation into a privileged working (anti-)method. Discussing *Inside Mœbius*, the book that served as his testament, he explained: "There is no script, nor any intention of telling a story. I simply set the characters in motion through my drawing, and whatever mental state I am in serves as the backdrop. I therefore emit some kind of reactivity in response to the pressure of the world around me."[13]

One of the characteristics of ad hoc invention is that it always depends on a rereading of the elements already established and available. Today's writing (or drawing) is controlled by what was written (or drawn) yesterday. It is therefore worth paying particular attention to the elements that were put in place from the outset, in the two opening pages, thrown down on the paper with no preconception about anything that was to follow.

What this amounted to was, first, a title: *Le Garage hermétique de Jerry Cornelius*.[14]

This could be read as a warning: reader, you are embarking on a *hermetic* work, and you are bound to get shunted off into *sidings* [*voies de garage*].

But it is above all the character of Jerry Cornelius (Lewis Carnelian) that catches our interest, this hero who shares Christ's initials, and whom Mœbius—following a number of authors from the British new wave—borrowed from the science fiction writer Michael Moorcock. A kind of hip James Bond that Atalante, who published the French version, introduced as follows: "a secret agent without a mission, a very rich and talented dandy, an oddball womanizer, irreverent and amoral. But, at the same time, a disaster-prone rocker from the London suburbs, moonstruck wanderer through a disintegrating world. Is he immortal? He saunters insolently through a chaotic universe that is hardly any different from our own."

It was not only the name of the protagonist that Mœbius took from the Cornelius "tetralogy" of novels, published between 1968 and 1977. Moorcock's comic tonality pervades the atmosphere of *Garage*. Right from the fourth line of the first novel in the saga, called *The Final Programme*, mention is made—a troubling coincidence—of a "French explorer."[15] Jerry Cornelius himself "didn't read anything except part of the comic supplement"[16] and is given to typically Mœbiusian utterances like: "the cosmologies mingle and absorb each other."[17]

The chief similarity between the two works lies in their conception of space. Exploring the "fake Le Corbusier château"[18] of his father, whose interior is a "complicated maze,"[19] Cornelius goes through one door after another. The first one enables him to enter a cliff made of plastic; another sends him through a library; a third is hidden inside a Picasso painting.[20] Similarly, there are innumerable doors, thresholds and openings of all kinds in *Garage*, punctuating it with a succession of boundary crossings. It is precisely this motif that is featured in the cover illustration of the album (just like the analogous one of *The Man from the Ciguri*): Grubert is coming toward us, emerging from an opening cut into a wall, an opening in the form of a comics panel that seems to allow two worlds to intercommunicate.

The resonance of this motif perhaps serves to explain and justify the "profession" attributed to the hero, as well as his outfit. Grubert is an explorer, a boundary crosser—and the heir to the characters from popular fiction who so fascinated the teenage Mœbius.

In the subtitle of the first episode, "Dangerous overhaul" ("Dangereuse révision"), it is easy to read a contraction of the words *rêve* (dream) and *vision*, which sum up well what is about to unfold. And, with hindsight, engaging in "dream vision" cannot fail to strike us as dangerous indeed. In the end, *Garage* speaks to us of nothing other than the struggle for power: the narrative grows out of the successive victories or defeats of the forces involved, their provisional alliances and their secret manipulations. Hidden behind the protagonists are more powerful entities, whose status is ill defined (e.g., the Nagual, the magician Tar'Hai, and the Bakalite troops) and who, although they are rarely actually shown, combat each other using proxy champions. Can these entities be likened to divinities, some benevolent and others malevolent? A remark by the author could invite this interpretation: "Religions are systems built on visions. They are revelations that have arrived. How? Through dreams, especially guided dreams and waking dreams—let us call them 'professional' dreams."[21]

The final card in Mœbius's initial pack is a metaphor, that of the machine and the engineer. In spite of a costume that makes him look more like an avant-garde mime artist, the character who monologues in these two opening pages is retrospectively designated in the second episode as "Engineer Barnier" and described as "very upset because his cable box exploded" (1:7). This "cable box" is a machine whose purpose remains obscure (it is supposed to be "launched toward the stars") but whose design, Barnier assures us, is "completely revolutionary" (1:5).

We will choose to see the mysterious machine as a metaphor for the story itself, and its workings. The fact that it explodes at the end of the episode can be taken as a clear indication that the storyline begun here was not going to be pursued. But, again, in the light of a retrospectively informed reading of the complete work, we may feel that it is by no means insignificant that this machine was intended to reach the stars. We should not forget that *Garage* ends when Grubert gets out of a train at Opéra metro station. The "stars" could then be read as the *corps de ballet* of the Opéra Garnier. (*Barnier* is only one letter away from *Garnier*, after all.)

This may seem like mere wordplay on my part. But this is something that Mœbius has never disdained, and when a journalist reproached him with his taste for "pathetic word games and puns," he replied: "I got a taste for it when I discovered *Impressions of Africa* by the surrealist writer Raymond Roussel."[22] We should recall that the genesis of this book is the link between the words *billard* (billiard) and *pillard* (plunderer).[23]

The circularity that links the end of a book to its beginning is a common device (we will meet it again, notably, in the next chapter, devoted to *Watchmen*). It is one form of what I have called braiding effects, which, over and above the need for breakdown of the action, establish additional and conspicuous relations between contiguous or distant panels. Braiding effects are, in general, a characteristic of works that are particularly highly wrought on a formal level. They operate both on the linear mode of reading and on the non-time bound perception of the page, and book, as network. Braiding might then seem antithetical to the idea of improvisation. This is not necessarily true since, as we have seen, even a story that grows like ivy is permanently constrained by material that has already been set down and accumulated. On rereading his own work, Mœbius was able, consciously or unconsciously, to exploit certain details that had originally been included somewhat randomly.

We will cite two examples taken, again, from the first episode.

On Engineer Barnier's back there can be seen concentric circles in the exact shape of a target. Later, the character that the engineer will meet and follow like his own shadow is none other than the Archer. Their closeness will reach its natural conclusion amid the raging waters. When he loses the helmet that he had never taken off, Engineer Barnier reveals a luxuriant head of hair, and turns out to be a woman. The Archer is on the point of kissing her (4:6). The arrow seems to have reached the target.

A second example: the cable box, Barnier explains, has a "crystalline structure" (1:5). Crystals will soon make another appearance. Beginning in 1:26, the exact moment when he is "ready to enter the second level," Major Grubert never lets go of a mysterious Gladstone bag, a graphic attribute that adds

The two pages that appeared in *Métal hurlant* 6, where it all began

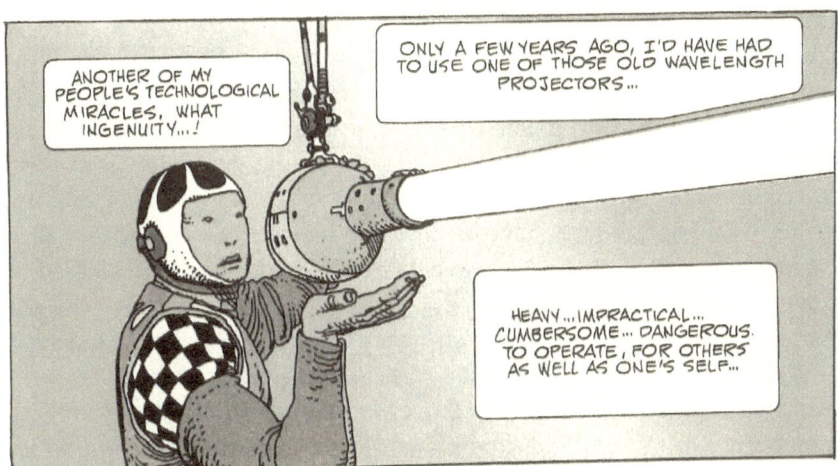

the final detail to his idiosyncratic persona, halfway between adventurer and country doctor. He keeps hold of it throughout most of the book, until the moment when he hands it over to Graad, the gatekeeper of the first level. When Graad opens it for the first time, a "fourteen-faceted crystal" comes out of it (3:26). It is this crystal, when attached to the cable box, that enables them to make the crossing.

It is useful to recall that between 1978 and 1985 (corresponding to the period of the creation of *Garage*) Mœbius had joined an "Iso-Zen" sect led by Jean-Paul Appel Guéry.[24] Throughout his work during this time, two symbolic motifs proliferated: on the one hand, the crystal and on the other, the star.[25]

After reviewing the "foundations" of the narrative edifice, that is to say the elements introduced in the first episode, and after noting how they are indeed a source of subsequent developments, we will now describe the ways in which the story evolves and feeds off itself up to the point where Mœbius decides to bring it to an end.

I think that we can distinguish three essential dimensions that work together as the driving force of narrative invention. *Garage* is a play upon the conventions of the adventure serial, a metanarrative, and a "coded diary," to quote Mœbius from his foreword.

To put it another way, *Garage* was able to renew its momentum and proliferate for three years by seeking to secure its own perpetuation, by interrogating and thematizing its own workings, and finally by enabling Mœbius to hold a dialogue with himself.

It could be said that these three dimensions comprise a *poetics*, in the sense defined by Umberto Eco: "the organizing rule that the artist proposes; the work that is to be completed in the way that the artist, explicitly or implicitly, conceives it."[26] On this basis, *Garage* grew like "a novel that invents itself," to borrow an expression from Alain Robbe-Grillet.[27] And, to append a third quotation, we could also say that we derive from the book a pleasure that exactly corresponds to aesthetic pleasure as defined by Hegel, which depends exclusively on the "way in which imagination presents itself, and the way in which it presents only itself."

The term "serial" defines, in the first instance, a mode of production. The serial writers of the nineteenth century, often accused of spinning their material out, were embroidering within a predetermined structure. For Mœbius, there is no guiding thread; there is instead the desire to create surprises, to surprise himself, and to keep his narrative options open in order to allow for every possible twist and turn and every sudden new direction, and there is also the need for urgency and speed to spur him on. "From one month to the next, I sometimes forgot what I had drawn in the episode I'd sent the previous month. Other times, I would only remember the deadline at the last minute and I'd send off two pages that I'd improvised in one night. It was wonderful!"

The serial corresponds, secondly, to a mode of publication. *Garage* enabled Mœbius to maintain a continuous presence in the magazine. It was published in installments, in short sections, fitted in between more substantial pieces in the pages of *Métal hurlant*, rather like a secret notebook, and marginal to the other commitments that had a claim on his time.

In this respect, it is useful to look closely at the parallel production of Giraud/Mœbius, in order to see whether the successive episodes of *Garage* constituted, in one way or another (by transposing, opposing, compensating for or exceeding it) a kind of response to what he was drawing at the same period, month after month—or to what he was not drawing. For example, the first years of working for *Métal* correspond to a five-year break in *Blueberry* (between *Angel Face* in 1975 and *Broken Nose* in 1980[28]); in fact, it is clear that elements from the Western have turned up in *Garage*. There is Samuel Mohad's cowboy hat (1:14), the typical Blueberry swearword "Damned!" (1:17), a small railway station that resembles the one in Durango in *Angel Face* (1:18), settings that seem borrowed from the Mexican desert, and, above all, the pages where Lark Dalxtrey seems to land in the middle of the Wild West (from 3:11).

The album constantly reminds us of the conditions of its own production in the form of separate episodes that appeared in a magazine. Its original serial format is emphasized by the frequency of reiterations of the title, and of synopses and signatures, even if the conventions of the serial are sometimes derided, as on the page where the obligatory "story so far" is matched by a predictive "story to come" (1:26). Moreover, most of the synopses are parodic. To take a few examples: "Anything can still happen in the airtight garage" (1:9); "Our story so far: No story so far today!" (1:23); "L.C.'s garage is airtight" (2:15); "It is written (Luke 12:2) that there is nothing covered that shall not be revealed, neither hid that shall not be known" (3:9); "you ain't seen nothing yet!" (3:11); not to mention the caption box that contains only the words "Our story so far" (2:13). Other instances conform reasonably well to what might be expected of a straightforward synopsis. Certain examples offer a lyrical or ironic paraphrase of the situation. But one of them completely overrides the function of the synopsis and explains how *Garage* came into being: it was with the help of "thirteen expansion generators, using the Gruber effect" that the Major, like an alchemist turning base metals into gold, had "transformed an insignificant asteroid [...] into a vast and complex world" (2:17). *The Airtight Garage* has not, then, been created *ex nihilo*; it is the result of the spectacular transformation of a pre-existing object. We will be given no further clues as to what the "expansion generators" might be.[29]

In addition to the synopses, another element that signals that we are reading a serial is the reappearance of the title on the first page of each new episode: "The Garage Hermetic of Lewis Carnelian" is repeated like a refrain, but in different lettering and sometimes spectacularly (see in particular pages 1:7, 2:7, 2:15, 3:21, 4:16). Page 2:21 is the most interesting in this respect: Barnier and the Archer are walking in front of a gigantic title that acts as a backdrop and seems to be sculpted in the rock. This is a device that rather obviously refers to the opening pages of the episodes of the famous *Spirit* by Will Eisner, a collection of which was published that same year, 1977 (Mœbius's page bears that date), by Les Humanoïdes associés.

The serial is, thirdly, a mode of narration. Mœbius only exceptionally makes use of the cliff-hanger at the end of an episode, although he sometimes does observe the convention that so many masters of classic comics have exploited before him. There is an example on 2:20 in the words of Lark, who has just been teleported: "What happened . . . ? Where am I . . . ?!"

In *Garage*, episodes more often break off at a point that is narratively insignificant. Occasionally, the final sentence serves as an action plan and points towards future developments. Right from the first episode, even though it was never intended to be continued, Mœbius took pleasure in parodying this narrative logic. The second page ends on these words from Barnier: "Everything has to be fixed before Lewis Carnelian gets back!" (1:6). The third episode ends on a question typical of the rhetorical devices of the serial: "Will the Major's spy fall into the trap that Lewis Carnelian will undoubtedly lay for him . . . ? You'll find out when you read Star Billiard . . . our next episode" (1:10). *Garage* is unique in that all the elements (titles, synopses, racking up of suspense at the ends of episodes) are integral parts of the page, and so punctuate the reading of the album, which gives it a certain ludic and parodic tonality.

By definition, the serial is an extravagant format that does not stint on décors, characters, or sudden reversals. The reader of *Garage* will not be disappointed. From the cosmos to the inside of a space ship, steppes with pseudo-Egyptian pyramids, deserts, oceans, a heavenly garden, a city with highly decorative architecture, and machine rooms, the action transports the characters from place to place, taking in a great variety of settings.

Mœbiusian inventiveness has free rein in another area: that of names. The vehicle that Carnelian drives around is called "Beetroot 2000," the characters are given the most unlikely names: Sper Gossi, Orne Batmagoo, Torpeniczel Chot, and so on. Mœbius even invents an incomprehensible language ("Drom stokeo stornilili . . ."), which is used first by the submarine crew, then by the cowboys (this is *Blueberry and the Aliens*), and later in a text in a caption box attributable to a narrator (3:18) and by the Major himself (3:23), as if by contamination.

Some proper names are easy to decipher: for example, the place called "feuille de Rizla" (Rizla paper)[30] can only be a reference to a famous brand of cigarette papers; others are private jokes. When the Archer turns out to be called Yetchem (3:17), only a few readers are likely to have noticed that this is the name of one of the contributors to the fanzine *STP*, which appeared between 1977 and 1979.

For the Major's main enemy, Mœbius chose the name of a mythological being of Mesoamerican origin. In pre-Columbian cultures, the Nagual was supposed to maintain order in sacred spaces.

Grubert himself has a mythical dimension, but he seems to belong to the world of popular adventure serials. He comes from the same family as the Monk in *Ballad of the Salt Sea*. The reader may judge. According to the Archer,

> in fact, the only thing we know for certain is that he was born in 1958 A.D. in Western Alemania [*sic*]. [...] Then he was reported missing during the Vietnam War. He had accidentally stepped through a trans-time circle in Angkor and, curiously enough, had stepped out into the nineteenth century, where he was taken in by a Brahmin from Pondycherhi [*sic*]. There, he was initiated to the equivalent of a phase IV level and worked for thirteen years in the secret laboratories of spatial magic. [...] Soon ... he teamed up with another explorer by the name of Lewis Carnelian. While upon a routine flight at the edge of the nebula Hakbah of Saligaa, they discovered the wreck of the "Otra," the famous mythical ark and mother ship of the great ancient ones. [...] It was during their exploration that the Major discovered the secret of immortality! (2:22)

An itinerary that leaves Engineer Barnier, like the reader, in a state of incredulity.

As well as describing *Garage* as an adventure serial, I have also called it a "metanarrative." We will consider this now.

It is entirely clear that Mœbius projected himself into the character of Grubert, who is nothing more than the diegetic embodiment of his own creative power, his fictional double. He confirms this interpretation himself in the preface to the new edition that came out in 1988, which ends with this sentence: "Expanding universes make it possible to imagine anything we like—for example, that all the stories I have written belong to the world of Grubert, or to a world that is governed according to the same principles, the universe of Mœbius."

As a demiurge constantly in orbit, the Major occupies, from his space ship the Ciguri, the symbolic position of the author who looks down upon and controls his work. *Garage* could, then, be read as a variation on the theme, frequent in fantasy literature, of characters who rebel against their creator and try to free themselves.

This serial seems to come to an abrupt end, as the hero escapes through the back door. This conclusion is, however, significant in a number of ways. By exchanging his helmet for an ordinary trilby, Grubert becomes anonymous again. He seems to enter our reality just at the moment when readers are invited to distance themselves from the fictional world they had projected themselves into. The Major ends up on a platform in the Paris metro, a perfect metaphor for the network, the intersection of narrative threads, a setting that seems to invite the reader to go back and browse through the album in all directions, alert to every *connection*. And, finally, the closure of the book is ensured, and signaled, by the name of the station: Opéra, the very word for *works* in Latin.

There are multiple references to comics. The most obvious is the fact that *Garage* includes so many comics genres. It is of course a work of science fiction (explicitly labeled as such on 2:17), but it contains pages in a style that is cartoony and almost "big-foot" (1:17–18, with a parodic reference to *Arzach*, in the form of the featherless white bird that shits on the Major's head); a Western sequence referred to above; a transformation of Grubert and Cornelian into superheroes (beginning on 3:27) during their confrontation, which takes on the aspect of a Manichean struggle between a black angel and a white angel (4:11); and, finally, a return to reality, to the everyday, to the urban setting that he had used in his memorable *White Nightmare* (1974).[31] And we should not forget that the character of Orne Batmagoo is dressed as a musketeer (3:21).

There is also the president of the city of Armjouth who employs "image capturers" who send him pictures in real time of everything that happens in the city, pictures that are then placed in a horizontal row, like comics panels (3:16).

Without attempting to provide an exhaustive list of every detail that has a reflexive dimension (like the Mickey Mouse head that decorates Grubert's helmet on 3:22), we will mention some dialogue extracts that seem to offer a commentary on the story that we are reading. The Major confesses, "What I love about the airtight garage is the infinite variety of passages between the levels" (1:23). And the fiancée of Mohad the spy exclaims, on looking out of the train window, "This whole area is remarkable ... except for the usual details, the impression of reality is striking!" (1:20), a judgment that seems to apply to the large image on the previous page, toward which her head is turned.

Garage is, ultimately, as its author has admitted, a "coded diary." Grubert, as we have said, is dressed in an explorer's outfit during part of the story. And the territory that he is exploring is not a hostile jungle or an impenetrable forest but, all at once, the space of his dreams, the extent of his powers, the potential of drawing and the unconscious of the author. What differentiates Mœbius from Giraud is precisely the fact that the former "works hand in hand with his unconscious."[32] Of course, lacking access to Mœbius's unconscious, the reader does not possess all the keys necessary to decode *Garage* in this light.

Perhaps it is also a way of exploring the map of its author's erotic desires, since, as we know, exploration is a metaphor for the sexual act.[33] The traveler is a thief, a seducer, and a voyeur in his soul. *Garage* is full of sexual innuendo, like the "seesaw hose," which we are told is an "essential component" (1:10), or the animal of some kind represented in an oval picture (2:25); and let us not forget Malvina, the Major's fiancée, who is a nymphomaniac—"great Malvina, deluxe sexual sorceress" (2:20)—who has the power to teleport a man with a single kiss. One of the most thrilling images in the book is the one, already mentioned, in which Engineer Barnier, gripped by the Archer's powerful arm, loses his (as the reader has assumed) helmet, revealing a woman's head of hair (4:6). Rarely have we seen a more unexpected and spectacular metamorphosis than that of the "little electron manipulator transformed into a nymph," in Thierry Smolderen's apt formula.[34] Even if we tell ourselves with hindsight that the rather anachronistic fur coat that Barnier had been wearing right from the beginning offered a clue to the character's femininity, it was a clue that we failed to read. Curiously, the Archer's mouth also becomes strangely feminine at that moment, and it seems as if we are leaving these two characters at the moment when their embrace is about to be sealed by a lesbian kiss.

Smolderen has devoted a discussion to the "autobiographical data" that permeate and inform *Garage*, and I refer the reader to it.[35] He describes certain characters as "thinking machines," that Mœbius created, he claims, "to represent some theoretical model drawn from his reading[36] or to reflect whatever he was meditating on at the time."

Smolderen is adamant, moreover, that "The intrinsic force of an image or a sequence is the more powerful for being an expression of psychic depth and intensity." This observation alone is not sufficient to explain the versatility, the plasticity of Mœbius's style. *Garage* offers a complete catalogue of all the ways in which this style is manifested. "There is not one Mœbius but several Mœbiuses, different each time," warned the master in *The Story of My Double*. "They possess the same infinite variety of emotions and sensations as life itself."[37] When he began *Garage*, Mœbius had only just emerged from the shadow of Giraud. For *Arzach*, which immediately preceded it, he had opted for a very controlled technique and a homogenous style.

With *Garage* he really explores for the first time all the graphic resources that Mœbius's universe offers him; it is clear, with hindsight, that the book has a programmatic dimension: it contains within it, in embryo, all those that were to follow it. As an example, we can look more closely at one tiny panel, the seventh, on 1:13. This robot (Star Billiard) sitting motionless in the desert in a meditation posture is none other than the central character of *40 Days dans le désert B*, which Mœbius would draw twenty years later.

The modulations of the graphic line and the vagabond pen flow naturally from an approach to creation that is both ludic and musical. The spreading of the work over a long period enables each sequence to take on the rhythm, color and orchestration that best suit it. *Garage* lends itself particularly well to this treatment, because of its division into short, almost autonomous sequences, differentiated as much in spirit as in style.

The feminine transformation of Barnier and the Archer

Star Billiard meditating in the desert

Mœbius was, then, one of the first to reject one of the main dogmas of classic comics, the maintenance of a homogenous style throughout the narrative. He even disregards the supreme rule, which demands that the characters should at the very least go on looking the same. In this book, for the duration of one scene a cartoony Grubert appears, transformed into his own caricature (1:17–18); his later metamorphosis into superhero renders him unrecognizable (4:11); he changes appearance again to escape into the metro, in a business suit (4:29); and a fifth version of the character is wearing evening attire in 1:15.

The layout is sometimes dense to the point of excess, sometimes open and airy; there is intermittent use of mechanical cross-hatching; the image is by turns pared down in the form of a rapid sketch (Mœbius's "musical scratches," as Pierre Sterckx nicely put it) and, conversely, minutely descriptive—or "grandiose and even pretentious."[38]

This graphic inconsistency had great impact on early readers of Mœbius, most notably young artists who were profoundly marked by it. Among them was the Italian Andrea Pazienza, whose meteoric career began in 1977 with his own *Garage, The Extraordinary Adventures of Penthotal*.[39] Later on, the hybridization of styles and sometimes techniques would become a major resource of modern comics. I will show later in this book how Mœbius's innovation was spectacularly re-appropriated by Dominique Goblet in *Pretending*

The motley inhabitants of the Garage

Is Lying. "The artist working in comics is more of an artist than anyone has ever been before in the history of art. Why? Because he or she has to draw entirely without a model and from memory. The drawing has to be rich, living, meaningful, and with all the complexity of reality."[40]

This "ideal" drawing that Mœbius refers to shines through in his representation of the figures who populate *Garage*: a colorful, cosmopolitan crowd, originating from all over the universe. Humans, animals, hybrids, and robots mingle together, often exuberantly dressed.

The creator of *The Incal*[41] and *The Aedena Cycle* also explains, "Mœbius's method consists of using drawing to put himself into different states of perception. To plunge into what the surrealists called the 'waking dream' or the 'fixed explosive': a lucid dreaminess like a light trance. A Pythic state."[42]

Reaching this state of consciousness demanded some preparation. "In order to breathe, some part of me needs to listen to jazz, smoke marijuana, and read science fiction and surrealist writers."[43] The artist has never tried to hide this: weed has been a determining factor in the development of his personality—as it was for most American underground cartoonists. "I discovered weed the first time that I went to Mexico in 1955. It unlocked a lot of things in me and turned out to be a fantastic crutch for my perception."[44] When Mœbius writes in the foreword to *Major fatal* that, during the *Métal hurlant* period, "scripts poured out of the smoke," that has to be understood literally as cannabis smoke. And it was not only the scripts: smoking was the prerequisite for the "automatic drawing" that Mœbius claimed to practice. The day when he decided to break his habit, he invented "Le Désert B," a play on words on *désherber* (to weed; to cut out the weed).

The chances are that the consumption of marijuana goes some way to explaining the detachment toward his own creation that Mœbius affects

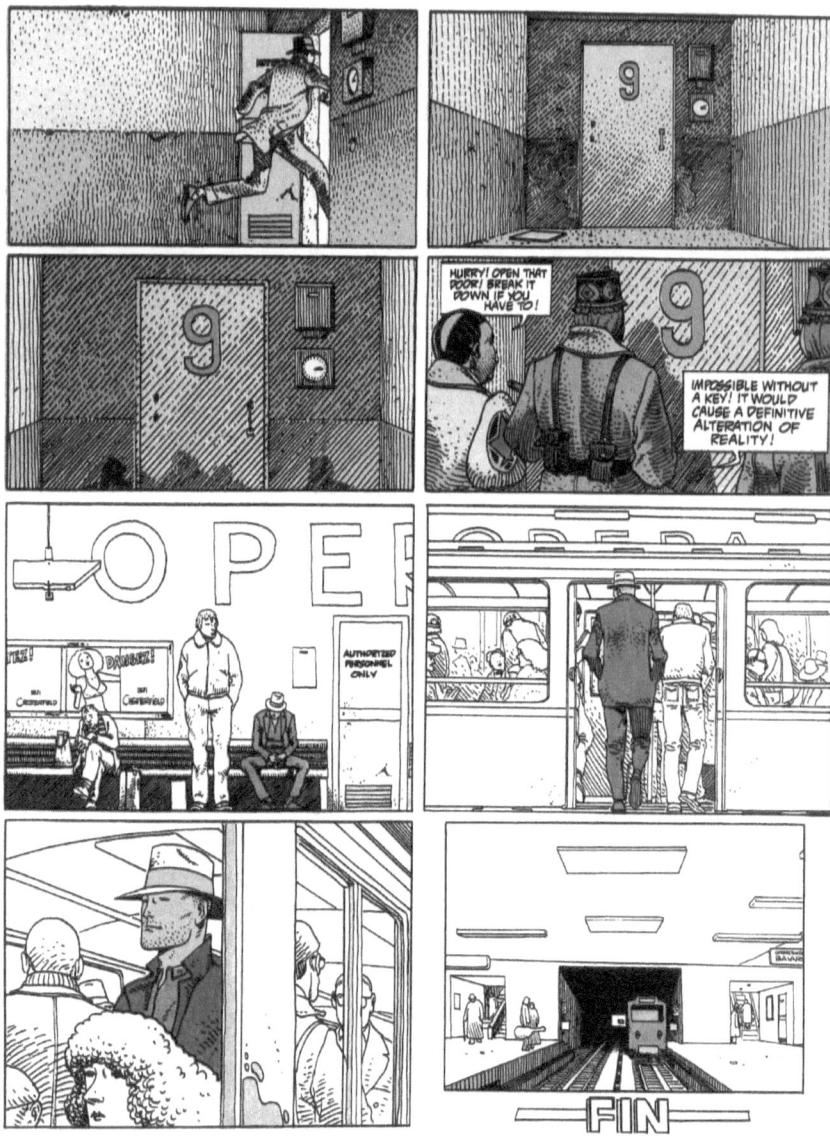

throughout *Garage*. This detachment takes the form of permanent irony. Some of the most impressive drawings are defused, as it were, by the witticisms that are interspersed through the text. The vocabulary employed does not shrink from heavyweight concepts and at times seems about to veer into metaphysics: destiny (4:7), world order (3:31), and alteration of reality (3:30) all crop up, but at the same time a voiceover can be heard. Just as the Master of the High Level is holding forth with explanations, it whispers, "it's all rather confusing"

(4:25). Elsewhere, Cornelius describes the garage as Grubert's "little private zoo" (4:16). And one of the most surprising moments occurs when Samuel Mohad and his partner make love inside the giant robot Star Billiard, which is their living space and their vehicle. A silent, rather comical panel shows the robot looking disconcerted and embarrassed at what has taken place (1:13). In fact, we learn forty-two pages further on that Mohad had stayed on board the Ciguri, and that the figure we had taken for him was only an "android duplicate" (3:7). This is retrospective irony: one robot was copulating inside another one.

I make no claim to have illuminated all the obscure recesses of *Garage*. For example, I do not know the meaning of the figures and numbers that punctuate the narrative, particularly salient among which are the series made up of six (the number of the room in 3:5), seven (on Grubert's helmet in 1:23), eight (the dragon curled over on itself at the entrance to Armjourth in 1:24), and nine (on the last door that Grubert goes through, before ending up in the metro, in 4:29).

But although one would need to be fairly bold to put forward an overall interpretation of this teeming, disconcerting adventure serial, I am tempted to shed some light on its deeper meaning by quoting this declaration from its author: "All of Mœbius's work aims to expose the acute neurosis that stems from my feeling of not belonging socially or even historically to the world in which I live."[45] The author of *Arzach* and *Airtight Garage* felt different at first because of his family circumstances (at school, he was the only child in his class to have divorced parents), and then, very soon, he felt singled out and isolated by his exceptional gift for drawing. By entering the field of comics, he made a choice that, in his view, further cut him off from the world, since "comics makes you marginal, like a poet or a child."[46]

Garage, which is the freest work he ever wrote, seems to me to be caught in this tension between the desire to assert himself completely as a poet and the desire not to cut himself off from reality, but instead to commit to it, just as Major Grubert does at the very end when he bids goodbye to the dream world and steps back into our world.

ALAN MOORE and DAVE GIBBONS
Watchmen (1987)

BACKGROUND

The British comics scriptwriter Alan Moore, who has been a dominant figure in English-language comics since the 1980s, was born in 1953 and achieved his first major success with *V for Vendetta*, a somber depiction of the near future, imbued with a climate of fascism. He turned more and more to the American comic book market, and became a contributor to DC Comics, for whom his first assignment was the series *Swamp Thing*, which he propelled to new heights of popularity. It was for the same publisher that he produced *Watchmen*, in association with his long-time collaborator, also British, Dave Gibbons (creator of *Harlem Heroes*, *Rogue Trooper*, and *Doctor Who*). The impetus for this original creation came from Dick Giordano, vice president of the company, who had suggested to Moore that he might revive a few characters from the defunct Charlton Press, whose rights he had bought up; the two men eventually decided to create new characters out of the old ones.

Watchmen began publication in 1986 as a miniseries of twelve comic books. John Higgins was the colorist. The work is made up of 338 pages,[1] not including forty-two pages of appendices. It was a huge critical and commercial success, and was the first comic book to receive the prestigious Hugo Award for science fiction. It won the award for best foreign album at Angoulême in 1989. A film adaptation, directed by Zack Snyder, came out twenty years later. In 2012, DC Comics published a prequel, in the form of a collection of stories entitled *Before Watchmen*, with the same protagonists—but without Alan Moore. Moore, after notching up a series of successes (*From Hell*, *The League of Extraordinary Gentlemen*, *Promethea*, and *Lost Girls*[2]), is still writing but is spending more and more time on the practice of magic. He is also part of a performance art group.

Watchmen has been through a number of French editions, mainly those published by Zenda,[3] Panini, and then, in 2012, Urban Comics, who made the wise decision to adopt the excellent translation produced for Zenda by thriller writer Jean-Patrick Manchette.

PLOT

It is 1985. A man is attacked in his apartment and thrown out of a window. He is a mercenary employed by the US Army under the nom de guerre "the Comedian." He was formerly one of a loosely knit group of masked crime fighters, the Watchmen, officially dissolved in 1977 after vigilante activity was prohibited by a new law. One of the Watchmen was a veritable superman, a quasi-divine being[4] known as "Dr. Manhattan." As a young physicist, Jon Osterman had been the victim of a laboratory accident that had turned him into a creature with almost unlimited powers, and blue skin. He too has been enlisted by the US authorities, an ultimate weapon who guarantees their invincibility.

The other former members of the group, a woman, Laurel (Laurie) Jane Juspeczyk (known as the "Silk Spectre"), and three men, Daniel Dreiberg (known as "Nite Owl"), Adrian Veidt ("Ozymandias"), and Walter Kovacs ("Rorschach"), are supposed to have renounced their activities as vigilantes and avengers. But Rorschach has never really given up and he is convinced that the murder of the Comedian marks the beginning of a campaign to pick them all off, one by one. He leads the investigation, recruiting Nite Owl and the Silk Spectre, who become close and have a romantic relationship as the story goes on.

Meanwhile, Dr. Manhattan, whose targeting by a cabal seems to accredit Rorschach's version of events, has chosen exile on Mars, and loses interest in all human affairs. Following his withdrawal, the Cold War intensifies, and seems bound to escalate into a nuclear war between American and the Soviet bloc. The entire plot of *Watchmen* is structured as a countdown that leads inexorably toward an apocalyptic outcome. In the twelfth and final chapter, a mass murder (in which three million New Yorkers lose their lives[5]) does indeed occur, but its cause is markedly different from the one that everyone had been led to expect. The combined efforts of the other Watchmen, and of Rorschach in particular, and the eleventh-hour return of Dr. Manhattan have not been able to prevent Ozymandias from carrying out his insane project: the simulation of an alien invasion (killing enough people for the threat to be taken seriously) so that humanity, on the verge of a fratricidal war, would bury its differences and reunite against a common pseudo-enemy.

WATCHMEN BECAME AN INSTANT CLASSIC AND A CULT BOOK. Few comic books have been so celebrated, analyzed or parodied. This chapter cannot of course cover every aspect of such a very rich work.

While most of the works in this book fall outside traditional genres or venture onto new terrain such as autobiography (e.g., those of David B., Goblet, and Bechdel) or a scientific imaginary (e.g., that of Harder), *Watchmen* fits squarely into the mythology of one of the great "native" genres of mainstream comics, superhero adventures, while at the same time questioning it and revisiting it so radically that for some time afterwards it almost seemed impossible for anyone to go on turning out the same kind of stories.

Critical literature has often emphasized the dark side of Alan Moore's story, its hyperrealism, its detachment, its extreme violence, and its unremitting grimness.[6] This tonality is not unrelated to the fascination that the work exerts, even if some readers find it morbid and are put off by it.[7] The unvarnished portrayal of "ultraviolence," to use Anthony Burgess's term from *A Clockwork Orange*—including, among other scenes, the interrogations carried out by Rorschach in the New York underworld (1:15–16), his retaliation to the prisoners who attack him in his cell at Sing Sing (8:14–17), and the way in which Veidt disposes of the man who has come to kill him in chapter 5 (5:14–16), not to mention the Comedian's behavior in Vietnam (2:14–15)—is one of the points that Moore has in common with Stanley Kubrick, for whom he professes the strongest admiration.

Watchmen was conceived during the presidency of Ronald Reagan. In Moore's view, America believed itself to be invulnerable, an attitude that led it to the worst excesses. He explains: "At the risk of doing a depressing comic book we thought that it would be nice to try and ... yeah, try and scare a little bit so that people would just stop and think about their country and their politics."[8]

Darkness and violence are merely superficial effects, however, and it seems essential to me to emphasize the extent to which Moore completely recasts the myth of the superhero.

A superhero is usually defined as a highly improbable character, a being whose existence can only be accepted on the basis of the conventions that underlie the reading of all fiction, that is to say "the voluntary suspension of disbelief," in Coleridge's term. Moore's reworking of the myth sets out, in various ways, to lend credibility to the figure of the superhero.

For one thing, there are six Watchmen, and only one of them has real superpowers: Dr. Manhattan (the explanatory backstory of the laboratory accident is a well-established classic of the genre). In the case of this vigilante squad, then, superpowers cease to be taken for granted and are shown as an exceptional, extraordinary phenomenon.[9] In order to make it clear that, with

ALAN MOORE and DAVE GIBBONS, *WATCHMEN* 51

The Comedian. (Here, and on following pages, we include the covers of the first French edition, for which Dave Gibbons had produced original artwork.)

one exception, his characters are merely mortal, Moore astutely chooses to open his story with the murder of one of the members of the group who, as a result, is portrayed only in multiple flashbacks. And, in the final chapter, Rorschach's refusal to compromise will cost him his life.

Secondly, Moore poses the question as to whether the escapades of these crime fighters are compatible with the law (following the traditions of the genre, each one has a nom de guerre, and so a double identity and a costume). Can a government tolerate the existence of these police auxiliaries with no legal status, a kind of semi-occult parallel militia, a law unto themselves? Of course not. And so the masked avengers are declared illegal in 1977, and required to cease their activities.

Moore then questions, with a perspicacity and a harshness that are unprecedented, the motivation of these men and women who have chosen to devote their lives to fighting crime, putting on a disguise to do so. One of them (Veidt) is a megalomaniac utopian, another (Rorschach) is a psychopath, another (Laurie) is carrying on a family tradition—she has succeeded her mother, inheriting her costume and the identity of the Silk Spectre—and the others each have their own story.

Fourthly, Moore wonders how the public would react to the exploits of the "superheroes." Can we assume that they would be seen as protectors, even saviors, and be greeted with adulation? Not at all: on the contrary, they inspire fear and dread just as much as, if not more than, the evildoers that they combat, as attested by the nagging question "Who watches the Watchmen?" borrowed from the Latin satirical author Juvenal.

Finally and above all, through the character of Dr. Manhattan, Moore demonstrates the effects that the very existence of a being with such wide-ranging powers would inevitably have on geopolitical equilibrium and on the course of history. In an article analyzing the defining features of the superhero, Harry Morgan and I wrote, "The powers of the superhero raise two questions: where do they come from (the question of origins) and to what use are they put (the question of objectives)."[10] Moore brings innovatory responses to this second question. The existence within its ranks of a character with almost unlimited powers has enabled America to win the Vietnam War (2:13.2). President Nixon has been re-elected several times by dint of a change in the Constitution (4:21.1) and the stifling of the Watergate scandal (9:20.4), and in spite of having had three heart operations (3:1.4). The country has reduced its dependence on oil given that Dr. Manhattan has, among other capacities, that of synthesizing lithium (4:15.5–6); and the list goes on.

Furthermore, while Dr. Manhattan is shown, like Superman, to have relationship issues, Moore focuses in particular on the emotional fragility of a character who is condemned to be the sole member of his species, and on how the resulting sense of his own difference will lead him to disassociate himself from humanity, once it has disappointed him.

Ultimately, it is no exaggeration to claim that *Watchmen* is the first comic to take seriously the logical implications of the existence of superheroes.

Over the last few years, Moore has been more and more critical about the direction that the genre has taken. In 2013, he declared:

> I hate superheroes. I think they're abominations. They don't mean what they used to mean. They were originally in the hands of writers who would actively expand the imagination of their nine- to 13-year-old audience. That was completely what they were meant to do and they were doing it excellently. These days, superhero comics think the audience is certainly not nine to 13, it's nothing to do with them. It's an audience largely of 30-, 40-, 50-, and 60-year-olds, usually men.[11]

And in 2014, he returned to the fray by proclaiming that, in his view, a passion for superheroes "seems to indicate a retreat from the admittedly overwhelming complexities of modern existence."[12] Of course, we can make the obvious objection that if there is one work that has done what was necessary to ensure that superhero comics should no longer be considered as children's literature, it is surely *Watchmen*.

Moore has definitively blurred the Manichean binary opposition between superheroes, traditionally the champions of good, and the supervillains whom it is their job to combat. Concealing the villain within the team designated as heroes is an inspired move, a brilliant dramatic twist.

Evil is inside the team.[13] Throughout the story, the Watchmen mistrust each other, keep each other under surveillance, and attempt to destroy or neutralize each other. Moreover, it should be emphasized that, although they have on occasions collaborated in the past, they have never operated explicitly or deliberately as an organized group. Their founding meeting, recounted in chapter 2, which was supposed to constitute them as an official team—on the model of a previous group, the Minutemen, that had been active between 1940 and 1949—ended in a fiasco (2:9–11). It is the public who give them the collective name of "Watchmen."

The six characters whose development we follow do nonetheless correspond, as Paul Gravett points out, to "archetypal superheroes: the near-omnipotent superman, the perfectly evolved man, the wondrous woman, the ordinary man gifted in science, the vengeful vigilante, the patriotic soldier."[14] The art of Moore lies in his ability to awaken all kinds of echoes in the reader who is a comics fan, while confounding expectations by exceeding or undermining genre stereotypes.

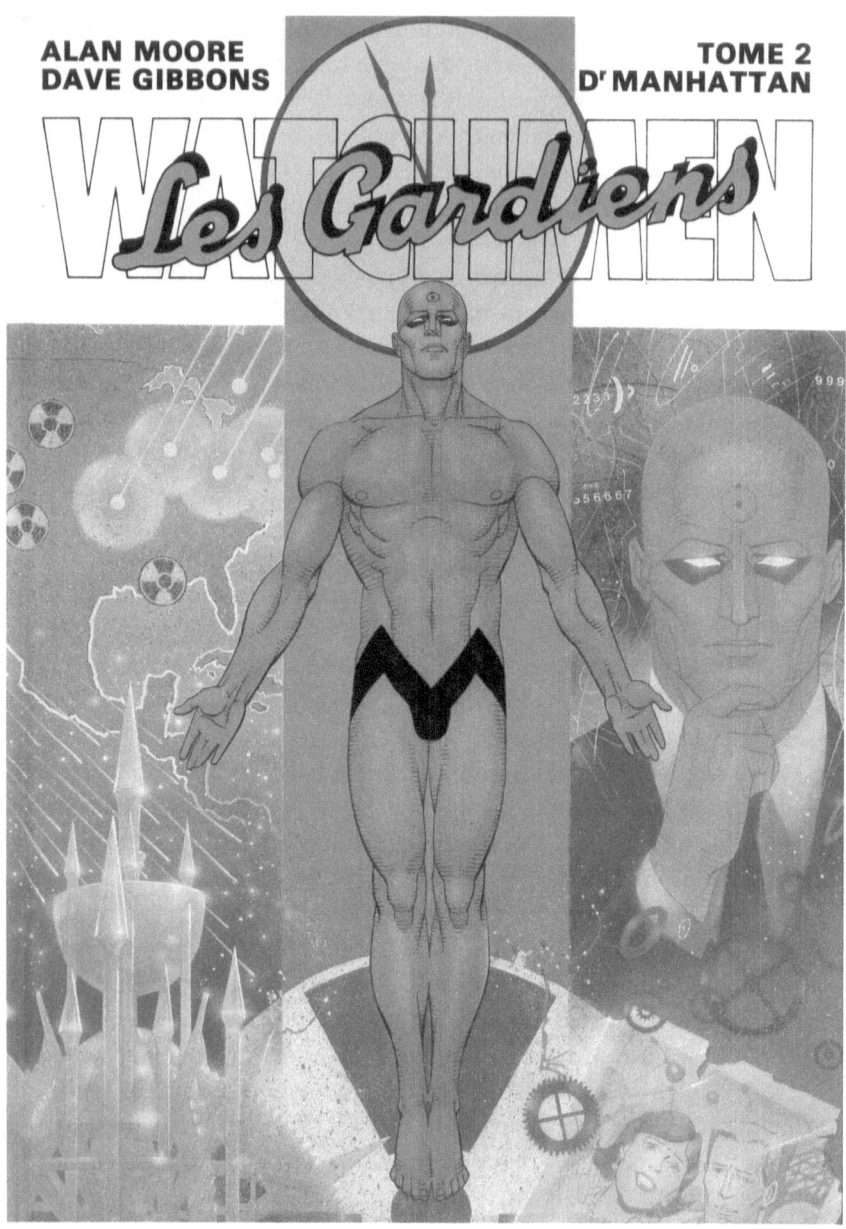

Dr. Manhattan

By inventing their own characters instead of taking over an existing series that had already passed through the hands of multiple authors, Moore and Gibbons freed themselves from a number of constraints. Notably the one that Moore considers as the worst, the fact that "in every story, nothing can ever have any long-term impact on the world, because it's the same world that's inhabited by all the other characters determined by the editorial policy of the publisher."[15] The Watchmen are distantly based on somewhat bland and obscure former Charlton Comics heroes, hybridized with other sources. For example, Rorschach is a synthesis of a masked detective called "the Question" and Steve Ditko's ultraliberal, Manichean and "objectivist"[16] character, "Mr. A." The Silk Spectre is the successor of "Nightshade" from the Charlton stable, but borrows rather more from the "Phantom Lady" from Quality Comics in the 1940s.[17] But the six Watchmen, freely reinvented by the authors, transcend their models. It is noteworthy that Moore opted for a different approach in *The League of Extraordinary Gentlemen*, when he brought together characters enshrined in popular literature, deeply embedded in the collective imagination.

The figure of the superhero is usually made up of a certain number of tensions or internal conflicts that have been pinpointed by Charles Hatfield: first, the contradiction between an often violently expressed individualism (the quest for power) and an altruism that turns violence to socially responsible ends by protecting the weak; second, the contradiction between being situated above the law (superheroes meting out their own justice) and a certain deference to the authorities; finally, a contradiction between self-effacement (Clark Kent) and flamboyance (Superman).[18] The author also notes that the exacerbation of masculinity is typically taken to extremes that verge on a parody of machismo. All these canonical elements of the genre are to be found in *Watchmen*.

The figure of Ozymandias/Veidt is perhaps, in its ambiguity and excess, the most striking incarnation so far of the tension between individualism and altruism. By building up an industrial and financial empire, by retreating from the world while playing at being a celebrity the better to disguise himself, by drawing up secret plans that require his collaborators to sacrifice their lives, and by subjecting the world to his will alone, this man, who believes himself to be the heir to Alexander the Great, chosen by the gods, and the master of the game, believes that, without any consultation with anyone else, he can resolve the problems of the world. "Given correct handling, **none** of the world's problems are **insurmountable**," he maintains at an early stage of the story (2:11.1). Is he mad or is he a genius? Both, probably. He is isolated by his intelligence just as Dr. Manhattan is by his omnipotence.

As regards their positioning in relation to the law and the authorities, the Watchmen tend, on the whole, toward insubordination. Dr. Manhattan and the Comedian serve under the star-spangled banner, the former most probably out of patriotism and the latter—who belongs to the family of modern mercenaries popularized by cinema, such as Mad Max, Dirty Harry and Rambo—because he is on the government payroll. But the episode of Dr. Manhattan's escape to Mars shows how fragile is the hold of the oath of allegiance that he has sworn. All the others are laws unto themselves. Veidt acts as if he is above the law (with his grand strategic maneuvers and his mystifications on a global scale), while Rorschach—like Nite Owl and the Silk Spectre, who tag along with him—is beneath it, carrying out an inquiry in the underworld, where even the police no longer dare set foot.

It is firstly through Rorschach that Moore renews the dialectic between self-effacement and flamboyance in a highly interesting way. The term "flamboyance" is literally appropriate in its designation of the flame-haired character. His costume is the antithesis of the usual superhero outfit: no cape, boots, or tights, just a grubby raincoat, a scarf, striped trousers, and a fedora. As an outline shape, Rorschach can pass unnoticed, whether on or off duty (he can be seen walking down the street incognito in the third panel of the very first page; I will come back to this). Although Will Eisner's Spirit went around in a business suit with only a domino mask to hide his face (an accessory that the Comedian would adopt in an even more minimalist version), Rorschach hides his entire face behind a mask made of a special fabric containing moving blots that shift around as he changes his expression, always in a strictly symmetrical pattern.[19] This mask is in fact revelatory, since we may venture to interpret it as a metaphor for his psychological instability. In combination with his swift and brutal operating methods, it turns the vigilante into a menacing figure. Without a face, without eyes, with a distorted voice (Laurie refers to "that horrible monotone **voice**" [1:23.2]), the nihilistic pariah that Rorschach has become has few remaining human qualities.[20] Less is more: the low-key costume has maximum effect.

The other character who illustrates this dialectic is—we inevitably return to him—Adrian Veidt, alias Ozymandias. Deception became second nature at an early age for this gifted child; as a school pupil he made sure to achieve only average grades so as not to arouse suspicion (11:8.2). Although his nom de guerre betrays his megalomania (Ozymandias is the Greek name for the Egyptian pharaoh, Ramses, the king of kings), the way in which he puts himself on permanent display all the better to conceal himself is remarkably skillful. Behind the supposedly retired vigilante, the circus acrobat turned businessman who markets (among other things) electric cars, diet plans, bodybuilding methods, perfume, and replicas of himself in the form of action figures—beneath his pretty-boy looks, his faded blond hair, and his kitschy violet and gold costume[21] (Rorschach calls him "pampered and decadent" in

1:19.2), no one suspects the preposterous scale of the project that he is hatching in his laboratory. While Bruce Wayne and Clark Kent are, respectively, disguises for Batman and Superman, here we are up against a far more elaborate and seductive deceit.

One of the greatest achievements of Dave Gibbons is to have made the duplicity of this Janus-faced character at least plausible, if not visible. Matthew Goode, the actor who plays Veidt in Zack Snyder's film, is far less convincing. But this is no doubt a matter of the ontological superiority of the medium of comics over cinema: the degree of abstraction of the drawings means that the characters, no longer made of flesh and blood, are more easily molded to adapt to the varying affective projections of the reader, as the story develops. Whereas the actor struggles to suppress a permanent simper that resists transformation into an expression of forcefulness and dominance.

As a final comment on the characteristics of the superhero highlighted by Hatfield, I would argue that in the case of Edward Blake, the Comedian, it is not sufficient to refer to machismo and the exacerbation of masculinity. Laurie Jupiter discovers that her mother had been raped by the young "Eddie." And another scene shows him as a cynical mercenary who cold-bloodedly shoots a young woman who is expecting his child, at the end of the Vietnam War.

But Moore also points to the intrinsic masculinity of the fantasy of omnipotence that underpins the mythology of the superhero. Out of the six Watchmen, only one has repudiated the escapades of the "masked avengers," denouncing them, with hindsight, as stupid, dangerous, and childish: it is significant that this should be none other than Laurie, the only woman in the group. What comes through from the words that she speaks in the first chapter, "I've spent [...] ten years running around in a stupid **costume**" (1:25.5), is a kind of female common sense, quite simply a grounding in reality that is lacking in her male "colleagues," who are ensnared by nostalgia for childhood games (Daniel) or a cynicism that is perhaps just another name for despair (Edward), or are blinded by faith in their own impunity and belief in their mission (Veidt, Rorschach). In the words of one of the supporting cast, the pathetic "Captain Metropolis," "**somebody** has to save the **world**" (2:11.7), don't they?

Having shown up the sphere of operations of the crime-fighters for what it is, a masquerade that is both grotesque and dangerous, Moore and Gibbons celebrate, as a counterpoint, the purely human values of love, spontaneity, trust and simplicity through the love affair between Daniel and Laurie. In chapter 3, Laurie leaves Dr. Manhattan after an argument. She finds solace with Daniel. In chapter 5, he invites her to come and stay in his apartment, on the basis that they are "**friends**" and "in the same line of **work**" (5:10.6).

She corrects him: "We're both **leftovers**" (5:10.7). It is Laurie who initiates the physical relationship, in chapter 7, to the music of *Unforgettable*, the song by Irving Gordon: "It's incredible that someone so unforgettable should think I am unforgettable too" (7:13.8–9). Together, they spring Rorschach from prison in Sing Sing. And so, not only does the love that blossoms, grows, and deepens between them have the power of transforming these two "leftovers" into "unforgettable" people, but it also reinvigorates the two retired vigilantes, who draw energy and efficiency from their newfound intimacy. In the twelfth and final chapter, Jon teleports himself and Laurie to Ozymandias's fortress in Antarctica. She is reunited with Dan there. And, leaving the two exceptional beings, Ozymandias and Dr. Manhattan, to their final showdown, the two lovers rediscover the vulnerability and the nobility of their human condition when they embrace each other: "I want you to love me because we're not dead" (12:22.4). An epilogue (12:28–30) portrays them leading the life of a normal couple, going by the names of Sam and Sandra Hollis.

Watchmen, without any doubt the greatest superhero story ever written, offers, then, a highly critical vision of the genre, its imagery, and its implied values. The work is also formally very distinct from the dominant aesthetic of comic books: no speed lines, no dynamic or chaotic page layouts, no onomatopoeia. Moreover, *Watchmen* is at the intersection of other genres: love story (we have just discussed this), crime mystery (it begins with Rorschach's determination to track down the Comedian's murderer), science-fiction epic (journey to Mars, scientific extrapolations, and not least the fact that the plot is set in a uchronic universe[22]), and political comic, which covers nuclear weapons, the danger inherent in the savior figure, and which above all poses, as we will see, the key political question of responsibility. A more precise description of the genre of *Watchmen* would be that it is a futuristic political thriller including superheroes.

The magnitude of the work is, obviously, one of its greatest assets. It began as a miniseries made up of twelve comic books, reissued as a very dense 380-page graphic novel. This was a format that gave the authors the freedom to treat their subject in depth and detail. The story takes its time, sometimes digresses, and fleshes the characters out, and each chapter is enriched by additional material (extracts from books, articles, reports, and correspondence) that, without being indispensable for understanding the work, enhances it by bringing in complementary perspectives.

In a work that demands a far greater investment from the reader than the majority of comics, the relationship to time, appropriately enough, is central.

As well as being watchmen, the Watchmen, are, just as literally, watch-men, just as the Minutemen were before them.

Rorschach

Dr. Manhattan has a very particular perception of time. Firstly, he can duplicate himself, and so live in several present moments at once—for example, he can make love to Laurie while continuing to work on his scientific experiments in the room next door (3:4–5). And he is, simultaneously, still in the past, in all the successive moments out of which his memory is woven, and already in the future, about which he is prescient. Chapter 4 follows the incessant temporal oscillation of his mind, as he recapitulates the course of his life in his quest to decide whether his memories link him closely enough to ordinary mortals to promote empathy with them, or whether he has become "totally indifferent" (3:28.1). This meditation takes place on Mars, "a place without clocks, without seasons, without hourglasses . . ." (4:26.2). This results in a very unusual narration, in the form of a temporal jigsaw puzzle, made up of jumps forward and backward and sudden elisions.

From the realist standpoint adopted by Moore, the superhuman nature of this "child of the cosmos," his capacity for exploring space, time, and the secrets of matter, is bound to result in ways of behaving and thinking that differ from those of mortals, and so have to be conjectured. Moore has tried to see the world through the eyes of a superman, and has tried to make us share this experience, which represents an unprecedented achievement in superhero literature, something that has perhaps been insufficiently emphasized.

Incidentally, we may note that Dr. Manhattan's nudity (a radical way of showing the costumes of the other superheroes for what they are: childish dress-up) is another bold stroke, even though it is unostentatious, and the color blue, which does not evoke flesh, attenuates the impact of the nakedness and diminishes realism.[23] The superman is drawn naked on his first appearance in the story (1:20–23), but Gibbons avoids showing his genitals. Subsequently, Dr. Manhattan is shown wearing a black suit or black underwear. Frontal nudity is on display from the third chapter onwards (3:20.4), once he makes a complete break, and frees himself from all the conventions that prevail among humans. (We should note that this coincidence is ambiguous. It is not Dr. Manhattan who retains a certain modesty while he is still living among humans, but the artist, who, perhaps hypocritically, makes sure that his nudity is not offensive.) He remains naked until the end, and most especially in chapter 12, which marks his return to Earth, a chapter in which he appears more godlike than ever—even if he has not been able to stop the large-scale massacre perpetrated by Ozymandias.

In *Watchmen*, historical time, as we have said, is divergent, having gone off at a tangent from the course of time familiar to us. As we will see, the plot allows for biographical time, that of life histories. And finally there is narrative time, which is itself double. The first scene bears the date October 12, 1985, while the attack on New York carried out by Ozymandias occurs on November 2, a month later. All the events that we follow along with the characters take place within this period. But this same stretch of time is also condensed: the device of the countdown signaled by the movement of the hands on the large clock face makes it symbolically equivalent to the last few minutes before midnight.

This reduction in time corresponds, moreover, to a reduction in diegetic space. The story may send us off to many different places, from the nuclear bunker of the American armed forces to Adrian Veidt's Antarctic retreat, taking in a bar in Arizona and the planet Mars on the way, but most of the action is situated around a New York intersection at Fortieth Street and Seventh Avenue near a cinema, a fast-food restaurant (Gunga Diner), an "Institute for Extraspatial Studies," and a cab company (Promethean Cab Co.). This is the crossroads where Rorschach habitually walks up and down, his trajectory always passing by the newsstand where, day after day, all the news is concentrated, recapitulated, and commented on.

The countdown figured on the cover of each episode as well as at the bottom of each final page by the inexorable progress of the minute hand on the clock face—not to mention the watches and wall clocks that proliferate through the story[24]—propels the plot forward and gives a sense of urgency to the characters' gradual elucidation of what lies in store. Even so, it is not until the end of chapter 10 that Rorschach and Nite Owl, after many twists and turns, understand that it is Veidt/Ozymandias who is their enemy.

This linear time, which structures the plot, is the exact opposite of the perception of Dr. Manhattan, for whom, as we have seen, past, present, and future are simultaneous, and this contrast reinforces his remoteness, his alienation from the events that are brewing.

The dramatic mechanism of the countdown to the apocalypse (the newspaper headlines are more and more alarmist about the immanence of a nuclear war between the Western and Soviet blocs) has its origin in the "Doomsday Clock" (quoted in 1:18.4) that, since June 1947, has appeared on the cover of every number of the *Bulletin of the Atomic Scientists*. The clock, drawn by Martyl Langsdorf, is metonymically reduced to the final quadrant, to the last fifteen minutes before midnight. The Science and Security Board of the magazine moves the minute hand forward or backward depending on the level of international tension and the risks of nuclear conflict.[25]

The layouts selected by Moore and Gibbons are also designed to reinforce the sense of the implacable march of time. Their basic template (from which they occasionally depart) is a nine-panel "waffle iron," in the term coined by the Belgian comics artist André Franquin to denote a regular layout. They claim that their decision was influenced by 1940s and 1950s EC Comics. In fact, as I have shown elsewhere, every drawn story has a basic rhythm, a beat,

Nite Owl

that is determined by the number and size of the panels: "When the layout is regular, so is the beat. The progression from one panel to the next is smoothed out in compliance with an immutable cadence. The 'waffle iron' is remarkably well suited to any narrative (or section of a narrative) that itself relies on the stability of some element, or in which a phased process unfolds. It is also ideal for materializing the inexorable flow of time."[26]

The other device that has a structuring effect is the alternation, usually quite marked, between the chapters that move the plot forward and those that linger over one of the characters, documenting in detail their past and their psychological makeup (for example, chapter 4 is devoted to Dr. Manhattan, 6 to Rorschach, and 11 to Ozymandias). Moore has explained how the greater depth in the treatment of characters grew out of exchanges with his collaborator.

> As we were fleshing out the characters in the course of our informal conversations and off-the-wall exchanges of ideas, we found ourselves being dragged into deeper and deeper water: it was no longer good enough to fill in the context of the life of a Rorschach or a Dr Manhattan, we also needed to think about their political views, their sexual orientation, their philosophy and all the factors that, in their world, had shaped those things.[27]

One of Alan Moore's outstanding attributes is the extent of his empathy for his characters. This is no doubt a quality shared by all writers of fiction, which generally leads—and *Watchmen* testifies to this—to a suspension of judgment. By revealing, in the form of flashbacks, the milestones of their personal biography, by offering each of them a big scene in which they make a confession or tell their own life story, by exploring the key relationships that have formed them (those of Rorschach and Laurie with their respective mothers, that of Jon with Janey Slater), and by allowing them to develop over the course of the comic itself, the scriptwriter gives us insights into the motivations of each of the Watchmen in turn, so that we understand and accept them. Even the fanatical Rorschach eventually finds favor with us once we understand what drives him, and his absolute intransigence then may actually be appealing. It is only the Comedian who seems to have no redeeming features. (He is even alleged to be the murderer of John F. Kennedy [9:20.5], whom Moore would manifestly have preferred to Nixon as "president for life.")

We cannot fail to notice that the chapters devoted to character portraits have the effect of slowing the plot down somewhat. Absorbing as they are, they nonetheless hold up the forward progress of the story, and so counteract the effect of the countdown. This suspension of the narrative plays its own part in maintaining suspense. By creating tension between the two structuring devices, Moore and Gibbons make the reading of *Watchmen* even more addictive.

On close inspection, the text of the work turns out to be pervaded by two repetitive motifs: symmetrical motifs and circular motifs (the circle being itself a symmetrical form).

Symmetry is explicitly thematized by the title of chapter 5, "Fearful Symmetry."[28] Its panels are indeed symmetrically arranged (in relation to their size and their positioning on the page) on either side of the double page that occurs in mid-chapter, which displays the enormous initial V for Veidt, divided in two by the centerfold—at the same time as an image reflected in water. There is in effect a spatial palindrome at the level of the chapter as a whole. Rorschach is also emblematic of the notion of symmetry, through his costume and the test that bears his name. But further recurrent motifs have a markedly symmetrical character: the Jolly Roger, commercial logos (like those of the fast food outlet Gunga Diner and the Pyramid Deliveries firm), butterfly wings, and so on.

The most resonant of these motifs is undoubtedly that of the couple: a man and a woman, face to face, in silhouette. Members of a street gang spray-paint them onto a door, and then onto a wall (5:11.5 and 5:11.9) at an angle to the comic's most prominent location, the intersection. This image recurs several times in the final chapters (see 11:9.6, 12:5, and 12:7.2–3); then the municipal cleaners paint over this piece of street art in 12:31.1. It takes on greater erotic connotations in certain of its occurrences, echoing the relationship between Daniel and Laurie; through the complementarity of the sexes, the authors take pleasure in emphasizing what it takes to make a human life. But this double silhouette, through derivation or contamination, also enters into a systematic series of echoes with other images: the silhouettes of Rorschach's mother and her lover (6:3.2–3), the symmetrical inkblots on one of the Rorschach test cards, and of course the evocation of a couple irradiated at Hiroshima.[29] It is Rorschach who first alludes to it: the silhouettes on the wall remind him of "the people disintegrated at **Hiroshima**, leaving only their indelible shadows" (6:16.6). In chapter 7, it is the very moment of this disintegration that is directly represented in Daniel's erotic dream (7:16.15–16). This vision is sufficiently haunting to be repeated, identically, on the following page.

In the context of *Watchmen*, the image of a body that has disintegrated immediately resonates with one of the most spectacular moments in the story, the disintegration of Jon Osterman in the test chamber (4:8.4), an accident that will bring Dr. Manhattan into being. And this unusually large image is also repeated when Ozymandias attempts the physical elimination of his only rival (12:14.4). More than 220 pages separate these two occurrences, but distance does not diminish the power of this remarkable visual rhyme.

Laurie

How should we interpret this insistence on symmetry? It seems to me that it has two meanings in this comic. Firstly, it refers to the sterile and anxiety-producing standoff between two opposing blocs, the East and the West, facing each other down during the Cold War. And then to a fertile and happy face-to-face encounter, that of man and woman, whose union produces life. Moore is also undoubtedly suggesting that the "solution" imagined by Veidt/Ozymandias is just as harmful and criminal as the "evil" that it seeks to combat. Symmetry is, then, what holds the balance between symbolic scales weighing not good and evil, but evil and evil. (This equivalence recurs elsewhere, moreover, at a lower level, between the methods of a Rorschach or a Comedian and those of the criminals.)

Let us move on to the circular motifs. As well as the clock and watch faces, the paradigm also includes the symbol for radioactivity, the hydrogen atom on Dr. Manhattan's forehead, the anatomical drawing inspired by Leonardo da Vinci (in the appendix to chapter 4), the concentric circles on the radar screens, the snow globe, the full moon, the portholes on "Archie"—Nite Owl's Owlship—and Nite Owl's goggles, the pumpkin, the Nostalgia perfume bottle, the watch cogs, the piece of machinery that Dr. Manhattan builds on Mars, the passageway that leads to Ozymandias's retreat, and the sphere before which he meditates in the final pages. However, out of all the circles encountered in *Watchmen*, the most salient is the "happy face" badge (or smiley, the most popular of all emoticons) that is an element of the Comedian's costume. To say that *Watchmen* is haunted by this badge would be an understatement: it is present on the first and last pages, and appears at regular intervals throughout the work, every time the fate of Edward Blake is evoked in flashback (1:11.3–4; 7:3.2), or whenever the authors give us access to the premises of *New Frontiersman* magazine, whose messenger boy, Seymour, invariably wears the same T-shirt decorated with the happy face symbol (7:12.1; 8:10.1–6). More surprisingly, it is also visible on the surface of Mars (9:27.1–2). Many readers must have thought the authors were being facetious, but the red planet does indeed have an officially attested crater—Galle, nicknamed the "happy face crater," whose rock formations configure an almost perfect smiley.

The importance given to this symbol demands interpretation. We can, in the first instance, note a certain analogy with the equally emblematic mask from *V for Vendetta*, a previous work by Moore, drawn by David Lloyd.[30] Behind this (similarly smiling) mask—called a Guy Fawkes mask because it bears the features of the English revolutionary who hatched the gunpowder plot in 1605—is the anarchist V, who is trying to overturn the fascist-leaning regime in Britain. In *Watchmen*, the badge is associated with a character who himself has fascist leanings, Blake. Although it is logical for a comedian to wear a mask (and I think a badge can be assimilated to a minimalist mask), and although Blake is disfigured by a scar that seems to stamp a kind of grin onto his face (Laurie: "And his scar . . . it always looked like he was sneering" [9:21.4]), the happy face symbolizes above all his "philosophy." For this cynic, the world is just a gigantic farce, which exempts him from any sense of responsibility.

On page 26 of the final chapter, the badge returns, associated with a reminiscence about a masochistic character ("Captain Carnage"), who liked to be beaten up.

On Mars, it appears just at the moment when Dr. Manhattan, at the end of his discussion with Laurie, changes his mind about the value of human life (9:27.1). And it is as if the planet itself were giving a broad smile of approval to this about-turn, which heralds the return to Earth of a potential savior, and which gives a positive resolution to a metaphysical debate that was on an unproductive track.

Cynicism, masochism, hope: the happy face symbol does not have a fixed meaning. It has, to use a term from psychology, a variable valence, sometimes positive and sometimes negative.

Its appearance in the opening panel should be read in conjunction with the text above the image. In this first extract from his journal, Rorschach says: "This city is afraid of me. I have seen its true face." This true face is, the badge suggests, one with a hypocritical smile, a false bonhomie that is rectified by the bloodstain, revealing its true violent nature.

As we have seen, the red smiley badge is only one of the manifestations of a more generic motif, the circle—which intrinsically possesses a number of connotations essential for understanding *Watchmen*. The circle can be seen firstly as a symbol of confinement, particularly within a system or form of inevitability: a single mind-set that literally goes around in circles. In this case, it concerns a war that seems unavoidable, since the leaders of the two blocs do not know how to escape from the deadly spiral that they have locked themselves into (even if only by building up a nuclear weapons arsenal). "War is a monstrous failure of imagination," wrote Kafka. Now, imagination is not something that Ozymandias lacks. Whether it is for good or evil, his solution for breaking the deadlock that humanity has arrived at is, as he himself says, an example of lateral thinking (11:10.2), a way out of the circle.

But, on the other hand, the figure of the circle suggests the failure of his initiative. For the circle symbolizes repetition, eternal recurrence, movement without beginning or end. The progress of the hands over a clock face is a case in point: when the two hands meet to indicate midnight—when the "apocalypse" happens—time does not stop. It continues, and the hands set off again, at the same rhythm, to complete another circuit. Ozymandias thinks he has definitively eliminated the risk of clashes between nations. Seeking the

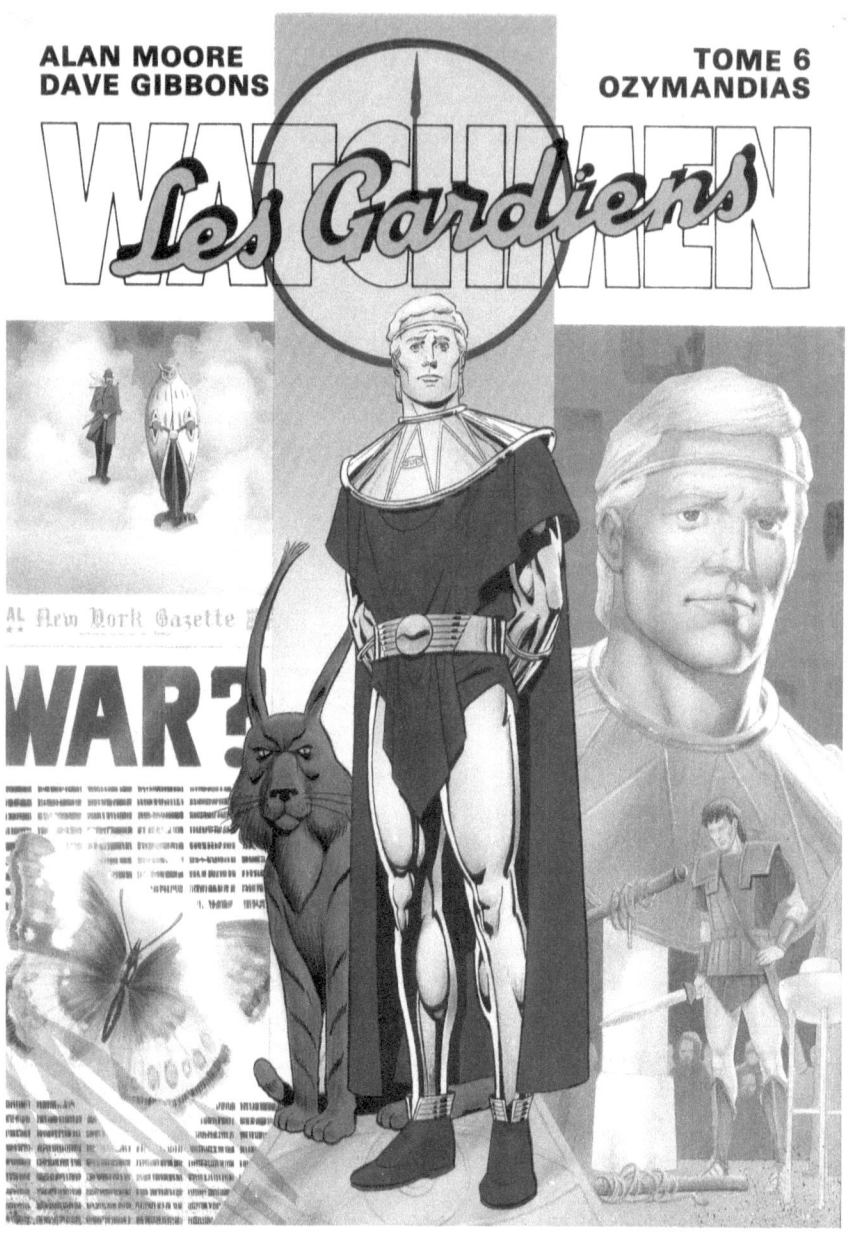

Ozymandias

approval of Jon, he asks: "I did the right thing, didn't I? It all worked out in the end" (12:27.4). And Dr. Manhattan rightly retorts: "**Nothing** ends, Adrian. Nothing **ever** ends" (12:27.5). The final panel of the work suggests new developments that will not go in the direction that Adrian, the sorcerer's apprentice, had hoped.

The circle makes manifest, by its very form, the idea of a story that is circular, looping back on itself. And *Watchmen* has several loop effects, both at the level of the opening chapter (whose final page corresponds to its opening page) and at that of the whole book. The happy face badge appears in the first panel of the first page as well as in the last panel of the final chapter, this time as a motif printed on Seymour's T-shirt. In the first case, it is stained by a spatter of blood, that of the Comedian, and in the second case it is spattered by ketchup. Each stain is shaped like a hand on a clock face.

However, the conspicuous repetition of the motif from the badge acts here mainly as a signal that invites the reader to notice a more discreet rhyme or loop, which applies to a different element. I am thinking of course of Rorschach's journal, whose first words coincide with the opening of the story, and which reappears in the final panel, no longer in the form of a text but as a physical object: the book in which Rorschach has been writing throughout his investigation.

Other extracts from the journal are made available to us at regular intervals (1:14, 1:16, 1:19, 1:24, 2:25–28, 3:6, 3:11, 3:18, etc.). Fearing for his life, Rorschach brings his journal to an end on November 1, 1985. We see him (10:22.6) posting it, and we see it arrive, two pages later, in the office of the *New Frontiersman*, the far-right magazine of which he is a faithful reader. Seymour reads the first few words of it, which correspond to the opening panel of *Watchmen*. So the two stories, that of Moore and Gibbons and that of Rorschach, almost coincide. They present two versions of the same events.

Rorschach anticipates the effects of the probable publication of his journal in the pages of the magazine, the global impact this will have, and the ensuing scandal. In the final lines, he writes: "If reading this now, whether I am alive or dead, you will know truth: whatever precise nature of this conspiracy, Adrian Veidt responsible" (10:22.5). The final panel, which shows Seymour's hand about to pick the journal up, invites the reader to anticipate in turn, and to prolong the story beyond its apparent ending. Thanks to Rorschach, the "whistle blower"—the only character who refuses to remain silent once the crime has been committed and discovered (12:20.7–9 and 12:23.5)—the truth will out, the so-called "attack by beings from another world" (11:25.4) will be denounced as a mystification, and the hostility between nations that was temporarily halted will be unleashed again. Ozymandias will have lost, because *nothing ever ends*.

It is significant that the final chapter is the only one not to include an appendix. The appended document is a virtual one: we are led to suppose that it is Rorschach's journal.

Not content with addressing us via his journal, Rorschach traverses the third panel of the opening page of *Watchmen* in person and bare headed, but still incognito, because at this stage we are unfamiliar with his features and ignorant of his identity. Just as he will do on numerous subsequent occasions, he is walking up and down the streets carrying a placard that proclaims "The end is nigh." Rorschach is predicting the end of the world, but at the same time he is telling us that the end of the book is close to the beginning, that we should make the connection between the two extremities of the work.

The insistent recurrence of symmetry and the plethora of circular motifs are, as we have seen, far from being mere formal games. These braiding effects provide us with essential keys for arriving at a deeper understanding of the themes of Moore and Gibbons's story.

And on closer investigation, it becomes clear that one braiding effect (already double, since it concerns both the badge and the journal) can hide another, or be superimposed on it. The first page of *Watchmen* is structured by a "zoom out" (which has in fact begun on the cover of the episode), the field widening from one panel to the next as our viewing position becomes ever higher. An identical "camera movement" occurs on the last page of the first chapter (this is the first of the two loops back mentioned above). This repetition does not concern, on this occasion, an iconic motif or an object within the diegesis, but a dramatic device or rhetorical figure: proof that a braiding operation can apply as much to elements of enunciation as to elements of content.

If readers detect this other striking repetition, they can, again, work out its explanatory function: the zoom out makes visible the structure of the plot, which constantly expands its scope, since the narrative takes us gradually from the murder of one man to a mass murder, and from a New York crime scene to the fate of the entire planet.[31]

In an article about *The Cage*, Martin Vaughn-James's experimental visual novel, I wrote that braiding was, in that case, "the privileged vehicle of the narration," since the reader was invited to carry out "a very volatile kind of reading that, by shifting back and forth, will bring to light the greatest possible number of relationships among all the pages, and make them resonate."[32] Although less immediately perplexing, it is now clear that *Watchmen* is a book that invites the same degree of participation.[33]

Ultimately, the central theme of *Watchmen* (already addressed in *V for Vendetta*) is responsibility. The word appears, in a key position, on the final page, when his editor appeals to Seymour: "I'm asking you to take **responsibility** for once in your miserable life" (12:32.6). Matthew J. Pustz claims that "Moore criticizes Manhattan's withdrawal from human affairs as well as Ozymandias's direct involvement and Rorschach's absolutes."[34] But the truth is that Moore is not criticizing anything. He does not make judgments. Each of his characters believes that they are right, follows their inclinations, and acts according to their own rationale. The scriptwriter orchestrates this plurality of viewpoints, dramatizes them, and creates tension among them. If he has any message to deliver, it is this: no one can claim to be the sole holder of truth; human life has value, and the world, in spite of the evils that plague it—chief among which is endemic violence—is worth saving.

In chapter 4, Veidt declares, "Our scientists are limited only by their **imaginations**," and Dr. Manhattan adds, "And by their **consciences**, surely?" (4:21.5). Veidt certainly has more imagination than conscience (to say nothing of his megalomaniac delusions about being the heir of Alexander the Great and Ramses II). Manhattan thus corrects Veidt at two apposite points of the story. But, since he is no longer truly human, he cannot be a model for ordinary mortals. And he has, in any case, his own responsibility for what happens. The questions that he asks a little further on—"Which of us is responsible? Who makes the world?" (4:27.2–3)—can only be answered in one way: we make the world, all of us, citizens of Planet Earth, and we share responsibility for it. *Watchmen* shows how changes in the global situation result from an intermeshing of decisions taken by multiple agents.

The image that symbolically sums up the exercise of responsibility, the making of a decision with no possibility of going back on it, is that of the finger that presses a button. Ozymandias's finger is shown to us twice, in close-up, exerting its fateful pressure (11:5.5 and 12:14.2). President Nixon is also shown sitting next to the nuclear weapon control panel (10:3). And chapter 7 had already introduced the symbol of the fatal button, in the mode of semi-parodic foreshadowing (7:2.6 and 7:27.12).

To the density of the network of visual references woven by the braiding effects there corresponds a similar density at the level of the text. Jean-Patrick Manchette, the French translator, praised the "shimmering language that makes Alan Moore a great writer." In his view, "the literary accomplishment of *Watchmen* is rare, even in literature."[35] Narrative voiceover, first-person narration, stream of consciousness, prolepses, and analepses—Moore uses all kinds of literary techniques, too many to set out in detail here. As from the fourth, the chapter titles are taken from quotations inserted at the end of each episode. These include texts by William Blake, Nietzsche, Shelley, the poet Eleanor Farjeon, Einstein, Jung, Bob Dylan, John Cale, and the book of Job.[36]

Several critics have likened *Watchmen* to the work of Philip K. Dick, since both have in common the rewriting of the history of America and the world in the postwar and Cold War periods.

Beyond this immersion in literature, the "shimmering language" very often involves a play on the double meaning of phrases and inscriptions. The sign "We fix 'em" (1:9.8) informs us about the activity of a garage, but applies simultaneously to the superheroes who have been "put out to grass" (1:9.5), but who will soon be back in service. The warning given by the army intelligence agent Forbes, " . . . and try not to get in any tight corners," is addressed to Dr. Manhattan, who has just arrived in a television studio, but also applies to Daniel and Laurie, who have headed down a dark side street where they are about to be attacked (3:11.4). When Dan and Laurie begin to embrace on a sofa for the first time, the television rebroadcasts an acrobatics display by Ozymandias in a charity fundraiser. Veidt says, "I haven't done this in a while" (7:14.4), words that could equally well be spoken by Daniel, who had ceased to have any sexual life. There are manifold other examples.

The richness and the artistic achievement of *Watchmen* arise out of the extraordinary precision of the relationships woven at every stage between text and image. There is nothing in the drawings that is incidental; everything signifies. In the texts, every word has been weighed and selected. Moore and Gibbons work in perfect harmony, offering a dazzling demonstration of the particular capacity of "talking" comics—that is, the possibilities opened up by the collaboration between two modes of expression.

In a scene that undoubtedly has metanarrative intent, the scriptwriter and artist show another couple about to make love: the writer Max Shea and the painter Hira Manish. Unfortunately, the nuptials between writing and the visual arts come to an abrupt end when an explosion kills both lovers (10:18). It is, in its very definition, the art of comics itself that is put to death. The explosion was programmed by Veidt. We told you he was the bad guy.

DAVID B.
Epileptic (1996–2003)

BACKGROUND

Pierre-François Beauchard, known as David B., was born in Nîmes on February 9, 1959. He attended Georges Pichard's classes at the École Duperré, in the Applied Arts section. The first album bearing his name was published by Glénat in 1985: he wrote the script for *No Samba for Captain Thunder* for Olivier Legan.[1] He subsequently produced an album for Bayard Presse for which he was both artist and scriptwriter: *The Accursed Stamp*.[2] He worked mostly for children's magazines, while producing one-off stories for *Chic* and *(À Suivre)*.

He was one of the co-founders of L'Association in 1990. He became one of the most assiduous contributors to their journal *Lapin* (scripting the whole of volume 10), while at the same time publishing *The Yellow Dwarf* and *The Four Wise Men* with another small press, Cornélius.[3] His album *The Pale Horse*, in which he transposed his nightmares into comics format, made a major impact in 1992.[4] Four years later, the first volume of *Epileptic* continued in this autobiographical vein. The chronicle of David B.'s childhood and adolescence extended over six volumes, ending in 2003, and was acknowledged as a pinnacle of achievement in comics autobiography. The fourth volume was awarded the prize for best script at the Angoulême festival in 2000. A collected edition in a single album appeared in 2011, six years after the English version published by Pantheon.

Since then, David B. has been a prolific comics author with a highly varied, mainly fictional, output (*The Square Tengû*, *Reading the Ruins*, *Along the Dark Paths*, and *Incidents in the Night*).[5] As a scriptwriter he has collaborated, most notably, with Christophe Blain, Emmanuel Guibert, Pauline Martin, and Hughes Micol. He is also, with Jean-Pierre Filiu, the author of a three-volume documentary in comics format: *Best of Enemies: A History of US and Middle East Relations*.[6]

PLOT

The six albums that make up the original edition of *Epileptic* are of unequal length and amount to 361 pages in all. The French title alludes to "le haut mal" (literally "the high malady"), a name once given to epilepsy, a neurological illness that afflicts Pierre-François's older brother Jean-Christophe. The two boys have a younger sister, Florence. The family lives in Orleans. Jean-Christophe's first epileptic seizure occurs in 1964. It inaugurates the "endless round of doctors" (1:10/10) who attempt to treat the boy. Doctors, neurologists, surgeons, psychiatrists, anti-psychiatrists, acupuncturists, homeopaths and faith healers take it in turns to study his case, without being able to solve it. The childhood of the future David B. is punctuated by his brother's frequent and spectacular seizures, which occur without warning, and by the multiple expedients to which his parents have recourse in their search for a cure. Bewildered, credulous, and drawn toward esotericism, the family experiments with macrobiotic Zen, spiritualism, clairvoyance, and alchemy; consults mediums, lamas, and magnetic healers; goes on a pilgrimage to Lourdes; and calls in an exorcist, all in vain. Except for a few brief periods of remission, these extravagant remedies have no effect: Jean-Christophe becomes more and more cut off by his illness, and less and less able to lead a normal life.

Epileptic recounts what it was like to grow up in a family whose attention was focused on this sick brother toward whom David B. had ambivalent and wavering feelings. In addition to this family chronicle, whose cathartic dimension is obvious, the author provides a fascinating account of the genesis of his own powerfully oneiric artistic imagination. David B. demonstrates a rare capacity for representing the invisible and the unsayable in the language of images.

ON THE COVER OF THE FIRST VOLUME, the two boys are drawn side by side, from the front, gazing out at us. This kind of direct address, confronting the reader, is a common device in comics. Gotlib, in particular, was fond of using it: Gai-Luron, Professor Burp, the ladybug, and Gotlib himself, as actorialized narrator (a narrator who is also a character within the story world) all "look us in the eye."

In the case of David B., the device evokes a family photograph that might have been taken by the parents: "Boys, come and stand side by side for the photo." But it is also part of a series that progressively evolves. In fact, on the covers of the following five volumes, the same composition is repeated: the two boys continue to face us, their arms dangling, with Pierre-François on the left of the picture and Jean-Christophe on the right. The variations in their

The covers of the French edition in six episodes. © David B. & L'Association. Courtesy of Matthias Rozes.

clothing (shirt, pullover, and T-shirt) are hardly noticeable, neutralized by their uniform yellow color.

This repetition materializes the passing of time: the boys grow (they wear glasses from the second volume). And while Pierre-François gradually becomes a teenager and then an adult, metamorphosing into David B., Jean-Christophe keeps the same dazed expression, the same blank look, until volume 6, when his weight gain and the many scars resulting from his falls bring about a spectacular physical transformation.

By drawing himself next to his brother,[7] David B. affirms his family relationship, his fraternal solidarity, at the same time as showing, by recording the progression of the illness, a difference that becomes accentuated, an irremediable separation between them.

At the same time, the background changes. The parade of frequently disturbing fantastical figures that runs across the entire cover (back, front, and flaps) grows ever larger. Drawn as silhouettes, the figures form a solid mass, invasive and threatening, until, from volume 4, they spread over the whole

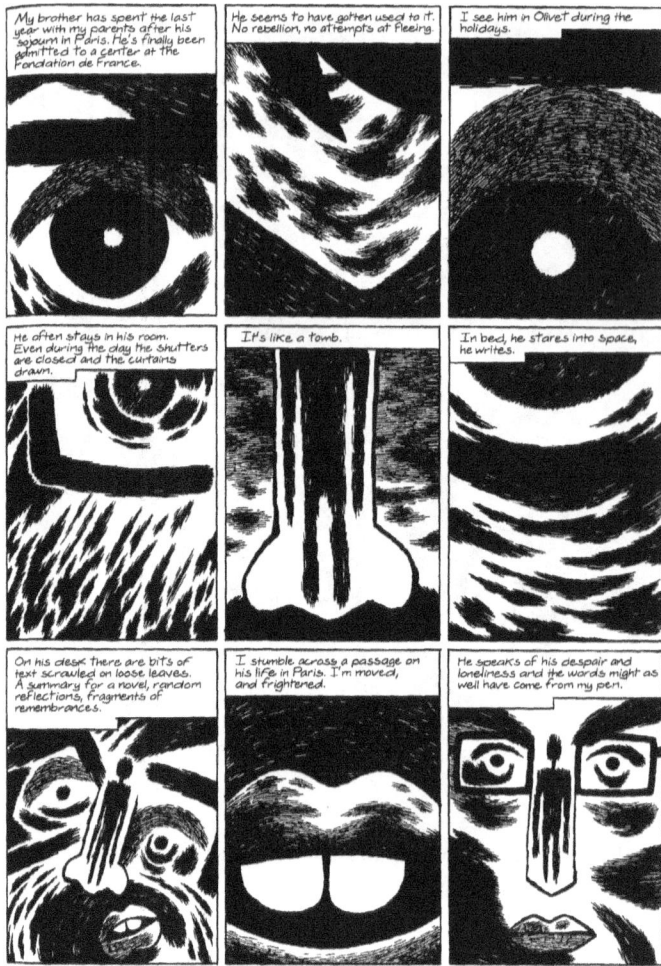

Epileptic, 316

height of the cover and then gradually become transformed into a flat black surface. They are a materialization and condensation of David B.'s imaginary, which continuously expands and grows richer. Out of this monumental design emerge the monsters that haunt him—Genghis Khan, various skeletons, a doctor, and birdmen, to name but a few—and in among them is his grandfather.

The division into six volumes was not planned in advance: "I had promised three volumes [...] without having done a detailed breakdown. I quickly realized that there was more subject matter than I had envisaged at the start. It's the kind of project that feeds on itself."[8] It is, then, possible that the six covers were also conceived of as the project went along, even if the author had certainly established the general principle from the outset. When we look at them now, they form a sequence that emphasizes the coherence of the whole and resumes, in a sense, a narrative whose structure is chronological overall.

But the front-view portrait is by no means confined to the covers. It is a major element of David B.'s visual rhetoric. There are a few early and striking examples in the first volume: the sudden appearance of Jean-Christophe on page 1, the father represented as a figure of authority at the top of page 3, Pierre-François in tears on page 6 and emerging from a dream on page 16, and Jean-Christophe as Hitler on page 20. Among the examples scattered throughout the remainder of the work, particularly noteworthy is the couple identified as "The B.s" (3:51/162).

All these faces turned toward us give an impression of forcefulness: they seem to interpellate us, and we scrutinize them in return, as if to wrench some truth from their muteness, beyond whatever words they pronounce. In no other work of David B.'s is such insistent attention given to faces. And, above all, to the face of Jean-Christophe, the brother who is so distant and so close, a face David B. unceasingly interrogates in search of a response or an explanation.

Is it because there is no justification to be found for such intolerable suffering that, in the final volume of his chronicle, the artist takes hold of his brother's face and deconstructs it, aggresses against it and makes it the central motif of some of his most arresting compositions? I am thinking of three pages in particular. On page 6:41/316, Jean-Christophe's despair is expressed through a fragmented face, the face of a zombie, in which an empty eye socket and rabbit's teeth are prominent. On page 6:67/342 a dream is transcribed in which David sees his brother's face become deformed, as if struck by invisible blows. Nine panels trace this progressive deterioration, this descent into chaos, until the head takes on the appearance of a cabbage. And on page 6:85/360, Jean-Christophe no longer has his own features. Instead, "all the faces in the world" stamp themselves on the empty head of a dead man.

When, one day in 1994, after a fairly long separation, David B. rediscovers his brother with a body that has become monstrous, "enormously bloated from medication and lack of exercise," and a face that is puffy, toothless, and covered in scars, he feels profoundly shocked. This encounter is referred to twice. It forms the opening scene of the first volume ("It takes a moment for me to recognize the guy who just walked in") and it recurs on page 65 of the sixth and final volume (340). On the first occurrence, the author is sparing in his comments. David B. has placed the scene in this opening position because of its violence: a boy no longer recognizes his own brother. The reader is immediately pulled up short. The second occurrence, which closes the work by coming full circle, allows the author a final meditation on the nature of his feelings toward Jean-Christophe.

Epileptic, 266

Having arrived at the end of the cycle, the reader cannot fail to be aware that the author was torn for many years between the desire to save his brother, to protect him—sometimes against himself—and the desire to kill him (see for example 3:20/131 or 5:50/ 265). But *Epileptic* ends with words of reconciliation: "I've sought brotherly ties in every friendship I've ever struck up" (6:83/358); "Your drawings were beautiful" (6:84/359); "I figured that at some point / My face would be yours" (5:85–86/360–361).

In their childhood years, the relationship between the two boys was one of complicity. One thing in particular brought them close together, a common passion for drawing.[9] This runs in the family: "Both of our parents teach art" (1:11/11) (the father in a high school, the mother in a teachers' college). *Epileptic* reproduces a jointly created drawing: the cover of an album in which their sister Florence was "tortured on every page" (ibid.). But when, seven pages further on, David B. recounts that he and Jean-Christophe spent their time "drawing battle scenes" (1:18/18), it is he alone who is shown working on a gigantic sheet of paper where two opposing cavalry regiments are furiously skirmishing, and it soon becomes clear that the activity described initially as a shared one has in fact become the refuge and the means of escape of the healthy child: "It's my own form of epilepsy. I expend the rage that boils in me" (1:19/19). In a scene that is quite amusing, David B. recounts how, when he was given some tests to do in a psychopedagogical institute, he began by deviously drawing "something stupid, the kind of image I'd never do on my own: a family on vacation" (1:36/36). But the mask quickly drops and he reverts to type: the second drawing is "an enormous massacre," which puzzles the psychologist (ibid.). The time will come later when the subject of choice of the young Pierre-François will be "samurai fight scenes" (2:7/58).

Epileptic, 279

The graphic production of the author during this initiatory period focuses obsessively and exclusively on violence, fight scenes, battles, and fantasy warriors. Of course, these are by no means absent from his later work. Whether it takes the form of a Western (in *Hiram Lowitt et Placido*, with Christophe Blain),[10] of a pirate tale (in *Captain Scarlet*, with Emmanuel Guibert),[11] of wars in the Middle East (in *Best of Enemies*), of the *Veiled Prophet*[12] that sows death, or of a metaphorical evocation of the butchery of trench warfare (in *Reading the Ruins*), David B.'s work abounds with images of savagery and death. *Epileptic* provides an insight into this fascination. Ever since a childhood in which he had had to "look horror in the face," the future artist was consumed with "rage." A rage that took hold of him, in particular, "when people told [him] that there was no explanation for this phenomenon, and that they could offer no simple or effective solution."[13] The word keeps returning like a leitmotif: "There is a rage inside me that I mitigate with my constant drawing. When my rage spills over, I take the saber my great-grandfather brought back from Indonesia and I go down into the woods. There I take a tree stump and chop it to bits" (3:22/133). It recurs in the final volume: "Actually I'm furious [enragé]! So there!" (6:4/279).

On more than one occasion, as *Epileptic* testifies, Pierre-François/David directs his rage back at his brother, and behaves aggressively toward him, deliberately provoking epileptic seizures (see for example 5:12–13/227–28, a scene that goes back on the promise made on page 1:37/37. He resents Jean-Christophe for not fighting harder against his illness, and he resents having had to take on, within his family, the role of "the one who doesn't cause any problems" (ibid.) or having always taken a back seat and sacrificed himself for a brother who, in the end, would "never get better" (6:5/280).

(The warrior fantasies that he expresses in his drawing are a manifestation of this rage, but they are also a product of a fragmented grasp of his family history. Half a dozen striking pages [1:22–27/22–27] are given over to his maternal grandfather's memories of World War I. The impact on the family of World War II and the Algerian War is also referred to. The author belongs to the first generation not to have been called up to fight: his own war takes place within the family home, wreaks emotional devastation, and spills over into his drawings.)

Indeed, this rage is given ever more forceful graphic expression as the work develops and David B.'s talent matures. There is a turning point in his writing at the beginning of the fifth volume (216). The line becomes thicker and more powerful and the artist departs from the simple binary opposition of black and white in order to introduce hatching and dry brush strokes. At the beginning of volume 6 (276), the line becomes thicker still. David B. now emphasizes the most intense moments of his story by using effects that increase the vigor of his drawing and impel it toward an expressionism that is not detectable in his subsequent output. The violence of the situations and the ferocity of the emotions are dramatically conveyed by images that grab the reader by the throat.

However, at the time, the inner tumult of the young Pierre-François was usually repressed. In front of his parents, he showed another face, permanently sarcastic and mocking (see in particular 3:45/156).

Furthermore, the future David B. takes refuge in his inner world, and invents fictive interlocutors. This world is constructed from his dreams and the books that he reads. Living in a family whose everyday life is already quite unconventional (they are not like the "normal people" who go to the supermarket: see 3:15/126), sharing his mother's fascination for Jewish culture, dragged along into the milieu of alternative medicine, sects of various kinds, esoteric speculation (the father predictably reads *Planète* [Planet], the famous magazine edited by Louis Pauwels and Jacques Bergier, whose slogan was "Nothing strange is alien to us!"), the boy perceives no watertight border between "reality" and the world of spirits, between the invisible and the imaginary. The garden and the woods become his kingdom, and nighttime is his sanctuary: "The 'normal' world could not help us, so we might as well turn to mysterious forces . . . I felt that the garden really was filled with their presence. Like all children, I made up characters and invented invisible friends for myself—as

Epileptic, 85

I couldn't have any other kind of friend—and I imagined them just as I later drew them."[14]

From an early age, he maintained, "I no longer fear ghosts, witches, vampires, devils" (1:16). Belief in the fantastical was a way of waging the "battle" with different weapons. It was a refusal to submit to the vicissitudes of a reality that had become oppressive.

More than an "invisible friend," Gabriel, the maternal grandfather, appears to have been the most influential guiding figure and protector. Pierre-François lost him at the age of eleven. His death is recounted in 2:21–24/72–75. The child thinks that the profile of his face, in death, looks like a bird.

From then on, the grandfather haunts the remainder of *Epileptic* in the allegorical form of a long-beaked black bird wearing a suit with a stiff collar. He is one of the "ghosts" who provide an escort for the boy, particularly on his nighttime escapades (2:33–34/84–85). Pierre-François's mother also tries to get back into contact with her late father by using a Ouija board, but the communication is blocked by "lower spirits": the grandfather disappears behind an army of grinning skeletons (3:37–38/148–49).

When Pierre-François discovers fantasy literature, and devours, in particular, the books in the "Marabout fantastique" collection (Meyrinck, Singer, Alfred Kubin, and the Belgian masters of literary fantasy, Jean Ray and Thomas Owen), he feels that only they can "make sense of the skewed reality in which [he] live[s]" (4:21/184); and the three characters from Jean Ray's *The Last Canterbury Tales*—a dead man, a magical cat, and the devil—are integrated into his select contingent of imaginary friends (4:22/185).

But the future David B. is above all an artist. His natural bent is to transform the fantastical into images. His ghosts all have at least a silhouette or precise shape, if not a body. "In the service of self-expression, I find drawing infinitely more rewarding than spiritualism" (3:42/153). Drawing is the vehicle that enables him to explore his fantasies, his fears, and his grief without risk, to lend them substance and a face, to exorcise them, and to become familiar with them. The characters that he draws are nothing more nor less than "guardian angels" (3:46/157).

The further the reader progresses through *Epileptic*, the more it becomes clear that its real subject matter is not quite what it had seemed to be. David B. is ultimately less concerned to reconstruct his family history than to recount how his experience of that history marked and shaped his artistic imagination.

It could also be said that *Epileptic* is the result of a kind of retroactive loop: what he went through in his childhood led David B. to take refuge in his graphic imagination; later, it was because he had cultivated this graphic imagination that he was able to convey his life experiences in a way that was formally original. And, in his case, it seems appropriate to describe this as a successful alchemical process: the suffering of the past has been converted into "gold," it has been sublimated into a major work, full of power and beauty. Time, experience, the acquisition of skills, and arrival at the belief that he had the right to represent his family and speak of his own suffering—these were stages he had to pass through in order for the alchemy to work. At the age of twenty, David B. already wanted to "tell the whole story" but he did not yet know "how to draw it" (6:15/290).

Several important phases of David B.'s development of self-assurance and autonomy are recounted. On page 38 of volume 3 (149), his decision is made: "I'm gonna be a cartoonist." Volume 4 opens (164) on the symbolic moment when, at the end of 1970, he decides to change his first name. (His adopted name, David, later takes on deeper significance for the young artist when he finds out about the persecution of Jews and the Holocaust [4:9/172].) On page 15 of the same album (178), the author tells us that he has begun to write down his dreams—a practice that, as we will see below, becomes the basis of his future work and permeates *Epileptic*. The final volume sees David B. move to Paris, where he takes classes in Applied Arts at the École Duperré and thereby escapes from his toxic nuclear family environment. And, while the artist does not linger over the early years of his career ("a sterile period"), he mentions, as a fulfillment of his artistic ambition, the creation of L'Association publishing house, which "saves" him (6:52/327).

Epileptic is chronologically ordered, although it includes some prolepses (references to events that will happen later) and analepses (accounts of events that had happened previously), which enable him to escape from the rather banal format of a strictly linear account. The point of the analepses is to delve further back into his family's past, as far as his grandparents and great-grandparents. As well as the evocation of his grandfather Gabriel's World War I experiences, there are pages devoted to the Indochina campaign in which Gabriel's father fought in the 1880s (2:37–38/88–89) prior to his return home and his marriage. David B. follows this thread of the family history through to Gabriel's wedding with Fernande, and then goes backwards in time to tell the story of Fernande's father, a clog maker. This digression into the past covers seven pages. The paternal grandfather is referred to in his turn in 4:6–8/169–171. He had belonged to an extreme right-wing movement between the wars.

Epileptic begins with a prolepsis. The opening sequence is set in 1994, two years before the publication of the first volume. But from page 2 on, the story gets properly under way with a starting point three decades earlier, when Pierre-François was five years old, and then the album takes us through his childhood.

Sometimes prolepses and analepses are combined: it is in a story that his mother tells him in 1996 that David learns the details of Gabriel's adventures in the trenches in 1914–1918 (1:21–28/21–28). The book in which he illustrates these events appeared barely four months after they had been recounted to him. We can deduce that this historical sequence had not been part of the original plan, but that its interpolation into the autobiographical narration was the result of the keen interest awakened in the author by these revelations.

Although it is the mother who is responsible for the retrospective account of World War I, it is, conversely, also the mother who somewhat brutally interrupts another seven-page analepsis in volume 2, insisting, "No, David, I don't want you to tell that story" (2:43/94). She is particularly apprehensive about the raising of a delicate subject: his great-grandmother's alcoholism: "The readers will think your brother's illness is in some way hereditary." David B. replies, "Epilepsy has nothing to do with heredity!" (ibid.) He has nonetheless, just like his sister Florence, long feared catching the illness, and is constantly watching out for early symptoms (4:1–2/164–165).

Having the minutest details of this family story revealed to the whole world has been very painful for David B.'s mother, who reacted angrily to these disclosures. The artist restricts himself to this single allusion to his mother's disapproval, and he does not dwell on it. He has, however, admitted that "there are things that I didn't recount because she had forbidden me to do so."[15] And—just like Dominique Goblet, Jean-Christophe Menu, or Fabrice Neaud—he has had to face up to the consequences of creating art from personal memories, and to accept that it has a "scandalous" aspect that has upset those close to him: after the publication of the third volume of *Epileptic*, he went for several years without seeing his parents, who broke off contact with him.[16]

Epileptic, 76

In other proleptic scenes, David B. comments on the past with his sister (3:49/160), or transcribes conversations with his mother (4:36–38/199–201 and 4:49/212). These are the only moments where he associates us with the work of investigation that he carried out with his family to reconstruct the past as accurately as possible, in order to check some detail or other. These insights into the creative process (which take up much less space than, for example, the conversations between Art Spiegelman and his father Vladek in *Maus*) are also the only instances that attest the distance that he has taken up in relation to the events reported in *Epileptic*. Within the story itself, this distancing is deliberately eliminated; as Catherine Mao has observed, "David B. undertakes to reimpose as far as possible the child's vision of events, and never to be judgmental."[17]

The narrative is punctuated by his brother's epileptic seizures. It is by definition difficult to render in static drawings the jerky, uncontrolled, violent movements that jolt the body of the unfortunate Jean-Christophe. David B. initially attempts to vary his portrayals: he emphasizes the change in the facial expression and the rolled-back eyes (1:8–9/8–9), then the whimpering, drooling, and hunching up of the arms (1:32/32), and then the loss of balance and falling (1:39/39). These different symptoms recur in different combinations. They gradually give way to the representation of a typical posture of a convulsed, disjointed, petrified body that serves as an emblem of the pathology.

Elsewhere, David B. gives form and shape to the enemy by introducing two visual metaphors: the black mountain with an inaccessible summit, and more importantly, the dragon, a demonic creature that incarnates the "High Malady." (This symbolism goes back to the Middle Ages, when representations of Apollo, the god of healing, could be found with a dragon or a griffin beside him as a symbol of illness.) Like Saint George or Saint Michael, Jean-Christophe is portrayed, sword in hand, triumphing over the vile creature: "He's cured" (1:51/51). This is, of course, only a short-lived remission. The

Epileptic, 140

dragon returns (2:20/71), attacks him, strikes him treacherously from behind, rolls on the ground with him, and twists him into knots (2:25/76). On the penultimate page of the second volume (110), the entire family rides the dragon, as if, by learning to live with the illness, they had tamed it. But the dragon looks stronger and more menacing than ever on the first page of the next volume (112). Henceforth, Jean-Christophe is almost always accompanied by his dragon. The day when he arrives at a center for people with disabilities in Brittany, the text reads, "They show him a locker where he can put his stuff" (3:29/140), but the only thing that he can be seen pushing into the bedside cabinet is the dragon, his intimate enemy. Not something that he possesses, but the creature that possesses him.

Later, the narrator affirms, "I can no longer distinguish my brother's illness as being separate from him. Epilepsy has merged with his body" (4:26/189). From that point on, the graphic representation of Jean-Christophe's body alters. It becomes less realist. Shadows devour his face. It seems as if the dragon, originally separate from him, has now become emotionally fused with its victim and is an integral part of him. Jean-Christophe himself turns into a kind of monster (5:38–39/253–54). In the last of the six volumes (the one in which the dragon has pride of place on the back cover), several consecutive pages (6:21–26/296–301) are characterized by an unusual compositional feature: the elongated, dislocated body of Jean-Christophe surrounds the whole page like a frame (or more precisely a hyperframe). On page 6:27/302, the dragon replaces him, taking its turn at serving as a frame.

The representation of chimerical or monstrous creatures has been a constant in art history. Monsters appeared in the earliest figurative art produced by humans. They swarm, like malevolent beings, through the medieval imaginary. Hieronymous Bosch owes his renown to them. In the comics field, the monster is usually to be found in genre stories: the *fantastique* and heroic fantasy. It is both unexpected and fascinating to encounter it at the heart of

Epileptic, 130

an autobiographical project, an account of personal life. The inclusion here of teratological imagery may be partly due to the fact that Jean-Christophe is himself perceived as a "freak," as Renaud Pasquier has noted.[18] But in certain sequences, monstrosity is projected onto the onlookers who gawk when a seizure occurs in a public setting (5:19–20/234–35) or sometimes onto David B. himself.

Just like the oft-repeated front-view portrait discussed above, the graphic transformation of a character into a giant is a recurrent device in David B.'s work. The first occurrence is on page 8 of the first volume, when an adult stands over the apprehensive Pierre-François. "Suddenly he appears! Looming over me! It's him!" The frightened child is no taller than the man's shoe. This disproportion translates his fear into visual terms. Seven pages further on, he is shown walking down the street surrounded by an army of figures who appear to be clones of the man who had intimidated him. He is, again, drawn to a smaller scale than they, as if to emphasize the tenor of the narrative text: "I may fear people, life, the future" (1:16/16). Jean-Christophe, on the other hand, develops an unhealthy fascination for Hitler and dreams that he is a "supreme leader," a dictator saluting "an eternal parade by an army that worships him," and David B. draws him as a giant to symbolize his power fantasy (1:20/20).

The simple and effective device of the matching of the size of a character with its dominant emotions is almost systematic. Another case in point, a little further on, is the head of the macrobiotic community in Artemare: he is seen in one panel sitting amid his flock, depicted as a giant because he is the leader; but in the next panel, where the text describes him as "a bit lost, surrounded by all these people who expect him to perform miracles," the relative sizes are inverted (2:2/53). What happens when another guru takes his place?

Epileptic, 253

He in turn appears as a giant staring down upon the members of his community, who all fit into his stockpot (2:6/57).

Beginning in volume 4 (164), Jean-Christophe is more and more frequently drawn as a giant (4:38–39/201–2, 4:48/211, 4:50/213). Gigantism is no longer, then, synonymous with power: the sick brother has quite simply become unreachable (like the black mountain peak that acts as a metaphor for his illness; henceforth Jean-Christophe is himself a mountain). His family fuss around him but their efforts are no more effective than a mosquito bite on a rhinoceros hide. In volume 5, the giant becomes angry (5:38–57/253–72). Now that he is oversized, it is all the more disturbing when he loses his temper. In a sense, he has indeed become a "dictator" who imposes his rule upon an entire family that is reduced to impotence. A striking image shows David dressed in a suit of armor charging the "dragon," his giant brother (5:55/270).

The image of the dragon can be related, moreover, to a whole series of other representations of animal forms. For example, the cat of Ray's *The Last Canterbury Tales* is not the only member of his species to appear. The character of Master N., a Japanese macrobiotic healer, is endowed with a face and tail that make him look like a tabby cat, as from his very first appearance in the book. "When I see him, he reminds me of a big cat" (1:44). His "replacement," a martial arts teacher, is also fitted out with a cat's head (3:5/116). Madame R., who has a macrobiotic shop in Paris where the family goes to shop, turns into a rat before our very eyes on account of her rapacity (2:15–16/66–67). I have already mentioned the bird-grandfather. In volume 5, the park becomes populated with a host of birdmen (5:17/232).

The dragon also takes its place within another series, this time relating to the symbolism of death, omnipresent in *Epileptic* and more generally throughout the work of the artist, who claims, "'That's my real subject.

Anxiety" (6:18/293). War and surgical operations both involve facing mortal danger. The dead are invoked in spiritualist séances. David B. harbors the secret hope that he will be able to "talk with Hell" (3:41/152). But his parents have, he finally concludes, only ever managed to speak to each other. All the family members, with skulls for heads, declare, in unison: "I hurt" (3:42/153). Then comes his younger sister Florence's suicide attempt (3:46/157). In a remarkable page in the final volume, just before symbolically cutting his neck open with a knife, David B. draws himself feeling the bones of his skull through his skin. "I'm trying to determine the shape of my skull. [. . .] I want those bones to pierce through the skin of my face, to break into daylight and for it to be over" (6:13/288). We can also refer to Jean-Christophe's "paranoid breakdown," in which he imagines seeing falling bodies and shouts out, "It's death! It's death!" (6:62–63/337–38). And, of course, there are the skeletons, who make regular guest appearances in David B.'s drawings and who are familiar, almost tame figures; yet, he seems shocked when he discovers, in a book about World War II, the terrible images of "pajama-clad skeletons" (4:9/172). The first panel of this page represents a single one of these: it floats like ectoplasm from a spiritualist photograph above the child reading his book, and one cannot help but be struck by the tense and convulsive posture that the artist attributes to it: it is identical to that of Jean-Christophe when he has a seizure—during each one of which he seems to die a little.

"Seeing him 'die' on a daily basis, you end up by feeling as if you've watched a lot of deaths, as if it were a massacre," David B. has explained. "The relentlessness of the illness makes it seem like willful destruction." This is why he formed a mental link between Jean-Christophe's illness and "the issue of genocide, the Holocaust."[19]

Concept images, which are not presented as the graphic transcription of a visible, tangible reality, but as the metaphorical, allegorical, or symbolic expression of psychic life (a feeling, a fear, or a nightmare), are not completely unprecedented in comics. We may recall most notably the hallucinations attributed to Arthur Même, the hero of Tardi and Forest's album *You Are There*,[20] from 1979: ants crawling over his body, waves of books threatening to submerge him—most of the drawings have an oneiric dimension.

In his symbolization of inner worlds, David B. explores a seam richer than that of his predecessors, but in using comics to depict elements of faith or occult knowledge, he is probably breaking completely new ground. This begins in the first volume with a page illustrating the doctrine of Yin and Yang, "two complementary but not opposed principles" (1:147/147). Further on, to explain alchemical lore, David B. has recourse to anthropomorphized laboratory retorts, animals, and books, rather than to the traditional symbols of ancient alchemy (4:44–47/207–10). In another passage devoted to Rosicrucianism, he

Epileptic, 203

uses its two major symbols, the rose (which represents the spiritual spark in mankind) and the cross, but these motifs undergo a series of metamorphoses over the next eight panels (the stem of the rose becomes a tree trunk, a column shaft, and so on) and he supplements them with all kinds of symbolic elements: Egyptian gods, knight in armor, owl, serpent, star of David, Book of Knowledge, and so forth. The artist produces syncretic images, from which there emanates a visual esotericism of his own, leading the reader astray through a dense forest where all the components of his imaginary mingle together (4:39–40/202–3). Similarly, the serpent, the owl, the cube, the swastika, the ladder, the book, and the skeleton are all deployed, along with other occult signs, in order to expound Rudolf Steiner's Anthroposophy (5:25–27/240–42).

This results in drawings that are impossible to paraphrase in words (what lies beyond "reality" also lies beyond language) and which exert a fascination upon the reader while also being quite intimidating: it seems clear that we are not in possession of all the keys that would allow us to interpret them, but it is by no means certain that all these rebuses can actually be decoded. Ultimately, the only referent of these graphic compositions is surely esotericism as such, the domain of "things hidden since the creation of the world."[21] This seems plausible, but, in an interview, David B. has explained that, in the above-mentioned sequences, the symbols were "not included innocently." And he added this enlightening detail: "They don't have an esoteric meaning, they have a meaning in relation to my family history."[22] A personal meaning, only superficially accessible to others who must rely on external appearances.

These compositions must also satisfy David B.'s criteria for visual appeal. "What interests me in symbols is their 'sign' aspect. In *Epileptic*, I try to draw in a way that resembles a sign."[23]

The prominence of concept images in David B.'s comics has exerted a direct influence over other artists who have also explored autobiographical subject matter: I am thinking in particular of Fabrice Neaud (*Journal*) and Xavier Mussat (*Flesh Color*).[24] It has been demonstrated how, on Neaud's pages, the drawing "seizes the virtual world of linguistic metaphor" and "foregrounds it" by literally illustrating it, but exceeds it by adding its own connotations. Sometimes the image from this virtual world "approaches the *fantastique*."[25]

David B.'s dreams are also the inspiration for several memorable sequences. The author recounts, in the opening volume of *Epileptic*, a dream that he had as a child while staying with his grandparents involving the Egyptian god of the dead, Anubis (this "apparition" of the god with the head of a dog, and more generally the fascination of the two brothers for Egyptian mythology, is perhaps the source of David B.'s attraction for creatures taking the form of animals). The young Pierre-François appears in the second and third panels. We see him first in bed, asleep, while the image of Anubis seems superimposed over him, illustrating the sentence "I was dreaming of Anubis, god of the dead" (1:16/16). But the exact nature of the following image is indeterminate: the young David is depicted both in his bedroom, raising his head from the pillow to sit up, and in a dream of which he now seems to be a protagonist, terrified by Anubis. This deliberate ambiguity returns in the fifth panel: although the child has woken up in the interim, Anubis is unexpectedly still there. And the image seems to be a reprise of the one in the third panel, which is doubly inverted from left to right and from black to white. If white symbolizes day and black night, this inversion is itself partly responsible for the boy's anxiety, and for that of the reader (who is interpellated by the child's gaze in the fourth panel): it materializes the blurring of the boundaries between the kingdoms of night and day, just like those between dream and reality.

Other dreams occur in the course of *Epileptic*—six in all. Dreams participate, albeit sparingly, in the narrative of remembrance as one of the components of subjective experience. David B. began to keep a record of some of his dreams when he was a teenager. The practice of systematically transcribing them into a series of dedicated notebooks began when he left the Applied Arts school in 1981. By following the instructions of specialized manuals, he trained himself to retain, on waking, an accurate memory of his dreams. A few of them, translated into the language of comics, furnished the subject matter of *The Pale Horse*. Dreams seem to have been his entry point into self-portrayal and personal disclosure. These dreams "can function like stories, little scripts, admittedly absurd, but with characters, a setting, a beginning, a middle, and an end. [. . .] I enjoy the exercise of translating that into comics format, because for me it is just that—an exercise."[26]

In the introduction to *The Pale Horse*, David B. wrote:

> At night, nightmares come galloping through our heads. [The nightmare] designates a nocturnal demon that takes on the appearance of an emaciated mare that weighs heavily upon the sleep of human beings. It is a representation of Death or the Devil from which we escape by mounting our own steed and setting off on a nocturnal flight that ends when we wake up. Every night, I struggle and I manage to escape death.

There is a dialectical correspondence between the white horse chosen as the emblem of this foundational book and the large black horse that features on the final page of *Epileptic*. This oneiric quality persists in the artist's later works: it is to be found, of course, in *Night Plots*,[27] a second collection of dreams, but it is also present in *Babel* (one chapter of which is called "Dreams")[28] and in fictional stories like *Urani*[29] or *Captain Scarlet*. *Incidents in the Night* is also based on a dream.

In a discussion of *Epileptic*, Laurent Gerbier has observed that the dreams that occur in it

> do not imply danger, fear, and a frantic escape bid, but have a much calmer tone; they essentially involve an encounter, an initiation in which the contact with the ghosts who appear in them is not frightening at all. The dream no longer means a nightmare: it is henceforth a means of contact through which are woven networks of symbols and echoes that inhabit the dreamer—that give him roots and a basis upon which he can feel at home in his world.[30]

David B.'s work is not only nourished by his memories: he also draws upon a wide literary culture. It is therefore hardly surprising that the motif of the book should be omnipresent in his work.

The first page of the sixth volume of *Epileptic* (276) shows the young artist in his student room in Paris, during the period when he was at the École Duperré. He draws himself literally sprawled on his stomach over his worktable, in a position that seems more suited to reading than to graphic creation. But that is precisely what the image suggests: the two activities amount to the same thing ("I stay in my room [...] inking in pages and devouring books"), or, at least, the substance from which David B. derives nourishment by "devouring" the books piled up higgledy-piggledy behind him is immediately reconstituted—I am tempted to say "spewed out"—onto the sheets that he feverishly covers with drawings (which, when he looks back at them, he admits he "can't make heads or tails of"). As if gripped by a power that exceeds it, David B.'s body seems to be the site of a process, a transmutation and a regurgitation.

The office of Raymond Abellio, as it is shown in volume 3 (3:23–27/134–38), is invaded by books, which take up all available space. For David's mother, who has written to him to request a meeting, Abellio represents, like Sartre and de Beauvoir, the incarnation of a mythical figure: the intellectual. As a result, these images seem more like the enactment of the myth (the intellectual surrounded by books) than like the portrayal of a real place.

This proliferation of printed paper leads on to the image of the sea of books, which occurs several times, most notably in the final sequence of *Epileptic*, perhaps as an echo of Tardi and Forest's *You Are There*.

I have already mentioned the prominence of the book (always drawn as thick, and open in the middle) among the symbols that unfailingly appear whenever David B. refers to grand esoteric theories (see for example the first, third, and fifth panels on page 5:25/240). For him, the book is obviously emblematic of the spiritual world and of knowledge and its transmission.

Epileptic, 276

In deliberate contrast with this sacralization of the written word, the artist takes a malevolent pleasure in including a scene that represents World War I soldiers shitting in books (1:25/25).

One of the few books actually cited by name is *Mein Kampf*, savored by Jean-Christophe (6:32–33/307–8). Beyond the fascination that the young man has with Hitler, much to the disapproval of his entire family, it is obvious that the words "My struggle" have a second meaning for someone who is battling every day against illness.

When asked about his influences in relation to comics, David B. cites first and foremost Hugo Pratt's *Corto Maltese*. He particularly likes the fact that Corto "is never really part of historical events. He's always on the margins."[31] This allusion to the margin may catch our attention, given that David B. has elsewhere spoken of his family in these terms:

> I realize that we were interested in anything that was marginal. Whether it was religion, where it was esotericism and heretics that interested us, or literature, where it was fantasy and science fiction that interested me. [. . .] In our tastes in whatever sphere, literary, cinematic, artistic, or theatrical, we were different from other people. When we went to Paris that's how it really was. I remember the films we went to see. Films that have never been rereleased and never shown on television. These were horrific things.[32]

And within this unconventional family, David B. was himself marginalized, as a result of the polarizing effect of his brother. Turning his experience into the raw material of an ambitious series of books must have represented a way of transforming his marginal position into a source of strength, as well as a way of coming back from the edge.

But Pratt's influence, acknowledged as equal to that of Tardi, operated primarily on the graphic level. David B. was impressed by the uncluttered line, the drawing that is a form of writing, and the balance between black and white. From *The Pale Horse* onward, he has made a virtue of simplicity. His drawing style eliminates unnecessary detail. He usually ignores perspective (the reader is sometimes reminded of a toy theatre made of paper cut-outs), which, as Ann Miller has noted, again recalls medieval imagery.[33] The creator of *Epileptic* seeks to extend into comics the lessons to be learned from all forms of early art, with its simplicity of design and optimal legibility—just like his lettering, which is exemplary in its regularity. His pen stroke, which seeks out the essence of his subject, combining a strong outline with a binary deployment of black and white, gives exactly the same consistency to ghosts and other products of the imagination as to real people. The drawings are less about bodies and more about silhouettes, diagrams, and symbols.

Epileptic, 232

As David B. learned to harness the uncompromising power of chiaroscuro, other models, such as, we imagine, the engravings of Vallotton or Masereel, may have loomed large. He does not allude to them, but he does make, within the work itself, a reference to Magritte's *Empire of Light* (5:17; 232). This picture that juxtaposes a blue sky and a house plunged into darkness is often cited as an example of the oneiric quality that pervades the work of the Belgian surrealist. It is understandable that David B. should have appreciated this canvas. In his own drawings, black and white and daylight and darkness are combined with no concern for realist coherence, but simply in order to enhance the visual impact and the legibility of the image, and to attempt to give expression to the inexplicable.

Epileptic is a work that is based upon a kind of reiteration—the seizures, the eternally disappointed hopes placed in one or another therapy, and the different refuges found by the author (in drawing, fiction, and the company of ghosts) reappear at regular intervals—but one whose interest never diminishes. Formally, it possesses clarity and coherence, the situations described are often striking, and, although it is rooted in lived experience, it is constantly open to departures from reality, leaving room for chimeras, fantasies, the imaginary, and the irrational. The strangeness of the events is thereby heightened. The reader is almost overwhelmed and, long after finishing *Epileptic*, continues to be haunted by it.

ALISON BECHDEL
Fun Home (2006)

BACKGROUND

Born on September 10, 1960, in Lock Haven, Pennsylvania, Alison Bechdel was a tomboy as a child and, unhappy with the stereotyped image of women in children's books, only drew men. It was in her first year at university that she discovered her homosexuality. The New York feminist journal *Womanews* began to publish her series *Dykes to Watch Out For* in 1983. It was syndicated in several dozen alternative newspapers and magazines, and has been collected together in some ten books since 1986 (mostly available from Firebrand Books). A leading light on the gay and lesbian comics scene, the author remained faithful to her group of characters until 2008.

In June 2006, Bechdel published her first graphic novel with Houghton Mifflin. The product of seven years' work, it is an autobiographical work called *Fun Home*. Starting the very next month, the French newspaper *Libération* serialized it over the summer. It was published in album form in France shortly afterwards, in the Denoël Graphic collection.

Fun Home achieved considerable critical and commercial success. In December 2006, it topped *Time* magazine's list of the best books of the year, across all categories. It was turned into a musical, which premiered at the Public Theatre of New York in September 2013.

In May 2012, Bechdel published *Are You My Mother? A Comic Drama*. While having a certain symmetry with *Fun Home*, this book does not have the same resonance, and is not, in my view, as convincing.[1] It concerns the relationship between Alison and her mother Helen (who is still alive), seen through the prism of sometimes intrusive psychoanalytic theories, in particular those of Donald Winnicott. More than the previous book, it probes the roots of the author's homosexuality: we are given to believe that it is because her mother stopped kissing her goodnight that Alison's sexuality was displaced onto her and onto women.

PLOT

Fun Home is a 236-page "family tragicomedy," an autobiographical narrative that goes back over a disturbing and defining period in the development of the author's identity. The Bechdel family lives in a neo-Gothic-style house, and the father runs a funeral home. Both parents are also English teachers, and the mother, in addition, is involved in a community theater, plays piano, and is writing a thesis. As well as Alison, they are bringing up two younger sons, Christian and John. It is a family whose members all have intense intellectual lives and cultivate their artistic talents.

In 1980, at the age of nineteen, Alison receives the news of the death of her father Bruce, in all probability a deliberate act. The tragedy occurs not long after she has discovered her homosexuality, which she has admitted to her parents. This sexual orientation ought to have brought her closer to her father, who, outside the bounds of his life as paterfamilias, was not averse to secretly seducing young men. The death of Bruce, at the age of forty-four, appears to be accidental, but he probably killed himself to avoid scandal. Two weeks earlier, his wife had asked for a divorce. In order to create this comic twenty years after the events, Bechdel delved back into her journals, which she had been keeping from the age of ten.

ALTHOUGH ALISON BECHDEL IS PRESENT IN HER BOOK AS NARRATOR and as character, it is her father, Bruce, who is the main protagonist of the book. The story revolves around the double enigma of his personality and his death. Like Dominique Goblet in *Pretending Is Lying* (a title that would not be inappropriate for the book by the American artist), Bechdel paints a rich, nuanced and fascinating portrait of her father. And, as in David B.'s *Epileptic*, alongside the manifest subject matter, another story unfolds, that of the awakening and affirmation of Alison's artistic vocation.

The first page is somewhat deceptive, in the sense that it appears to show a complicity and physical closeness between Bruce and his daughter, which, as we will discover, was in reality highly sporadic. We find out on page 19 that Alison does not know how to go about giving her father a kiss; we read, on page 68, that she is embarrassed by the very rare gestures of affection between her parents, and on page 67, that an "arctic climate" reigns in the family. And Bechdel conveys the isolation of the family members, each "absorbed in our separate pursuits," by using the windows of the house: seen from outside, each

The opening scene...

...corresponds to the closing scene

of them seems to enclose a separate cell, containing one of the protagonists (this device is used on pages 86 and 139).

The image of the young Alison balancing on her father's legs is nonetheless echoed in the final panel of the book, where she jumps from a diving board into his outstretched arms. These two images, which bookend the narrative, emphasize the centrality of the father/daughter theme. On the opening page, Bechdel refers to "the moment of perfect balance" as she hovered above him; the final page of the book declares, "he was there to catch me when I leapt."

Two of Bruce's other character traits are established right at the outset: his passion for literature, and his talent for interior decorating, as demonstrated by his refurbishing of the house (and also the yard, as we later discover).

I will come back to the question of literature, but while we are dwelling on the opening page, we can note a book on the floor next to Bruce, which

happens to be *Anna Karenina*. Most of the great works evoked throughout the book are commented on by the author. This one is an exception. Hillary Chute has made the perceptive suggestion that the reference to Tolstoy's masterpiece could perhaps be explained by its opening sentence: "All happy families are alike; each unhappy family is unhappy in its own way."[2]

A genuine domestic tyrant in that he imposes his taste on the whole family and forbids them to move the slightest object, Bruce Bechdel is a genius at salvaging and personally restoring junkshop finds, out of which he transforms his house into a stately home. His daughter refers to him as an "alchemist" (6), gifted with "remarkable legerdemain" (5), and sees in his restoration work his "greatest achievement" (4). She remarks, not without bitterness, that her father "treated his furniture like children, and his children like furniture" (14).

The reader who is not yet alerted to Bruce's sexual preferences could be inclined to interpret this particular talent as evidence of a personality whose feminine component is at the very least marked. But the reader may also wish to avoid giving into facile stereotyping. No, not all interior decorators are gay, any more than all male hairdressers. In this case, however, Bruce's talent is well and truly indicative of his sexual orientation, as the author herself will come to realize. Further on, it is with hindsight that she writes, "What kind of man but a sissy could possibly love flowers this ardently?" (90).

Other clues, whose significance will subsequently be revealed, are scattered in the early chapters. For example, Bruce is shown reading a work by the art historian Kenneth Clark on *The Nude*, the cover of which is adorned with a male torso (it is in fact Michelangelo's *David*, although Bechdel's drawing does not make that clear) (15). This is the first naked male body to appear in the book; the second is the corpse (44) that Bruce is preparing in the embalming room of the funeral home. Entering the room, Alison is shocked by "the strange pile of his genitals," but her father, accustomed to the nakedness of corpses, betrays no sign of discomfiture.

The recurring figures of deceased people (others, naked or dressed, can be seen on pages 49, 91, and 148) signal the theme of death that haunts the book, above and beyond that of the father, which represents its dramatic climax. *Fun Home* is a comic that unceasingly foregrounds the sexualized and mortal condition of its protagonists. The body takes on a much greater importance than usual in a medium where it is often reduced to a silhouette and a costume, and knows neither aging nor physiological needs.[3] Later in this book we will consider another album in which characters are powerfully embodied: Craig Thompson's *Habibi*.

Unlike the ageless heroes of traditional comics, Bechdel draws herself at different stages of her childhood and adolescence. As she evokes the key moments of her family life, she sometimes represents herself as a small girl (for

example, when she recounts the stories her grandmother used to tell her), sometimes as a preteen, sometimes as a teenager, and then as a college student. These different periods of her life are interspersed according to the needs of the narration and, as a result, her graphic appearance fluctuates. Similarly, Bruce is shown during his military service or in the early days of his marriage but, apart from the evocation of the episode in which, as a boy, he got his feet stuck in a newly ploughed field (40–41), his appearance is far more stable.

Fun Home is a Bildungsroman, and the author emphasizes in a number of ways the ambivalence of the child whose body is starting to become adult. On the day when she records her first period in her journal (168), she is wearing a Bugs Bunny tee shirt, which marks her out as a child. She also stresses how limited her understanding can be, for example when she attends a play by Oscar Wilde (*The Importance of Being Earnest*) without picking up the allusions to homosexuality (166). One of the major topics of the book is the length of time it takes before her own "deviant" sexual preferences succeed in reaching her conscious awareness.

In general, events are not recounted in the book in the order in which they occurred. "A chronological structure wouldn't have worked, because I found myself wanting to say many different things about the different events," the author has explained.[4] In order to say these "many different things" she revisits the same traumatic events several times, in particular the death of her father, relentlessly seeking to understand what caused it (suicide or accident) and to make sense of it. It is in this spiral, obsessional structure that the difference lies between this highly wrought book and the diaries in which the sequence of events had initially been recorded. For example, the truck that runs Bruce Bechdel over appears for the first time on page 28 and then returns on pages 59, 89, 116, and 232. Similarly, the image of the family members offering their condolences that we see on page 27 appears in a redrawn version on page 125.

As Jacques Dürrenmatt has noted, the purely factual journal that has been kept since childhood "serves as the basis for reflection."[5] Hillary Chute explores this idea and observes insightfully that *Fun Home* is not a book about "what happened" to Bechdel's father, but rather about "ideas about what happened to Bruce Bechdel." It is even a book about hermeneutics, in the sense that the author arrives at the ideas "through an intense engagement with archive material."[6]

The title of the comic fosters a deliberate ambiguity between "funeral home" and "house of entertainment." The subtitle, "a family tragicomic," underscores the mixtures of genres. Bechdel continues in this vein with her next book, *Are You My Mother?*, subtitled *A Comic Drama*—that is to say, both a drama in comics format and a drama that is comical.[7] Moreover, on page 58, she refers to "*comic* relief in my parents' *tragedy*."

Humor is not, it must be said, the most salient characteristic of these autobiographical works, which seem to me to be suffused with seriousness. This is because the atmosphere that pervades the Bechdel family household is heavy with secrets and silences. Because tragedy strikes it, presaged by a metaphorical storm (176). Because death stalks the book. Because the author depicts herself as suffering from an "obsessive-compulsive disorder" from the age of ten (135), prior to developing a "compulsive propensity to autobiography" (140). Indeed, *Fun Home* can hardly be described as a comedy, and Bechdel's insistent use of the term is a little surprising.

It is, furthermore, a demanding book, in more than one respect. On page 206, Bechdel complains about the excessive concern for detail of the professor who lectures on Joyce's *Ulysses*: "Once you grasped that *Ulysses* was based on *The Odyssey*, was it really necessary to enumerate every last point of correspondence?" In fact, that sentence—was she aware of this when she wrote it?—applies perfectly to her own narrative technique. The whole book testifies to a fierce determination to pursue her inquiry to the bitter end, to dig deep into her subject and leave no stone unturned. Bechdel transforms comics, usually considered as an intrinsically elliptical art, into a device for x-raying her thoughts and emotions. As Dürrenmatt writes, she "refuses to consciously fictionalize anything whatsoever," and "it is through the meticulousness and rigor of an account that spares no excruciating detail, that she succeeds in transcending the particular to reach a kind of universality."[8]

The literary qualities of the book place their own demands. These are evinced firstly by the sheer amount of text. Unlike *Pretending Is Lying* by Dominique Goblet—the album (also an autobiography) that will be the subject of the next chapter—*Fun Home* is borne along by a verbal narrating voice, with only rare and barely noticeable interruptions. Out of the first 100 pages of the book, I counted no more than twelve panels where this voice was

I HAVE SUGGESTED THAT MY FATHER KILLED HIMSELF, BUT IT'S JUST AS ACCURATE TO SAY THAT HE DIED GARDENING.

HE'D BEEN CLEARING BRUSH FROM THE YARD OF AN OLD FARMHOUSE HE WAS PLANNING TO RESTORE...

...AND HAD JUST CROSSED ROUTE 150 TO TOSS AN ARMLOAD OVER THE BANK.

THE TRUCK DRIVER DESCRIBED MY FATHER AS JUMPING BACKWARD INTO THE ROAD "AS IF HE SAW A SNAKE."

AND WHO KNOWS. PERHAPS HE DID.

On page 89, the third reference to Bruce's death

BUT ALAS, 768 PAGES OF *ULYSSES* LAY BEFORE ME LIKE AN EXPANSE OF UNCHARTED SEA. THE CLASS MET IN PROFESSOR AVERY'S LIVING ROOM.

MR. AVERY HAD HURT HIS BACK, AND RECLINED ON THE COUCH MUCH AS THE WISE WINDBAG, NESTOR, MIGHT HAVE RECLINED WHILE COUNSELING YOUNG TELEMACHUS.

absent. All the other panels are overhung by one or more lines of narrative text, or include a narrative caption within them. It is extremely unusual for a narrator to exert so much control over a graphic story, to the point where its presence is inescapable.

This is why *Fun Home* is somewhat at odds with run-of-the-mill comics. It has a different kind of rhythm and fluidity. The reader does not glide from one image to another, but, continually, from a text to an image. It is rather like attending an illustrated lecture, in which photographs appear on the screen to illustrate each point (we will see later that photographs are a key reference point for Bechdel). Page 228 consists only of writing: the author's comments, split into four narrative boxes, are superimposed over the final page of *Ulysses*.

The literary qualities also take the form of an overabundance of allusions to all kinds of canonical texts. After Tolstoy (*Anna Karenina*) come notably Ruskin (*The Stones of Venice*), Kipling (*Just So Stories*), Camus (*A Happy Death*, which happens to be the book that Bruce Bechdel was reading just before he died, and *The Myth of Sisyphus*), Fitzgerald (*The Great Gatsby*), James

(*Portrait of a Lady*), Hemingway (*The Sun Also Rises*), Grass (*The Tin Drum*), Colette (*The Pure and the Impure*), Proust, Tolkien, Salinger, and Austen—without forgetting the examples of homosexual and feminist literature (Anaïs Nin, Kate Millett) or dramatic works (Alison's mother rehearses and acts in Shakespeare, Albee, Osborne, and Wilde). Some of these books are simply shown being held by one or other family member, or quoted in passing; but the fourth chapter is entirely dominated by Proust, the sixth is steeped in *The Importance of Being Earnest*, and the seventh and last is suffused with Joyce's *Ulysses*, Bruce's favorite book.

These texts, like those of Camus and Colette, effectively work as narrative filters.[9] Alison needs the nourishment of classics and needs to measure her own experience against the experiences described in them in order to understand herself and her family. Bechdel explains that she drew upon "these literary allusions not only because it was a useful device, but also because it was a technique for emotional distancing that I had learned from my parents. [...] It is in some ways easier to see my parents through the prism of the fictional characters that they resemble."[10] She confirms as much in the book itself: "My parents are most real to me in fictional terms" (67).

Hillary Chute has analyzed the complexity of the network of correspondences that Bechdel creates with these formative texts, and particularly *Ulysses*.

> In the final pages, there is slippage between Alison and Bruce Bechdel as they figure various Joycean characters: first, Bechdel presents Alison as Stephen and her father as Bloom. Next, Alison is shown as Bloom, contemplating his father's suicide. Then her father is suggested as both Stephen ("I'm not a hero") and Joyce himself, in his less palatable moments. When Bechdel has finished narrating the publication history of *Ulysses*, her book also ends: the end of *Ulysses* becomes the end of Bruce Bechdel.[11]

If we add that Bruce's memory betrays him when he mistakenly attributes to Bloom the words of his wife Molly, it becomes clear that a reader unfamiliar with *Ulysses* might get a little lost.

A second source of reference is interwoven with this first one: the legend of Icarus and Daedalus, his father. From the very first page, the game that Alison as a child plays with Bruce is called "an Icarian game." However, on the following page it is made clear that "in our particular re-enactment of this mythic relationship, it was not me but my father who was to plummet from the sky." It will not be Icarus, the child, who falls, but Daedalus, the father. This reworking of the myth will be echoed several times, up until page 221: "But which of us was the father?" On the penultimate page, however, it seems that

The images presented as photographs have a distinctive graphic treatment

Alison has re-assumed the identity of Icarus: "What if Icarus hadn't hurtled into the sea? What if he'd inherited his father's inventive bent? What might he have wrought?" (231). Perhaps he would have drawn *Fun Home*.[12]

We have seen how Hugo Pratt took pleasure in threading numerous literary references through *The Ballad of the Salt Sea*. But they were only passing allusions there to create complicity or to name-check some well-known authors. Bechdel does something else altogether: literature is indissociable from her thought processes, which are permanently nourished by it. There is no room for doubt: Bechdel takes for granted that her reader is an intellectual like herself. This assumption, it is hardly necessary to emphasize, is unusual in comics and still more so in American comics.

It is almost always her father who picks out books for Alison to read. One could argue that by writing *Fun Home*, she has in a sense repaid her debt toward him. Bruce has become what he would always have wanted to be: a character in a great work of literature.[13]

As well as these constant references to books, the author draws upon an extensive archive: her journals, as we have mentioned, but also photos, letters, road maps, extracts from dictionaries, drawings done as a child or teenager, passports, police reports, and other administrative documents. None of these documents is scanned: all are redrawn, all bear the signature of the artist's hand.[14] This desire for a unified graphic style induces her to go so far as to imitate her father's handwriting (224).

But there is more, beyond what the reader is able to detect: each panel is based on one or more photographs. Bechdel herself posed for each character, enacting all the roles, down to the least important bit parts, out of a concern that the bodily positions should be as accurate as possible. These photographic documents enabled her to bring precision to compositions that had already each been prepared by five or six preliminary sketches.[15]

In her next book, *Are You My Mother?*, the artist explains to her psychoanalyst (251–252) why her drawings have to be so meticulously planned, leaving nothing to chance or spontaneity: each line, she says, has to convey specific information. Bechdel sees the drawing as a *text*, in the full sense of the word.

This method certainly corresponds to the obsessiveness of the author. As far as I know, she drew *Dykes to Watch Out For* without needing to rely on photos, and her drawing was no less expressive; indeed, I would suggest that the opposite is true. What is unusual here is the effort that Bechdel puts into disguising the photographic origin of her images—unlike Shaun Tan in *The Arrival*. There are, however, photographs in *Fun Home* that are presented as such. And these are either drawn in a different style from the other images, using hatching rather than a wash (this is how Bechdel treats the family photographs that occur on the title page of every chapter, or those that appear within the narrative itself, as on pages 100–101 or 120), or drawn from the source document in the style of the other images, without any break in the graphic code (this is the case of school photos, passport photos, press photos, and magazine photos of celebrities, as on pages 35, 47, 48, 64, 72, 74, 85, etc.). So there is a complex interaction between the panels containing photographs that have obviously been redrawn, in a style that sometimes plays down their photographic status and sometimes emphasizes it, and the other panels, also based on photographs but not discernable as such.

Although Bechdel has taken this self-imposed detour via photography, she nonetheless maintains that there is "something inherently autobiographical about cartooning," because "a page's marks are a manifestation of the person making them."[16] And she uses the resources of comics in a very studied way, such as in her choice of blue gray as a wash that is both soft and cold, and that she describes as having a "bleak, elegiac quality to it."[17]

Bruce was as "problematic" a father to Alison as Vladek was to Art Spiegelman. This is a recurrent theme in comics, and one that we will meet again in the next chapter, concerning Goblet. As in *Maus*, the relationship is made up of both identification and distancing.[18] As in *Maus*, the death of the father interrupts a process that remains unfinished.

Alison identifies with her father in two different respects: artistic talent and sexuality. On the sexual terrain, Bruce's strategy of concealment complicates any attempt at closeness. When he is summoned to court (173), the real reason is hushed up, and Alison fails to understand what is going on. Even in the letter that he sends her after she has come out to both her parents, the confidence that he offers in return is merely implied (211). A panel on page 219 frames the father and daughter together. It is the most tightly framed close-up in the whole book. She is expecting an exchange, a one-to-one conversation where masks could finally be dropped. She looks directly at him, but he avoids her gaze, staring instead at ... the fork he is drying. Although the truth about her father was slow to be revealed, Bechdel anticipates knowledge that Alison does not yet have in the scene where the family dresses to go to a wedding (98). She is about twelve, but, adopting a Proustian term, Bechdel writes, "We were inverts." It seems that her father had already sensed the sexual preferences that his daughter would manifest later, as is clear from the scene in the luncheonette (118). But the "manic-depressive closeted fag" (125) and the butch intellectual will never be in sync, never really in tune. "And in a way you could say that my father's end was my beginning. Or more precisely, that the end of his lie coincided with the beginning of my truth" (117).

Those who turn the truth of their life as they see it into a book will not always meet with the approval of family and friends. Bechdel hoped to get her mother's blessing. The first time she mentioned *Fun Home* to her mother, she had already been working on it for a year. Her mother did not really understand what drove her to reveal all these "sordid family secrets," but she did not formally oppose it. With hindsight, Bechdel offers this analysis:

> I know I hurt her by writing this book. She made that clear, but she also let me know that she grasped the complexity of the situation. [...] I do feel that I robbed my mother in writing this book. I thought I had her tacit permission to tell the story, but in fact I never asked for it, and she never gave it to me. Now I know that no matter how responsible you try to be in writing about another person, there's something inherently hostile in the act. You're violating their subjectivity. I thought I could write about my family without hurting anyone, but I was wrong. I probably will do it again. And that's just an uncomfortable fact about myself that I have to live with.[19]

Fun Home is a book that is impressive in its lucidity, its sensibility, the complexity of its composition, and above all its fierce determination to seek out the truth, at whatever cost.

DOMINIQUE GOBLET
Pretending Is Lying (2007)

BACKGROUND

Dominique Goblet was born in Brussels in 1967. She studied illustration at the Institut Saint-Luc, graduating in 1990. She worked with the pioneering Frigo collective, which set up the independent press Fréon, the publisher of her first two books: *Spitting Images* (1997) and *Memories of a Perfect Day* (2000).[1]

Her work appeared in *Frigobox* and *Frigorevue*, journals published by Fréon—which merged with the small Paris-based press Amok in 2002, thereby founding Frémok—but also in *Lapin*, *Comix 2000*, and *Strapazin*. As well as an author of comic books, she is also a photographer and a painter, and she has created works on paper—including some very large-scale ones—that have been exhibited in galleries. She has also taken part in theatrical performances (Muziek LOD, in Ghent).

Pretending Is Lying was published by L'Association in 2007. This 140-page book was twelve years in the making. It was nominated at the Angoulême comics festival, and won the Töpffer Prize awarded by the city of Geneva.

Goblet has also contributed to the co-authored works *The Association in Mexico*[2] and *Wrestling Match in Vielsalm*,[3] an album created jointly by professional artists and artists with learning difficulties. In 2010, she published *Chronography*, the fruit of a collaboration with her daughter, Nikita Fossoul, over a ten-year period (1998–2008) during which they produced portraits of each other.[4] In the same year, she published *The Wolfmen* with Frémok, and in 2014 *Seeking LTR* with Frémok and Actes Sud.[5]

PLOT

Pretending Is Lying opens on Dominique's reunion with her father, whom she has not seen for four years: she is going to introduce him to her own daughter, Nikita. Her father, a retired firefighter, now lives with a new partner, Blandine.

This family gathering brings back a traumatic scene from Dominique's childhood. In order to punish her for being noisy and disobedient, her mother inflicted violent and excessive punishments on her. Her father, who declined to get involved, will later protest that he did not know what was going on.

This first story takes up chapters 1 and 3. It alternates with the account, in chapters 2 and 4, of an unsatisfactory love affair, in which Dominique's partner is unable to make a definitive break with his previous girlfriend. The young man in question is never named within the story, but the paratext enables us to identify him as Guy Marc Hinant. He informs us in an afterword that he had collaborated on the chapters in which he features.

PRETENDING IS LYING HAS BEEN CALLED A GRAPHIC UFO by some readers on web forums. It is a comic book that is formally atypical, startling and often innovative. The intertwining of two stories, the highly elliptical narration, the inclusion of insistent ghostly presences, the deployment of very diverse graphic styles and techniques, and a finale that consists of a series of painted, non-figurative surfaces are all authorial marks upon a work that breaks with the usual conventions of drawn literature. Dominique Goblet's approach to the medium is that of a visual artist, but it is likely that her other influences include music. Her partner Guy Marc Hinant is the founder of the Belgian independent record label Sub Rosa, which specializes in electronic and experimental music. He has also codirected, with Dominique Lohlé, documentary films on noise and the art of listening. There is undoubtedly a musical dimension in the construction of *Pretending Is Lying*.

Goblet's initial aim was to recount the violence that she had experienced as a child. "Weirdly, until I turned it into a book, every time I met someone I wouldn't let go of them until I'd forced them to listen to all the nightmare stuff that had happened to me. It was really weird, I couldn't help it, I couldn't stop myself from talking about all that stuff."[6]

This was a sensitive subject to deal with in the medium of comics, particularly since, in spite of the violence that she inflicted upon her, Dominique loves her mother deeply. "Very deeply. And I realized that, ultimately, that was the challenge: to recount something that was really violent, but to make you understand that in spite of that violence I loved my mother more than anything. And on top of that, to get you to like my mother—to make you empathize with her."[7]

The subject of this first part of the story could be summed up as follows: how can you have very hard things inflicted on you by someone and still love that person? In some ways, the other part of the story could be summed up in the same way. Dominique loves Guy Marc and cannot leave him, even though he makes her suffer through his inability to commit exclusively to her. It therefore appears that the two personal histories that alternate in the book are not only linked by the identity of the autobiographical protagonist; they also share an underlying structure.

The four pages that serve as a prologue are designed to establish the complicity between Dominique and her mother, whom the child sees as a magician. And the recollection of the punishment inflicted upon her in the attic, far from being insistent, is condensed into a single image, which occurs late in the book, over a hundred pages in. It is of course a very powerful image, all the more arresting in that it is only one of two, apart from the ghostly apparitions (see below), that take up a whole page.

Even if any spirit of revenge or resentment is avoided, the very fact of tackling the subject of mistreatment means facing the likely disapproval of close family and friends. David B., as we have seen, was estranged from his family for four years as a result of certain scenes in *Epileptic*. Dominique Goblet had to take a three-year break from writing *Pretending Is Lying* because she was seeing a lot of her mother during that time. She felt that by stating what had hurt her, she would cause further hurt herself.

Moreover, of the two parents it is the father who is the more prominent in the book. The mother appears only in the prologue and in chapter 3. It seems that all the household tasks fall upon her, while the father vegetates in front of the television. She is depicted as stressed out and therefore irascible, but we see that she is quick to regret her fits of temper; she may not apologize for the disproportionate "punishments" that she dispenses, but she shows real tenderness toward her daughter.

The father was already a haunting presence in *Memories of a Perfect Day*, in which Dominique searched for his name in a cemetery, but he was never actually represented in that book. We meet him here, argumentative and plaintive, a loud-mouthed Brussels native who mangles the French language and maintains his imposing bulk by downing beer after beer. Nikita nicknames him "Grandpa Mustache." He addresses Dominique with belittling Flemish nicknames: *Dom* ("Stupid") and *Nikske* ("Little Nothing").

Blandine, Dominique's new stepmother, who treats her with hostility, is made to look like a zombie by the artist. "She was very strange, what with the prescription drugs and the alcohol, scrawny and morose . . . she was a bit scary. And as I didn't want to let her into my life, I made her look more like a symbol than a human being."[8] So Blandine has a face that is faceless, lacking ears or hair, which evokes a skull or the character from Edvard Munch's famous painting, *The Scream*.[9]

The words chosen as the title of the book, *Pretending Is Lying*, are spoken by an angry Blandine, addressed to Nikita. She overreacts to an innocent remark by the little girl about a drawing that she has just done.

In the middle of the book there occurs a break. Two bister-colored pages, with a close-up image of the father drawn to resemble an engraving, bear the inscription "July 8, 1998—the day of my birthday—the firefighter is dead." An event that has taken place while the book is in the process of creation has intruded into its pages.[10]

Dominique's father did not, then, live long enough to read the comic in which he featured. His death, coming before the work was finished, recalls that of Vladek Spiegelman, who died before his son Art's work *Maus* was published or that of Chris Ware's father, who was unable to read *Jimmy Corrigan*. In all three cases the father of the author was not only a protagonist but also the intended first reader of the book.

Although *Pretending Is Lying* is autobiographical, conveying the perspective of its main character, the author herself, it is nonetheless noteworthy for its depiction of the father, a veritable "portrait" that captures his personality, his temperament, his physical, intellectual and moral qualities, and his way of moving and speaking, all of which add up to a multilayered and memorable figure. It is an uncompromising but empathetic portrayal.

The mother-daughter relationship is approached in the book through two "pairs" a generation apart: Dominique and her mother (who is not given a first name), but also Dominique and her daughter, Nikita. The child who appears in the prologue is Dominique; the child in chapter 1 is Nikita; in fact, the two small girls are obviously about the same age (Nikita is perhaps slightly younger) and the two sequences begin with an identical situation: the child is walking along the street with her mother. This provides a transition that may perturb the reader somewhat. Subsequently, Dominique looks a little older in the pictures that head each chapter, and Nikita returns, for a two-page sequence, as an older child. Her mother brushes her long blonde hair, puts her to bed, and explains to her, "You have to laugh at the things that scare you." The parallelism between the two small girls is accentuated by their first names: the end of Domi*nique* corresponds to the beginning of *Ni*kita (which Dominique sometimes shortens to "Nik"). And there are other doublings: Dominique's parents are divorced, and Dominique in turn is separated from Hervé, Nikita's father. Likewise, Guy Marc lives apart from the mother of his son. Finally, Guy Marc's father watches television while his wife cooks; the division of roles is the same as for Dominique's parents.

Angry with Nikita, Cécile is turned into a child's drawing. © 2007 by Dominique Goblet. Translation © 2016 by Sophie Yanow. Published by arrangement with New York Review Comics.

Chapter 3 opens on a flashback, a seventeen-page sequence that retraces the events that had led up to Dominique's banishment to the attic and punishment at the hands of her mother. We see the father in the house, busy watching a Formula One competition on television (the race took place on the Zandfoort track in Holland in 1973). When the punishment occurs, his attention is entirely taken up by an accident: the driver Roger Williamson's car rolls over and catches fire. The father is riveted by the events on the screen: "I've never seen such a thing!! What a mess!!" And he repeats again and again: "If I'd been there . . . I would've have gotten that guy out!" But this fireman who boasts about saving people has failed to come to the rescue of his daughter, and does not see (or refuses to see) what is going on under his own roof.

He repeats, three times in the space of seven pages, "You all abandoned me," referring to the day when his wife left him, taking their daughter. "But no Papa . . . It's you who abandoned us," Dominique replies to him—a sentence that is reprised seventy pages further on, to create a link between chapters 1 and 3.

In contrast to the reunion with the father, which actually happened just as Dominique recounts it in chapter 1, the parallelism between the motor-racing accident and the mistreatment of the little girl is invented. It is a narrative device, a form of mise-en-scène intended to display the father's personality. "I did some research on the net and I came upon this accident that could have corresponded with that time period," the author explained to Xavier Guilbert.[11] Her father often watched motor racing on television. All she had to do was "knit together" the scene of the accident and the scene of the punishment. This could be described as a "poetic collision."

Goblet crosscuts the images of the race on the screen and the events in the house over several pages. The raised voices of the quarreling mother and daughter annoy the father, who would like to watch his program in peace. Once the accident happens, there is no more crosscutting: the images show only the disaster, taking up the point of view of the father, who is mesmerized by the spectacle. The other drama continues to unfurl on the "sound track": the voice of the furious mother ("I'm going to tie you up!!! That's what we have to do with nasty little girls like you . . . We have to string them up!!!") is superimposed over the commentary of the sports reporter. This means that even if the father is later in denial, he must be able to hear the mother's words, since it is through his perception of the scene that we have access to it. And the two sequences of events converge when the mother says to Dominique: "Put your hands in the air!!" while the image shows David Purley, with his hands in the air, unable to help his fellow driver, who is trapped under the burning car.

His language and his body language, along with scrawled lettering, build a portrait of the father. © 2007 by Dominique Goblet. Translation © 2016 by Sophie Yanow. Published by arrangement with New York Review Comics.

Sound is prominent throughout this chapter. The noises that little Dominique makes as she plays (click clack with the scissors, tak tak with her foot) that exasperate her mother, the mother's shouts, the patter of rain drops and the rumble of thunder, the roar of the racing cars, and later Blandine's ranting all form a sonic accompaniment that the reader "hears" even if it is not accessed through an aural channel. The cumulative effect is anxiety-inducing.

One aspect of chapter 1 that has considerable impact is Goblet's work on lettering. When the father speaks, the handwriting is jerky, chaotic, and stuttering. Far from aspiring to transparency, the lettering ostentatiously makes its presence felt: it "bears the trace of a bodily presence," as Catherine Mao observes.[12] In comics, the lettering usually has a neutral appearance and its role is purely functional. But not here. Goblet has learned from modern painting, which "has massively reworked signs and scripts, subjecting them to visual reinterpretations that poeticize the letter or maintain its link to the hand."[13] The text itself becomes iconic, adapting itself to the father's intonation and the modulations of his voice, increasing in size when Blandine starts sounding off, and sometimes invading the whole surface of the panel. As Didier Pasamonik has noted, Goblet believes that "drawing is another form of writing; and similarly, she believes that writing has inherently visual qualities."[14]

We may recall Hugo Pratt's pithy formulation: "I draw my texts and I write my drawings."[15]

As if to harmonize with the lettering, the drawing in chapter 1 also undergoes a kind of disintegration. The effect is particularly noticeable on the page where Nikita comes to show Blandine the drawing that she has just done. Over four panels, the characters look as though they have been drawn by a child, implying that Nikita's "style" has contaminated the story, or that she has become its enunciator. Perhaps Goblet wishes to express the feeling of regressing to the state of a small and powerless child, uneasy at the conflict that has broken out. But the style is remarkably free throughout the entire chapter, with distorted bodily proportions (for instance, Dominique's microcephalic appearance in the first panel) and flexible rubberlike limbs (the father often appears to be dancing, contorting himself like the clubbers shown toward the end of chapter 2); the drawing is often very schematic though occasionally more descriptive.

In contrast, the account of the fraught love affair between Dominique and Guy Marc is much more serene in formal terms; the drawing is more realist, more elaborate, and more classic—apart from the fact that it is not inked in and so exploits all the sensuality of the range of gray tones achievable with a lead pencil.

This part of the book includes few dramatic events. It is a series of scenes from everyday life, shorter than those in chapter 1, some of which take place in Dominique's absence (such as the pages in which Guy Marc announces to his parents that he has met a girl, whom he describes as "special" and "really pretty"). Although the book includes a portrait of Dominique's lover, his character seems comparatively bland. The two pages over which he regales her in careful and comic detail with his recipe for tuna pasta—seemingly the pinnacle of his culinary expertise—reveal one aspect of his personality. His problematic relationship with time is another aspect: "It seems like I don't have time to do anything." "I need time for me and my son ... do you understand??" "I've got a ton of work waiting. I can't waste my time like this!"

While in the autobiographical works by David B. and Alison Bechdel it is the authors who take on the status of reciter—verbal narrator[16]—and make considerable use of an overarching narrative voiceover, there is no such instance in Goblet's work. Apart from a few introductory lines, the narrator stands back. Thought balloons are also used sparingly. I have counted four in all, in addition to a panel that sets out the thoughts of the autobiographical character. Apart from these rare cases of access to her inner life, Dominique betrays her feelings only through her facial expressions and through acting out, which are almost invariably highly eloquent.

Not only does Goblet decline to duplicate her story by adding a running commentary, presenting instead an unmediated version of events, but the narration itself is elliptical. It is conspicuously unencumbered by temporal, biographical, or contextual details. Her editor and confidant Jean-Christophe Menu says in his introductory text that time is the "true first subject" of the book; but it is the time of the book's making that he is referring to. The actions that Goblet represents are never situated within a precise chronology. No date is put on them, and the ages of the characters are left vague. The reader comes across a few mentions of time elapsed, such as "I haven't seen him in four years," "I was with him for eight months and he left me," or "It's been five days since we saw each other." But there is no way of knowing whether the incident of the punishment in the attic happened once or several times. One page abruptly reveals that Dominique is seeing a psychotherapist (she wants to know why she is always the one to be dumped), without making it clear whether this is a one-off visit or part of a long-term therapy, and for how long it has been going on. In the space of three pages, the reader is casually apprised of the existence of this therapist, and then of that of a bearded friend and confidant to whose identity no clue is given, and finally of the fact that Dominique runs a drawing workshop for adults. These scenes are like sudden flashes, windows opened and then immediately closed. Likewise, the epilogue, in which Guy Marc moves toward a reconciliation with Dominique after he has "finally moved," is not temporally located: we never know whether the time that had passed since their breakup was a matter of days, weeks, months, or even years. And although it emerges that the father has died, we are hardly given any information about what happens to the mother after her separation from her husband.

The narration of *Pretending Is Lying* is, then, full of gaps, with remarkably little concern to clarify the circumstances of the scenes that feature in the book or to situate them within a rational continuity, a coherent course of events, or a quantifiable temporal dimension.

However, the aspect of the book that has undoubtedly proved the most disconcerting to readers is the mixture of styles and graphic techniques. A patchwork of this type is not completely unheard of in comics. There is a striking example from as early as the nineteenth century, with Gustave Doré's *Dramatic, Picturesque and Caricatural History of Holy Russia*.[17] As Guillaume

Dégé writes, "all types of graphic form are assembled and intermingled: naïve and direct-style children's drawing, elaborate and explosive baroque drawing, shadow puppets, and abstraction, but also caricature, exuberant scribbles [...], and educational, quasi-scientific drawing."[18] And as we have seen, in *The Airtight Garage*, Moebius gave free rein to the whole range of variations in his own style.

Like a number of visual artists, Dominique Goblet has adopted the mixing of techniques as a working method. She says: "I like to vary techniques all the time, so as not to get bored."[19] In this book she uses red ballpoint, pencil, and paint. In chapter 1, the backgrounds are covered with linseed oil that has darkened over time, giving the pages an unusual patina.

Furthermore, Goblet borrows from the most varied graphic and visual arts traditions: she makes reference to icons, to prehistoric cave drawings of animals, to nonfigurative painting, to life drawing and drawing based on photographs, to television images, and even—in the prologue—to the "cute" style. Images containing no characters have an important place in her work: urban landscapes (a car park, the Belgian radio and television tower, a water tower, Brussels rooftops, etc.) and still lifes. The colors associated with one or other element are not stable: from one image to the next, the father's T-shirt or Dominique's hair may be black or white. And the page layout is unsystematic, with the number of panels per page fluctuating between one and seventeen, and the strips numbering two, three, or four.

The reader senses that this display of visual techniques not only has an aesthetic purpose but also serves to render certain emotions as accurately as possible. However, the author's intentions are not always easy to decipher. The meaning of the horned animals superimposed on the image of the father is not obvious (a devil or a cuckold?). And the page where he appears in the middle of a Byzantine pseudo-icon, where he seems to have taken the place of the Virgin Mary, is ambiguous. Does it correspond to the father's perception of himself (an exemplary parent, whose devotion verges on saintliness) or is this Dominique's ironic vision as she listens to him? There is no definitive answer.

Regarding the final pages, where figurative representation disappears altogether, I can only quote Catherine Mao: "the resolution seeks to *materialize* sound and breath, to give them something more than consistency: actual substance. To achieve this, Dominique Goblet first plays upon the extension of the visual plane: she opens up the frame until there is no longer a panel, and then no longer a plate, just a sheet of paper and color in which the eye drowns. [...] The work ends up as matter and spatiality, reliefs and flat color blocks, from which a few words spurt out, as if they were breathed onto the paper."[20] And who knows whether the swallows that fly across these final pages are harbingers of a new spring in the relationship between Dominique and Guy Marc?

This kind of aesthetic syncretism, which produces a collage effect, can of course be associated with what was called, first in architecture and subsequently in almost all areas of contemporary creative art, postmodernism. In the field of literature we could make a comparison with the changes of tone, style, and literary technique to be found in James Joyce's *Ulysses* and *Portrait of the Artist as a Young Man*.

Pretending Is Lying includes one last category of images: the spectral images. As we have seen, Goblet makes Blandine, her father's new partner, look like a zombie. She is, in addition, surrounded by a sort of malevolent aura, as if she were an apparition, a ghost or an ectoplasmic emanation.

There is a second group of images made up of the panels in which the artist materializes the threat posed to her relationship with Guy Marc by another young woman, Michèle. Dominique's bouts of ophthalmic migraine are symptoms of a refusal to see her, a refusal to face up to the situation—in vain. This third party is portrayed as an insistent ghostly presence, always there, all the more intriguing for the reader in that she "haunts" the book for about thirty pages before we get to meet her. Is it by chance that, on the third page of this long sequence, Dominique recalls a memory of her father, who "felt an icy liquid going through his body?" Dominique herself takes on, for the duration of one image, a ghostly consistency: torn between the two women, Guy Marc imagines that they are both with him. He feels their presence so strongly that he turns round to make sure he is alone.

Other ghosts, less easily identifiable, also haunt the book. They appear as full-page images, swallowed up by a darkness through which we can barely perceive a shape that is deliberately left indistinct and indeterminate. The haunting effect of these silent images, outside the text, pervades the book and confers upon it a strangeness, an unassimilable quality. These images are the graphic manifestation of psychic wounds that can never completely heal. They are also an intimation of the unsayable, the ineffable, the unrepresentable, of episodes shrouded in silence, of memories repressed. They are the mute surface onto which readers can project their own uncertainties.

The ghostly theme runs through the whole book. The author has chosen to characterize some of her relationships and impressions by means of this structuring metaphor, while at the same time using it to pursue her artistic exploration.

On the cover of the album, Goblet has drawn a static image with no narrative burden. She represents herself sitting holding a glass of wine, looking introspective, plunged into her thoughts and memories. Perhaps she is

Accompanying the couple, Michèle's spectral presence. © 2007 by Dominique Goblet. Translation © 2016 by Sophie Yanow. Published by arrangement with New York Review Comics.

reflecting on her book and what it will be like; or perhaps she is meditating on the title, whose enigmatic words hover above her.

The meaning of the title is doubtless to be found in the afterword by Guy Marc Hinant. He writes, "What is the proportion of fiction produced by the simple fact of focusing on the key moments of our lives?" And he goes on to conclude that the characters that represent Dominique and himself in this comic should not be confused with the real live people. They are "controlled avatars" bearing "similar names." Hinant is repeating here what many have said before him. Jacques Lacan, most notably, has insisted that as soon as we take up the pen, or even before, as soon as we formulate our story, we are creating a fictitious self. As Simone de Beauvoir says in *Memoirs of a Dutiful Daughter*, "My life would be a beautiful story come true, a story I would make up as I went along."[21] Or André Gide in *If It Die*: "Memoirs are never more than half sincere, however great one's desire for truth; everything is always more complicated than one makes out. Possibly even one gets nearer to truth in the novel."[22] Dominique Goblet would probably not describe her book as autofiction, that fashionable catchall category, but she has no illusions: she knows that the point of a book is not for reality to leap naked onto the page. The subject matter must be organized and recomposed; its "truth" is subjective and acknowledged as such: it is, after all, a work of art. Recounting and drawing are "pretending" and so inevitably "lying."

Moreover, Goblet does not claim sole authorship of her work. She enjoys sharing and collaboration. *Chronography* was cowritten with her daughter, and consists of portraits that each produced of the other, over a period of ten years beginning when Nikita was seven. Her contribution to *Wrestling Match in Vielsalm*—about the imagery of wrestling—again involved joint authorship, this time with Dominique Théâte, who suffers from mental illness. And in her most recent book, *Seeking LTR*, she shares the billing with Kai Pfeiffer.

Pretending Is Lying opens on this notification: "The text of chapters 3 and 4 was co-written with Guy Marc Hinant." What we have just read is, then—both unusually and unflinchingly, in that it recounts a chaotic relationship with its frictions, its deceits, and its inevitable share of resentment—a plural autobiography that allows room for the point of view of the other person. "To be honest, I thought that using these painful experiences as artistic raw material, doing it together and reflecting on it together would help us in real life to understand what had been going on and above all to transform any remaining resentment into complicity..."[23]

Another characteristic of Goblet's approach is her liking for long-term projects: ten years to create *Chronography*, and twelve years to get to the end of *Pretending Is Lying*. Many of the major comics of the modern era (*Maus*, *Jimmy Corrigan*, and the works of David B. and Jens Harder discussed in this volume) have required a gestation period, a long process of maturation and unremitting toil. Goblet appreciates the fact that independent presses allow her the luxury of escaping from the imperative of productivity that drives commercial comics publishing. *Pretending Is Lying* is a book that was given time to marinate, to settle, and the reader is also invited to take time to savor its poetry to the full.

SHAUN TAN
The Arrival (2006)

BACKGROUND

Shaun Tan, born in 1974, is an Australian painter and illustrator. A fine art and English literature graduate, he has published illustrated children's books as both writer and artist (*The Lost Thing* [1999] and *The Red Tree* [2001]) and has worked extensively in animation for studios such as Pixar and Blue Sky. His father is of Chinese heritage, born in Malaysia to immigrant parents; on his mother's side he has Anglo-Irish ancestors. His wife is Finnish.

He has always lived in the same place, but his Asian features have persistently provoked the question: "Where did your parents come from?" That was what begat the project that became *The Arrival*, Shaun Tan's first—and so far only—comic, a way of reflecting on what his forebears must have felt and an attempt to make their story his own. It took him four years to write and was published in Melbourne in 2006. The following year, Dargaud brought the book out in France under the title *In the Footsteps of Our Fathers* [*Là où vont nos pères*]. It won the Best Album prize in Angoulême in 2008, followed by many other awards worldwide. In 2010, Tan published a book about the making of *The Arrival*, under the title *Sketches from a Nameless Land*, which was published in French translation by Dargaud the following year.

PLOT

A man has decided that he must leave his wife and daughter behind for as long as it takes. With a heavy heart, he sets off from his home and his native land to seek a better future elsewhere, in a "New World," a single suitcase his only luggage. After travelling by train and boat along with other emigrants, he arrives in a large city where everything is radically unfamiliar to him, and finds himself thrust in among its residents, whose language he cannot understand. After a series of chance encounters, he gradually comes to grips with local conventions, does various short-term jobs, and makes friends. When he eventually feels completely integrated, he writes to his family and sends money so that they can join him. They have a happy reunion, and his small daughter is quick to show how well she in turn can adapt.

THE MAN HAS NO NAME. Neither does the country or the city that he leaves, nor the country or the city where he settles. And there is a reason for this: *The Arrival* is a silent album, with no word written or uttered. It is entirely narrated through the sequencing of pictures. There are no names, and not even an initial, as is the case for some of Kafka's heroes. There are no mustaches or glasses, no distinctive features. With his suit, his trilby, and his suitcase, he is an everyman. The man with no qualities, with whom anyone can identify. He looks like a commercial traveler. Tan has given the man his own, not especially ethnically stereotyped, physiognomy.

Although comics is generally acknowledged to be by its very nature a mixed, hybrid language, a meeting point between text and image, silent works are nothing new—there have always been many wordless short-form comics and strips. In the nineteenth century, Caran d'Ache conceived the project of a "novel in drawings," intended to be over three hundred pages long with not a single line of text. The book was to be called *Maestro*, but it was never finished, although about a hundred pages did get drawn. In 1930, the cartoonist Milt Gross actually completed a similar project, when he produced *He Done Her Wrong*. Within the same period, artists like Frans Masereel and Lynd Ward inaugurated novels in woodcuts, artists' books that imparted their subject matter, usually a story, at the rhythm of one image per page. It was not until the modern period that what could be called "pure graphic literature" returned, with works like *Arzach* by Moebius, *The Magic Lantern* by Guido Crepax, *The System* by Peter Kyper, *Dracula* by Albert Breccia, *Frank* by Jim Woodring, *The Worst Possible News* by Blanquet, *Prosopopus* by Nicolas de Crécy, *Flood* by Eric Drooker, *L* by Benoît Jacques or *Happy the Man Who* by Nicolas Presl,[1] to name but a few titles that should suffice to show the diversity of current work being created in this format. By awarding the "best album of the year" prize, across all categories, to *The Arrival*, the Angoulême festival has definitively legitimized wordless comics.

It is unlikely that Tan was familiar with his predecessors in this tendency, especially since he admits that he had no previous comics culture, and that he had only begun to rectify this (he cites Crumb, Clowes, and *Watchmen*), at the point when he decided that his book would be a comic rather than an illustrated book.

Many wordless graphic narratives have a dreamlike quality. This is perhaps explained by the fact that silence produces, of itself, an effect of detachment from reality. Silence makes the scenes played out before us seem unreal, because we know from experience that in real life they would include sounds, and the characters' actions would be accompanied by words. That being the case, it is tempting to use silence as a way of generating strangeness, to reinforce the unreal or fantastical aspect of the spectacle being portrayed.

This dreamlike dimension is very present in *The Arrival* right from the moment when the protagonist arrives in this foreign city, a huge metropolis with curious architecture inhabited by floating objects and imaginary animals, whose population observes strange customs and writes in an incomprehensible script. Tan has explained that the book took shape when he realized that the theme of emigration chimed with his preoccupations as an artist, and particularly his "fascination with surrealistic illustrated stories."[2]

This city appears so highly phantasmagorical in every respect that the reader begins to wonder if the newly arrived protagonist is really experiencing all these disconcerting occurrences or if he is dreaming. The bewildering environment not only gives Tan the opportunity to express his penchant for the fantastical but also acts as a metaphor for the sense of nonbelonging felt by the foreigner. He perhaps exaggerates, however, when he explains that, if the city in his imaginary country "might appear to be a confusing assemblage of bizarre architecture, mystifying symbols, strange vehicles and other less distinct forms," that is simply because "that's true of any city to a foreign eye."[3] This could no longer be said today, in the era of globalization, when the skylines of most big cities look alike and when a pizzeria or branch of McDonalds can be found on a street corner anywhere. The emotion expressed by Tan certainly corresponds more closely to what nineteenth-century travelers must have felt. It is, in that regard, interesting to note that the author situates the story in an imagined world that has not undergone any great mingling of cultures and where national, and even local, characteristics have been preserved in aspic. The strangeness that the city displays not only confers a poetic dimension onto the book but also acts as a metaphor, enabling readers to be as amazed as the protagonist of the story by what they see and to identify all the more with his bafflement.

It is the shock of this discovery of a new world and the presentiment, right from the outset, that integration will be difficult that are at the real heart of the book. From this point of view, the original English title, *The Arrival*, is certainly more appropriate than the vaguer, more ambiguous title chosen for the French edition, *In the Footsteps of Our Fathers*.

In relation to the silent narration, Tan has said, "I found that this absence of language also slowed down the flow of the narrative."[4] This affirmation may

Drawing as universal language

seem paradoxical, insofar as it is generally agreed that it is the text that detains the reader's gaze and provides a stable path across the page. Many readers leap from speech balloon to speech balloon and glide rapidly over wordless panels, which are thought to be low in information content and instantly intelligible. The paradox is only apparent, however. In a silent narrative, there is no longer an entry point giving access to meaning; meaning has to be sought out and tracked down through the patient, meticulous, investigative reading of motifs contained within the image and of the different levels of articulation with preceding and following images. *The Arrival* demands an attentive, alert reader who takes the time to see, to understand, and to feel.

The notion of drawing as a form of writing, as a language in its own right, is thematized within the plot and so acquires a reflexive dimension. Thus, unable to make himself understood by the residents of his adopted city in their language, which he cannot speak, the man expresses himself through drawing on several occasions. He scribbles a bed and a window onto a page from a notebook to indicate that he is in search of a roof for the night; elsewhere, he shows a pictogram of a loaf of bread; further on, he uses a sketch to evoke the dangers that led him to emigrate. And so, in the context of a silent comic, Shaun Tan inserts incidents attesting to the universality of the language of images.

Just as Tan did not invent silent comics, neither is he the first artist to have taken immigration as his subject matter. In fact, the Museum of the History of Immigration in Paris held a major exhibition on the topic from October 2013 to April 2014.[5] We will cite only a few key works: *The Four Immigrants Manga* by Henry Yoshitaka Kiyama, *Sudor Sudaca* by Muñoz and Sampayo, *Yellow Negroes* by Yvan Alagbé, *Little Polio Boy* by Farid Boudjellal, and *Portugal* by Cyril Pedrosa, without forgetting, of course, *Persepolis* by Marjane Satrapi.[6] So it is through its treatment of the subject that *The Arrival* is unique and remarkable.

For example, to return to the phantasmagorical dimension of the city, it is important to notice that this fantastic aspect is in tension with the documentary-like graphic treatment. We could call this a naturalistic style, which, without being photorealist, nonetheless conveys a realist illusion. Tan refers to a story that is "both real and abstract, some unclear genre between fact and fiction."[7] From this point of view, the album is in phase with the aesthetic of fashionable currents in illustration, "fantasy" and "pop surrealism," in which dreamlike scenes are represented with a refined and classical facture, and often executed with virtuosity.

Moreover, with their sepia tint, the images seem to emerge from the past, and to be drenched in a certain melancholy. In places, the reader has the impression of turning the pages of an old photo album (I will return to this point). As a result, it is difficult to associate the host city, which nonetheless embodies hope, with any kind of future. Everything seems to take place in the past, a past that is indeterminate, atemporal (although marked by the tragedies of the twentieth century), and not attributable to a precise period, because we discover there a large number of phenomena (for example, the means of transport) of which there is no historical record. To put it in a nutshell, it seems that this is a case—as with *Watchmen*—where we can refer to uchronia.

In deliberate contrast with the puzzling environment that awaits the man, the opening pages of the book, which depict what he is about to leave behind him, accord very great importance to everyday objects: a suitcase, a hat, a clock, a cooking pot, a teapot, furniture, and drawings done by his daughter are like so many reassuring reference points, familiar in both senses of the word.

Even if, as the text on the back cover makes clear, this comic is "the story of every migrant, every refugee, every displaced person, and a tribute to all those who have made the journey"—even if the author deploys all available resources in the attempt to treat immigration as a universal theme, it is no less important to individualize his hero sufficiently to make him not just a cipher but a flesh-and-blood person to whom the reader can become attached. His talent for making origami birds is the quirk that marks him out, along with the delight in playing jokes that is displayed by the revelation of one of these paper birds under his hat: a real conjuring trick, intended to make his daughter laugh at the moment of their separation.

The Arrival comprises 116 pages, divided into six chapters, devoted respectively to the departure, the journey, the arrival, the discovery of a new culture, the process of integration, and finally the reuniting of the family. A happy ending, indeed. The little girl, who wears the same woolen hat on the opening and closing pages of the book, and who seems not to have grown much older,

has adapted so rapidly and so well that it is now she who, on the last page, is shown giving advice to new arrivals, specifically to a young woman who is looking lost, suitcase at her feet and map in hand. At the little girl's heel is an animal identical in every respect to the one that the protagonist found in his furnished room and which became a companion, almost a mentor to him. The story could, then, start over again, this time from a woman's point of view.

The animal in question is featured on the front cover. It seems to be wagging its tail, while the man is looking down at it, perplexed. It is a weird creature whose body merges with its head and is adorned with rounded ears, while its paws, tongue, and tail are all pointed. On its first appearance in the book, it emerges from some kind of container and seems at first to be as frightened of the man as he is of it. But they quickly adjust to each other. Lacking the power of speech, it is unable to be a source of much assistance, information, or advice to its new master. Its raison d'être seems rather to be to alleviate his solitude and to enable him to form a first bond. Since every new arrival has one of these animals, it would seem that it is the municipal authorities who provide these four-legged friends—from a variety of species—as part of their integration policy.

As Tan puts it, "the relationship between man and creature in the book is a metaphor for one's connection to an environment."[8] The city in which the man has just opened up a new chapter of his life places a high value on the animal kingdom. Small, apparently autonomous creatures can be seen sitting on rooftops engaged in conversation; large sculptures are dedicated, it seems, to totemic animals (giant owls loom above a working-class area); some kind

A district swarming with totemic owls

of dragon is guarding a private residence into which our hero has incautiously stumbled; and then there are strange pocket-sized birds that look a little like sardines with wings, until they take flight and unfurl rainbow-colored tails that make them resemble children's kites, and move off in formation. (A family of these birds makes a nest on the man's windowsill.) The omnipresence of these birds works as an analogy, as the author explains: like their human counterparts, they also migrate.[9]

On the double page that shows the immigrants' first view of the city from their boat, the entrance to the port is given tangible form by two giant sculptures that face each other: two men, themselves representing immigrants, each arriving on a boat. They are shaking hands. The reassuring, somewhat idyllic image presented by this monument, the gateway to the city and in a sense its emblem, conveys a spirit of brotherhood and welcome. In this projected version of New York (if we allow that the reception center is modeled on Ellis Island), Shaun Tan undoubtedly betrays a certain naïve optimism. He describes an ideal city that has never existed, a sort of Promised Land for the migrants of the whole world, a haven of respect, peace, and prosperity. It is not insignificant that the two giant sculptures, facing each other, both incorporate an animal presence: one of the men is carrying his little (furry) companion in his arms, the other bears his (feathered) companion on his shoulders. The city is thereby displaying the close and privileged links that have been forged and encouraged between the human and animal populations. It is as if the idea of fraternity could be extended to creatures regarded as inferior. In a single image, Tan suggests many things, leaving it up to readers to follow one or another path and to seek, as the story unfolds, elements that will corroborate, complete, or contradict their intuitions.

In the home that the man left, there were no animals. (But his passion for creating origami animals—a technique that Tan himself learned from his father—no doubt testifies to a certain interest in other living beings.) When his family is reunited at the end of the book, it has admitted another member, the selfsame "weird creature" that has never ceased to keep the father company ever since his arrival. This detail alone suggests that even greater happiness has been attained.

Apart from relationships to animals, the host city has, as we have already remarked, other strange aspects: the architecture; the modes of transit that seem to defy the laws of gravity, including a sort of flying phone booth and a sort of flying boat, a hovering contraption halfway between the zeppelins of yesteryear and Mississippi steamboats—the kind of thing that someone who had never seen a plane would imagine; musical instruments; eating habits; and everyday objects. "I tried to think of strange equivalents to every common device, from clocks to mailboxes," says Tan.[10] Oddly, the clothing is only slightly out of the ordinary. The most unsettling element, for the newcomer, is undoubtedly the writing system. Tan has invented a new script by breaking the letters of the Roman alphabet into their component parts, and recombining them. The man is unable to read or understand anything in writing. He has literally become illiterate, and therefore a dunce, which will cause him a serious problem when he manages to get a job as a billposter—a nod to Vittorio De Sica's *Bicycle Thieves* (1948). He posts them, but back to front.

Tan has acknowledged that one of the sources of inspiration for *The Arrival* was *The Snowman* by the British author Raymond Briggs.[11] A small boy makes a snowman that comes to life and goes into his house, where it is baffled by domestic appliances like a refrigerator and a gas stove. It is this bewilderment that Tan bestows on his character.

The positive statement made by the giant sculpture at the harbor mouth is borne out by the rest of the story, which does indeed show how the immigrants, in their adoptive country, come together, help each other, get to know each other, and, of course, share experiences by swapping stories. Three such accounts are framed within the album.

In the first one, an Asian woman recounts how she was snatched away from her studies and set to work in a factory. She fled the country on board a train. The panels are presented as if they were photographs, with stained and tattered edges, stuck down onto the colored pages of a scrapbook. A few pages further on, the protagonist meets a father and son who look like regular Americans. The father has a strange story to tell. He and his wife had had to go into hiding and escape from a burning city seemingly being laid waste by giants bearing massive suction devices. Aided by a people smuggler, the couple made it onto a boat, which finally took them to their newly adoptive country. Finally, it falls to an elderly man to tell his tale. Sent to the battlefront as a soldier, he came back maimed to find his city in ruins and all life apparently extinguished. We understand that he too had no alternative but to flee.

Each of these three subplots is a variation on the same theme. They illustrate the definition of immigration displayed in the permanent exhibition of the Museum of the History of Immigration: it is a "collective phenomenon lived out in many individual ways." The flyleaves of the album, showing a mosaic of sixty portraits of men and women of all extractions, in the form of ID shots, for the most part inspired by photographs held by the Ellis Island museum, widen the perspective still further, and underscore the universality of the experience. "The unstated premise [...] that everyone in the city is actually an immigrant"[12] gradually dawns upon the reader.

The architecture of the host city includes conical structures that inevitably make us think of teepees. Was this Tan's way of indirectly alluding to Native Americans? Through them, he seems to have turned the question on its head: the indigenous people are indeed those who have stayed put, those who were already there and have witnessed the arrival of successive waves of others.

By extending his storyline to embrace the lot of others beyond his main character, Tan is suggesting that reasons for abandoning one's homeland are manifold: penury, hunger, mass unemployment, religious or political persecution, totalitarianism, environmental disasters, wars—the list goes on. The enigmatic image of giant Cyclopes armed with suction machines were

An extract from the Asian woman's story: a fake photo album

perhaps invented by the author to evoke ethnic cleansing. This large-scale composition, which occupies a double page, is undoubtedly the most horrifying of all the scenes that the book exposes us to, along with the images of the open mass grave and the ruined city that feature in the old man's story. In comparison, the protagonist's own story seems less dramatic, and the circumstances that lead to his departure are unclear. Some kind of threat hangs over him and his family, represented by the huge black spiky tentacles that infest the streets, but this is a graphic metaphor whose meaning is indeterminate. Could it be an economic crisis? Some other catastrophe? Or maybe simply an allegory of despair? By keeping the motivation of his central character vague, Tan gives his story a universal dimension: it stands for all the others.

We must return to the pseudophotographic status conferred on the images that convey the Asian woman's account. The slippage from images supposedly referring to "reality" into these pictures of pictures, with a documentary and memorializing value, is effected through an initial photograph, the one that appears on her entry visa, which she proffers in response to the gesture of the man as he shows her his own document. Tan zooms in on this ID shot, which functions as a way in to the three subsequent pages that make up the woman's actual story.

Everything is paradoxical here. There is a paradox in transposing something that the context shows to be an oral narrative, recounted to a travelling companion, into the form of a pseudophotographic story. There is a paradox in making it seem as though the scenes in which the young woman is being harassed or forced to flee could have been captured on film, when by their very nature, they must have passed unwitnessed. There is a paradox in including, amid these images that may plausibly be viewed as standard square photographic prints, a full-page image that has to be interpreted, more implausibly, as an enlargement. Besides, there is no particular reason why this woman's story should have been treated any differently from the other two stories framed within the main narrative, which are devoid of the photographic reference. Ultimately, the reader cannot escape the conclusion that there is no difference, as regards the graphic rendering, between these supposed photos (distinguished as such only by their border) and any of the other drawings in the work.

Benoît Peeters, writing on *The Castafiore Emerald*,[13] has observed of the photographs published by the fictional magazine *Paris-Flash* when it broke the news of the forthcoming marriage of the diva with Captain Haddock:

> These photos simultaneously validate the realism of Hergé's graphic line (the photos resemble the drawings) and, more insidiously, undermine it (the images do not resemble real photographs). Hence the rather strange effect of these two pages: the magazine has abandoned its own codes in order to conform with those of comics, while at the same time the representational system of comics is disrupted by its encounter with a different medium.[14]

The aesthetic of *The Arrival* is very far removed from Hergé's clear line, and yet, here also, its encounter with photography produces "a rather strange effect."

Throughout the book, Shaun Tan's style, which is realist, naturalistic, modeled, and marked by use of the whole range of gray scale, gestures toward photography. Since the images presented as photographs are not treated any differently from the other panels, their illusionistic force is increased: the authority of the real is conferred, by contamination, on the whole book. The fantastical aspects of certain motifs and scenes are validated and given the same truth value as the more banal, familiar aspects. The reader is therefore hardly surprised to note that the photograph that the protagonist takes with him when he leaves home—a photo that shows him, his wife, and their daughter together and which is his most precious source of comfort on his journey—seems to have a magic power: the power of conjuring up, at the bottom of his suitcase, the image of the absent wife and daughter, left on their own. It becomes an ephemeral miniature theatre made up of objects and dolls that haunts the immigrant like a mirage.

If the medium of photography and its effects are problematized in *The Arrival*, this is, of course, because Tan has made abundant use of it during the process of creating the book. He has explained his working method:

> I [...] spent about six months working on *The Arrival* in a simplified style, sort of half-way between realism and a cartoon. [...] Eventually, I tried a more photographic style, using carefully shot video images as reference. [...] For each page in the book I would storyboard a scene, organize shots for location and time of day, hunt for objects and appropriate clothes, discuss each scene with "actors," film dozens of short sequences, isolate the best image frames, and use these as the basis for each panel.[15]

The texture of the image is applied with a soft pencil, and the sepia tints are added digitally at the end of the process.

Shaun Tan, who shot the sequences in his garage, is not the first author to begin by creating an image bank and then to put together a kind of photo story as the prior stages in the production of a comic book. Jean Teulé, Frédéric Boilet, and Alison Bechdel have all used this method—and long before them, in the 1950s, so did the British artist Frank Hampson in his science-fiction series *Dan Dare*. While Teulé and Boilet (the latter more overtly as time went on) leave evidence of the photographic origin of their images in the final version, Alison Bechdel attempts to disguise it. Tan occupies a kind of indecisive halfway position; his story has a completely original, hybrid status, a poetic realism that is somewhere between dream and reportage.

The photos that comprise the raw material of *The Arrival* are not limited to the ones staged and filmed by the author. Archive photos have an equally important place, without necessarily always being faithfully reproduced;

A reinvention of the Great Hall on Ellis Island

they serve as a source of inspiration for the author and as a starting point for reflection.

> Many ideas for the book were inspired by old photographs of people and places that have long since passed away, and these have often been triggers for other paintings of mine. There is a sense of mystery already in historical records that has something to do with their distance and silence, so I need to work my imagination to build a lost world around these little fragments of memory. It's almost as though the absence of information demands the creation of fiction to fill the void.[16]

The archives that he has drawn upon most extensively are those concerning Ellis Island, situated in New York at the mouth of the Hudson, less than a kilometer to the north of Liberty Island. In the first part of the twentieth century, Ellis Island was the main entry point for immigrants arriving in America. The immigration services were based there from January 1, 1892, until November 12, 1954, and over twelve million people passed through. Tan reinvents the famous "Great Hall." In a full-page image, the gigantic Registry Room[17] is hung with banners proclaiming messages in the mysterious script. The upper part of the image consists of a large semi-circular *veduta*, displaying a cityscape toward which fly balloons transporting the immigrants who have received their entry certificates.

Although the artist relied heavily on photographic or video images in the process of creating *The Arrival*, the copious working documents that he has published, notably in *Sketches from a Nameless Land*, testify to the fact that he also drew upon many other tools and techniques: the drawings were worked on through free experimentation consisting of small sketches drafted with a light pencil and then more detailed studies, with hatching of varying degrees of thickness indicating the shades of gray, for which a precise graphic breakdown with explanatory notes appears in the margins. He also used stencils, collages, and folded paper, and he even made three-dimensional models and clay sculptures. For his first comic, Tan deployed a wide range of methods; he "cobbled together" a composite technique, and arrived at a result that was remarkable in its coherence and controlled artistry.

The layout is one of the most accomplished aspects of the book. Sophie Van der Linden, a specialist in illustrated children's books, explains that, in contemporary production, "the diversity and flexibility of the album are often both represented within the same work. During the course of the book, most illustrators vary the organization of the page," resulting in conspicuous breaks in continuity.[18] The experience that Tan has gained in this area shows through in the freedom with which he occupies the space of the page. A large number

of pages have the look of the "waffle iron," or orthogonal grid, with all panels having the same shape and size. But the number of panels on each page varies to a considerable extent. There are five regular pages with nine panels, thirty-eight with twelve panels (or sometimes eleven, when one panel is doubled in length), and others with four or sixteen panels. The flyleaves, as we have mentioned, feature an array of thirty small panels at each end. And rhythm is conferred upon the book when certain moments are given spectacular promi-nence, occupying a whole page (this is the case for twenty-four of them, an

exceptionally high number in a comic book) or a double page (of which there are nine instances). By varying the rhythm, by creating certain surprise effects, and by inviting a reading that is sometimes intense, sometimes analytical or contemplative, the artist has imbued his album with an almost musical dimension, without ever giving in to facile effects.

I will conclude on the first of the large "splash panels" occupying the whole page. It appears on a right-hand page, the third in the first chapter. The man and his wife are standing on each side of a table, their hands clasped on top of a closed suitcase. They seem resigned. This melancholy image brings together everything that makes up the home that the man is preparing to leave (except the child, who is in bed) and prefigures his departure. The objects that are represented (clock, hat, origami folding, children's drawings, cooking pot, and teapot) have all been previously introduced to us in separate panels on the first page, as if it were an inventory. They are collected here in a recapitulatory panel whose function is to freeze an image of domestic harmony that is just about to be undone. Some 115 pages further on, on the second page of chapter 6, and four pages from the end of the book, there is another splash panel that echoes this one, creating a loop, a particularly significant braiding effect. The framing is about the same; it is similarly frontal, and the table is in the same position in the middle of the composition. This time, the father, the mother, and the daughter are seated at a shared meal and looking happy. At their feet is the domestic animal that is now part of their household. It is the same scene, transposed into a joyful mode. The equilibrium of the family has been restored, as is evinced by the return of a certain number of identical objects: an origami folding, the man's hat, drawings (different drawings), and the precious photo. New objects have appeared, based on a different design principle, favoring circular, floral, and solar shapes. Shaun Tan invites the reader to navigate from one end of the book to the other and to compare, term for term, the two images, which condense the situations of departure and arrival. The end point of the book, the arrival, is a mirror image.

CRAIG THOMPSON
Habibi (2011)

BACKGROUND

Craig Thompson was born in 1975 in Michigan, and grew up in Wisconsin in a born-again Christian family. The Bible was the only book that his parents read or allowed in the home. Thompson studied graphic art in Milwaukee, self-published his first three comic books, with a very low print run, and then worked with Top Shelf Productions, the publishing company set up in the 1990s by Brett Warnock and Chris Staros. Top Shelf published *Good-bye, Chunky Rice*, the story of an adventurous turtle, which won Thompson the 2000 Harvey Award for Best New Talent.[1] A French-language version was published by Delcourt in 2002. It was later reissued by Casterman after the resounding success of *Blankets*, which had been published in 2003 by Top Shelf and translated into French the following year.[2] This multiple prize-winning comic book is centered on the author's adolescence, his religious upbringing, his first love, and his break with Christianity. Thompson has said that he felt justified in tackling personal subject matter after discovering Edmond Baudoin's *Piero*.[3] In 2004, Thompson published the travelogue *Carnet de Voyage*, a record of his journey through Europe and North Africa.[4]

Habibi, the result of four years' work, came out in 2011. It is a little thicker than *Blankets* (672 pages rather than 592). The cultural magazine *Télérama* described it as a "torrential saga" that was "graphically dazzling." *Elle* magazine declared Craig Thompson to be the Charles Dickens of comics. He is certainly one of the most prominent authors on the American independent comics scene.

After a collaboration with James Kochalka (*Conversations #1*), he is currently collaborating on a book with Baudoin.

PLOT

Habibi is set in Wanatolia, an imaginary Middle-Eastern country, at an indeterminate period during the 20th century. The narrator is a young Arabic woman called Dodola. She tells her own story and that of Cham, an African boy nine years younger than her, whom she renames Zam.

As a child, she is sold into marriage, and witnesses the murder of her husband. She is reduced to slavery, but manages to escape and takes Zam with her. They find refuge in a boat that is stranded amid the dunes in a sea of sand. To ensure their survival, Dodola's only recourse is to prostitute herself to the traders from passing caravans in exchange for food. They soon create a legend around her: she becomes known as "the phantom courtesan of the desert" (124) and her reputation reaches as far as the Sultan of Wanatolia, who orders her capture. Confined in his harem, she becomes his favorite and receives a new name: Sfayi, "pleasure giver." After she has been faced with the challenge of satisfying him for seventy nights in a row and has given him an heir, she is set a second test: she must turn a jug of water into gold. Unfortunately the ruse that she uses is discovered, and she is condemned to death.

Meanwhile, Zam has joined a community of eunuchs and has been castrated. He is sent out to earn money by prostitution, but is captured in his turn by the Sultan's henchmen. He joins the eunuchs in the "Palace of Tears." Although the harem is a forbidden space, he defies the rules and manages to enter it, just in time to save Dodola from being executed by drowning.

They are rescued by a fisherman called Noah, who assumes they are man and wife. Dodola falls seriously ill and is on the brink of death but recovers. They set out to return to the ship where they had lived before, but it is now buried in an ocean of garbage. They reach the capital of Wanatolia, a big modern city, and squat in the abandoned top floor of an unfinished high-rise building. Zam gets hired as a construction worker. Dodola decides to have a child with him, and only then discovers that he has been castrated. Zam considers suicide, but changes his mind (guided by the words of the prophet: "the Greater Djihad [...] is the struggle against oneself"). They have to leave their high-rise squat because construction work is starting up again. In the city they buy a small slave girl who becomes their adoptive child.

HABIBI IS A GRAPHIC NOVEL THAT TEEMS WITH LIFE. It is sensual, erudite, committed, feisty, cruel, and both contemporary and timeless. It is a compendium woven through with references to the great monotheist religions (religions of the book) that thoughtfully intertwines themes as diverse as slavery, freedom, water, food, ecology, language, writing, knowledge, love, the status of women, desire, motherhood, sacrifice, and faith. Thompson said of *Blankets* that he had "needed a heavyweight book to find an adequate space in which to express himself."[5] This is, self-evidently, even more true of *Habibi*.

It is also a graphic tour de force in that the artist borrows from artistic traditions that are foreign to his own culture—Arabic calligraphy and the decorative ornamentation of Islamic art—and succeeds in fusing them with the codes of Western comics in a visual syncretism that compels admiration.[6]

These borrowings are not gratuitous. They are not there simply to add local color, to heighten the exoticism. Calligraphy plays an important part in the story itself. Dodola's father is illiterate, but the husband to whom he sells her is a scribe. Although he subjects the child, far too young to be married, to the violence of a premature deflowering, he also becomes her teacher: it is he who instructs her in reading and writing. He enables his young wife to gain access to knowledge and to texts: the Koran (the sacred text) and *The Thousand and One Nights* (the quintessence of the art of storytelling), between which he establishes no hierarchy. The thieves who break in and cut his throat are, conversely, depicted as uncultured unbelievers who deny that books have any value.

Thompson does not explain how Dodola is able to go on educating herself, but he nonetheless shows her to be extraordinarily erudite, able to compare, with all the assurance of a theologian, the accounts of Abraham's sacrifice from the Koran and the book of Genesis (47).

The author offers an illuminating recollection of his own experience: "For ten years of my life, I read the Bible every day. We didn't have a radio or television and we never watched films on video or heard any music except religious music. On the other hand, comics were allowed because they were intended for children."[7]

Dodola, in turn, teaches Zam. The letters that she traces out for him on a sheet of paper in the nine cells of a square become his talisman. This square is reproduced on the page facing the title page of each of the nine chapters that make up *Habibi*: to every chapter there corresponds a specific letter that dictates its theme. Throughout the book, Thompson makes numerous references to the science of magic squares, refined by Arabic mathematicians between the ninth and eleventh centuries, who referred to them as "the harmonious arrangement of numbers." In *Habibi*, however, they can contain letters as well as numbers. The artist is aware that Islam had drawn upon ideas about magic and astrological beliefs borrowed from the ancient world (including the Greeks, Indians, Persians, Nabataeans and Sabians) and that it had adopted ancient cosmologies based on the interdependence of all the elements: stars of the Zodiac, planets, plants, minerals, colors, calendars, numbers, the human body, etc.[8] *Habibi* encompasses magical thinking, which inevitably lends a somewhat esoteric aspect to certain pages.

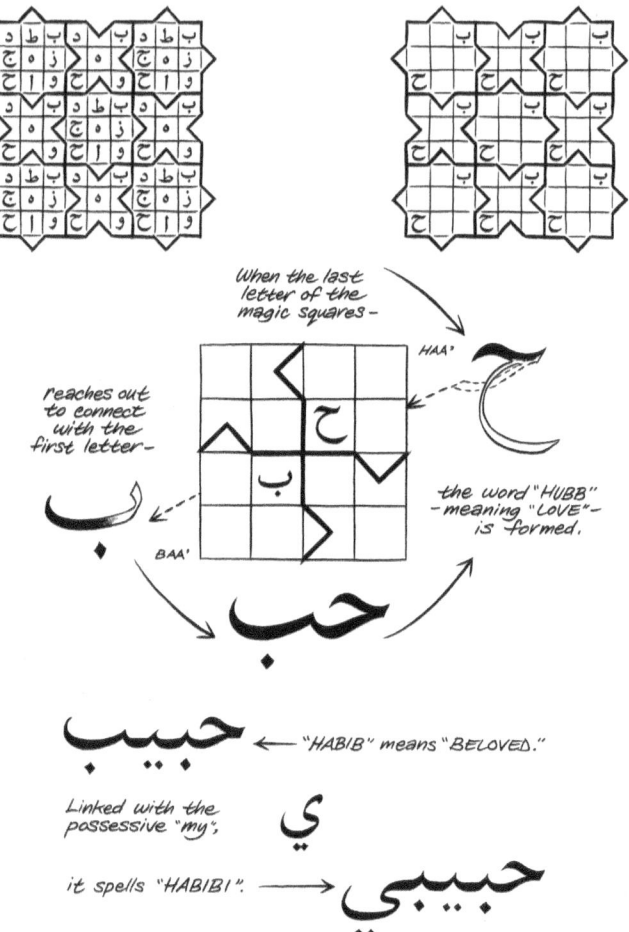

Writing protects, then; it gives access to knowledge; we even discover that it is a remedy for desperate illness (473–74), and that in other circumstances it can be assimilated to sexual energy (640). In Islam, writing is a liturgical act. Calligraphy gives visible form to the word of God, revealed to the Prophet. Writing originates with God. The first sentence of *Habibi* alludes to the "Divine Pen" from which "fell the first drop of ink."

But Arabic calligraphy is also a form of drawing. When "tangled up," the letters generate many ornamental forms, as is stated and shown on pages 38 to 39. And Thompson, the American artist, endeavors, with patience and fervor, to emulate the elegance of the abstract decoration of the Koranic texts. As he himself explained in the press pack issued by Casterman when the comic was launched in France, "The ornamental borders in *Habibi* draw inspiration

from illuminated manuscripts and were incredibly time consuming, taking three times longer to draw than the panels that they contain. [...] Arabic calligraphy has been called 'music for the eyes.' I find that perfect." The drawing of the letters, the rhythm of the writing, and the dance of the paintbrush all resonate, in various sequences, with a winding river, an undulating sand dune, the branches of a tree, and the contortions of a snake, giving rise to visual rhymes of all kinds.

Thompson favors black and white because he likes "the calligraphic look that you can get from black ink."[9] His brush stroke is not like Baudoin's, lacking the French artist's spontaneity, freedom, and vibrancy. It is a precise, descriptive stroke, deriving suppleness and power from the play of downstrokes and upstrokes. Black and white are equally proportioned on many pages, counterbalancing each other.

For Thompson, one of the functions of art is to capture beauty, to re-enchant the world, and comics can aspire to do that just as much as paintings hung in galleries, even if the medium has often seemed best suited to caricature,

derision, and the grotesque. Thompson resists this tradition. However, in spite of the aesthetic ambition that underlies his work, and notwithstanding the seriousness of the subject matter, and the gravity of the themes, he has no qualms about introducing visual gags (for example, the man hoisted into the air by a camel on page 69) or about including elements of caricature: the negative characters are frequently depicted with grimacing faces (see in particular the rictus grin of the slave trafficker [63–65], or that of the Sultan in a lascivious mood [259]). A *New York Times* critic (Robyn Creswell, in the edition from October 14, 2011) describes the sultan as "a *Mad Magazine* version of King Shahryar from *The Thousand and One Nights*." There is another grotesque character in the perpetually flatulent Goojez, the chief of the harem dwarves.

To the richness of the themes there corresponds, then, a graphic polyphony, or polygraphy, which sets up a tension between realism and caricature, narration and decoration.

In the press pack, again, the author explains that the September 11 attacks played a role in the conception of *Habibi*. "Islam was being demonized by the media and I tried to humanize it, to discover its beauty, and to understand it. [...] My research led me to discover Arabic calligraphy, geometrical designs, decoration, and architecture—all these artistic domains that have developed in such an incredible way on account of a supposed prohibition on figurative art." He has, he further elaborates, been particularly inspired by Sufism, "a form of spirituality involving religious ecstasy and mysticism."

Habibi can, then, be described as a politically committed book, if only because it deliberately runs counter to dominant American opinion. Its political commitment is also evident in its denunciation of the subjugation of women, the unequal distribution of wealth, and the environmental devastation of our planet. I will return to this.

For his evocation of the Arab Muslim world, Thompson drew on a period spent in Morocco in 2009, and the sketches of motifs that he made there, which became the subject matter of *Carnet de Voyage*. Several of the backdrops in *Habibi* are very close to drawings that appear in the earlier book; I am thinking of those that portray the Medina in Marrakech (31) and in Fez (106) and the Bahia Palace (43), not to mention the camels and sand dunes. And even if none of them are shown in *Carnet*, there is no doubt that Thompson must have come across water carriers like those he draws in *Habibi* (326), in Jemaa el-Fnaa Square.

However, the artist preferred to invent an imaginary country, Wanatolia.[10] This decision allowed him to avoid concrete reference to the political situation, known to be explosive, in the Maghreb or in the Middle East. It lends a general applicability to the events portrayed: without being rooted in a specific geopolitical reality, *Habibi* presents itself not as a documentary but rather as a folk tale or parable. The author refers to "a simplified fairy tale, with a castle at the top of a mountain." He also makes it clear that "*Habibi* does not take place in a particular location or at a particular time and borrows freely from historical fact and from fantastical stories."[11]

The desert, the souk, and the carpet sellers are all timeless background elements. The slave market, the harem, the baths (207), and the caravans all reference a more mythologized past. Several pages have visual echoes of nineteenth-century Orientalist painting, and certain works by Gérôme in particular are directly quoted, as is Ingres's *Bain turc* [Turkish bath] (210).[12] *Habibi* is at its most conventional when it exploits the sensuality and exoticism attached to these images.

The modern face of the country is also represented. It is gradually revealed: first a motor cycle (11), then a hydroelectric dam (142–43), the engine room of the boat (160), an industrial backdrop (290–92), modern apartment blocks, a fuel tanker (415), and, finally, the big city.

And this is a fable that addresses highly contemporary issues, extrapolating slightly by exacerbating the problems of pollution and access to water to a level even more acute than we know it to be.

Some commentators have reproached Thompson for perpetuating stereotypes, by featuring the harem so prominently (in chapters 2 and 4) and by including an orgy scene between the Sultan and his courtesans (259). This is notably the viewpoint of Kathleen Gros, who sees the comic book as "problematic." She points out that "the exclusively sexual connotation of the harem is a western construction," when in fact the harem was also a space where women could socialize with each other. She comments, "In Habibi, Dodola never finds much support or camaraderie among the women in the harem," and asks, "Why is Thompson's depiction of a futuristic East so firmly rooted in the past? It serves to further the trope of the 'timeless orient'—an erroneous portrayal of the East as unchanging, ancient, and behind the west in terms of progress."[13]

This criticism seems somewhat unjust to me. It does not take account of the fact that a fable, a folk tale, is entitled to take all kinds of liberties with reality. Thompson's Orient is primarily a mythical setting, a way of decentering the narrative. He cannot be accused of wishing to denigrate the Arab Muslim world. On the contrary, he extols its architecture, art, and calligraphy, and he has closely studied its sacred texts. Does he tackle science? He sets up an equivalence between Aristotle (250), "the father of biology," and Jabir Ibn Hayyan (251), "the father of chemistry," implying that Greco-Roman and Islamic cultures have made equal contributions to scientific progress. Through the character of Noah, he celebrates the legendary hospitality of Arabs and Muslims. Conversely, he does not touch on the issue of religious fundamentalism, and his portrayal of the Prophet is always very respectful. The capital of Wanatolia, revealed late in the story (538–39) as the setting for the epilogue, is portrayed as a big modern city that resembles Manhattan—even if its abandoned construction sites and its low-wage foreign workers suggest Dubai or Abu Dhabi. The women appear emancipated (615). The Sultan's palace, on the other hand, is a world that is closed off, an enclave where time seems to have stopped because the decadent and tyrannical monarch is concerned only with pleasure and lives for sex and opium. But Thompson's position is clear: he constantly contrasts the poverty-stricken people with the wealthy and powerful who evade the harsh realities of the world. This is an antagonism that quite obviously has universal relevance.

The mixture of spirituality and sexuality that characterizes *Habibi* was already to be found in *Blankets*. A number of episodes from the New Testament are evoked and illustrated there. But, in the earlier book, romantic relationships are very chastely portrayed. Craig and Raina seem to inhabit the ethereal plane of high emotion, in the throes of first love for each other. *Habibi* is infinitely more direct and crude. Emotions are still very important (*Habibi* means "my beloved;" the other pervasive word is *Bismillah* ["in the name of God"]) but there is no restraint on the depiction of sexual desire, pleasure, prostitution, or rape, in explicit and repeated images. Thompson explains: "As a child I was molested by a babysitter, but as a teenager I was also deeply affected by the rapes that someone else to whom I was very close endured."[14] It

Dodola encounters emancipated women in the capital

is clear that the sexual violence that the artist inflicts on Dodola—all the more troubling given his obvious empathy for his two protagonists—is a kind of exorcism, and is intended to shock the reader's conscience.

Habibi is a highly *embodied* comic book. The representation of the body is taken seriously and treated boldly. Rejecting one of the most deeply rooted traditions in comics, that of the immutable heroes who not only never age but always wear the same costume to maintain the consistency of their image, Thompson shows the transformation in the bodies of Zam and Dodola over the course of the narrative. They both age (the action stretches over twenty years) and their appearance changes. The metamorphosis is particularly spectacular in the case of Zam. From a small boy he becomes an adolescent, then a man. After being rescued from the streets by a group of eunuchs, he is castrated in his turn. The once-skeletal boy becomes obese. (In a beautiful image on page 628, in which Dodola and Zam embrace, they are portrayed at different ages all at once.)

The character of Dodola, often depicted as naked by an author who nonetheless avoids falling into voyeurism, condenses *all* the experiences and all the assaults on her body that can be undergone by a woman. Deflowering, rape, pregnancy, prostitution, attempted abortion, exhaustion, dehydration, illness—she is spared nothing. Future motherhood (endured while enclosed within the harem), far from being glamorized, inspires only "disgust" in Dodola (105). Thompson uses anatomical drawings of the female reproductive organs (81), and insists on the darkening of the skin, the tenderness of the breasts, the weight gain, the discomfort, the shortness of breath, the heartburn, and the feeling of detachment from the body.

There is another striking scene in the book (479) where Dodola, sick and stricken with fever and dysentery, expels the contents of her gut from both ends of her body. This body, cared for with unparalleled devotion by Zam, this body that has appeared throughout the book as seductive, an object of lust, is now represented, with unusual crudity, as abject.

The Orientalizing phantasmagoria of *Habibi* is balanced out by a realism rarely seen before in the portrayal of all these afflictions. Realism gives way to fantasy when Dodola's body is covered with writing (405), recalling Peter Greenaway's film *The Pillow Book*, and when she medicates herself by swallowing letters, which she spits out again once she is cured.

Thompson sets up an evident parallel between the female body and the planet Earth, both defiled and abused. "I think that humanity is destroying the Earth, and that the human race may die out," he has said, confessing his "nihilism."[15] The boat that has run aground in the sand dunes is a symbol of the impasse to which the actions of humans have led us. The title of the sixth chapter, "Drowning," is to be taken both literally (the protagonists almost drown) and in a more general sense: the human race is at risk of drowning under its own waste. When Zam and Dodola find their boat again, it is scarcely visible under a sea of filth. In the village, the illnesses spread by contaminated water have devastating effects. There are no more fish. "The city wells up with diarrhea and sludge. Raw sewage, factory residue, chemicals. Cyanide, lead, nitrogen sulfate. All manner of human waste" (448). And Noah, the fisherman, becomes a spokesman for the author: "Our species is destined to consume itself. There's already too many of us. We're horribly inefficient critters—greedy, yet wasteful—and expendable. The rich gorge themselves on our corpses. We've poisoned the earth, and we've poisoned ourselves" (505). The images of the river full of sewage are arresting. On that issue also, Thompson is hard-hitting. His book is definitely not for those of a delicate disposition.

The artist aligns himself, then, with the ideas of ecofeminism, a movement that is relatively young (the term appeared for the first time in 1974) and which is concerned both with the subjugation of nature and that of women, making a link between patriarchy, capitalism, and the destruction of nature. "Regarding women's bodies and nature as 'passive' [. . .] is a way of justifying their exploitation," according to Vandana Shiva, one of its key figures (the founder of Diverse Women for Diversity in 1998).[16]

Craig Thompson is not a recent convert. Already, in *Blankets*, he was asking his father whether they should not recycle some of their trash. And his critique arises out of a global political analysis: "Everyone, in the industrialized western world, is a passive participant in the exploitation of people from poor

The passionate bond between Zam and Dodola, from childhood to adulthood

The river is an open sewer

countries. That is the nature of capitalism and globalization, and of world trade, and of industrialization, and of wealth in general."[17]

Habibi focuses particularly on the problem of access to water, the most vital of all natural resources, a problem that becomes even more acute in a desert environment that is dry by nature. But this theme is only one of the manifestations of water as a structuring motif that permeates the entire narrative. Right from the opening scenes, Dodola's husband washes her feet with very pure water. On page 30, we hear about a river that has dried up, and on page 45 about a sacred well, a gift from Allah. A little further on, it is said that God created every moving thing from water (61). We also learn that Dodola is the name of a rain goddess (175). Cham is the name of a character from the book of Genesis, one of the three sons of the patriarch Noah, a survivor of the Flood. (Dodola changes his name to Zam because the sons of Cham had been cursed.)

The story is also suffused with bath water, amniotic fluid, water that must be turned into gold, drain water, water retained by the dam, punishment by drowning, mythological stories about sacred wells, and the water-bottling factory where Zam finds employment. Water is involved in everything that happens; it flows through the book, mingling closely with the narrative flux.

His treatment of the water motif is characteristic of the way in which Thompson interweaves themes, sets up rhymes, and structures his story like

When liquid becomes smoke

a vast echo chamber. There are correspondences between numerous scenes from different parts of the book. The slave market on page 653 refers back to the one on page 63. Dodola, the former slave, as favorite of the Sultan, is allocated her own personal slave, Nadidah. The theme of selling girls into marriage, which had been Dodola's fate, is picked up on page 352. There comes a time when it is Zam who bathes the suffering Dodola (443) as she had bathed him as a child (94–103). Zam rejects the child that she bore in the harem, but later tells Zam of her desire to have a child with him. And so on.

Furthermore, Dodola is a teller of tales who, throughout their relationship, comforts Zam with stories. Thompson takes pleasure in listing (pages 94–102) the many justifications for the art of narrating: to soothe Zam to sleep, to bring them closer together, to nurture his imagination, to distract him from hunger, to teach moral lessons, to show the complexity of life, to divert oneself from studies, and to retell their experiences. A treatise on narration, synthesized in a few pages and integrated into Thompson's own story.

Dodola's stories are mostly episodes from the Koran or the book of Genesis: scenes from the life of Abraham, Moses, Job, or Noah. In fact, most of these stories offer parallels with the experiences of the protagonists and metaphorically illuminate them. To take but one example, in the episode concerning Solomon and Bilqis, there is a triple resonance. The heroes fall in love with each other, like the sovereigns of old (564). But Zam feels rejected by Dodola once she has discovered that he is a eunuch and is therefore unable to be a husband to her, just as Solomon felt abandoned by Bilqis, who refused to sacrifice her virginity to him (572). Moreover, the consolation that Solomon seeks in polygamy (by taking "700 wives and 300 concubines") recalls, quite clearly, the behavior of the Sultan of Wanatolia. It is usually Zam who mentally creates these short circuits between reality and legend: his entire experience of the world is filtered through Dodola's stories. And it is by telling new stories, "a torrent of stories," that Dodola regains her health, sweeping her spirit "back to reality" (510–13).

Correspondences can also be observed between certain graphic motifs like that of the round window, which is found in contrasting contexts. There are first the portholes of the protective ship, the home and refuge of the heroes; then there is the circular barred window of the dungeon where Dodola is imprisoned on the order of the Sultan (221–24).

Let us look more closely at the river motif, around which Thompson has woven a remarkable braiding series. The first chapter is, indeed, called "River Map." The first occurrence of the motif is on page 9, in the form of a river of ink. Ten pages further on there appears an image showing a trickle of blood next to a hand, resembling the river as it flows across the panel. This image is a detail excerpted from another panel, which appears on page 22, where the widening of the frame enables the reader to identify the man whose throat has been cut. This is the husband who was imposed on the young Dodola. The ink used to sign the marriage contract (11) and the bloodstain on the sheet after her deflowering (13) are the same shade of black. The motif of the river returns on page 31; its serpentine shape is now explicitly linked to the letters of Arabic script. And this page is preceded by two scenes devoted to lessons in Arabic calligraphy, one given to Dodola by her husband (15) and one given to Zam by Dodola (37).

Let us look at the water that is figured on pages 44 (a stream gushes forth from the feet of Ishmael), 296 (four rivers extend from the base of the Lote Tree), 451–54 (the polluted river, an open sewer), and 571 (the water spilling out of the bottle). It can be seen that the different liquids follow the same diagonal, a composition that establishes these images as a series that is perceptually salient. Other serpentine forms—the umbilical cord, the snake—can also be likened to the river motif. Not to mention page 196, where the image from page 19 is repeated with the black and white reversed: the trickle of blood has become the smoke from a narghile.

This dense network of interrelated images converges on the syncretic panel that takes up the whole of page 475: a mixture of water and ink courses through Dodola's body, winding its way from her mouth to her stomach. The libation contains letters. In this way, the three major themes of life (blood), knowledge (ink), and ecology (water) are woven together throughout *Habibi* by a carefully arranged series of visual rhymes that ensures the coherence of the work. And this is perhaps where the notion of the "graphic novel" takes on its full meaning.

The story recounted in *Habibi* spans twenty years. With its picturesque settings, its multiple dramatic episodes, and its unashamed pathos, it has some of the qualities of a nineteenth-century popular saga and may indeed recall Dickens, as press reviews have suggested. Its backbone is the strength of the indissoluble bond between Zam and Dodola.

This relationship takes on different aspects as they grow older and are marked by the ordeals that they have undergone. Dodola is maternal at first: she is the elder of the two, an educated and resourceful young woman who takes care of the abandoned Zam and treats him like her own child. When Zam grows up, they become something like brother and sister. He wants to participate in the tasks that ensure their survival: she is responsible for providing food, he has the chore of fetching water. Then, gradually, the boy becomes aware of more ambiguous feelings. A skillfully handled sequence, in which several timeframes intersect (94–103), shows how Dodola, embarrassed by the way that he is looking at her, realizes that it is no longer possible for them to take a bath together. "When I grow up, I'll marry you," Zam says to her ingenuously (100). The boy witnesses the rape of Dodola (152–55) and becomes obsessed with the idea of possessing her in his turn.

Dodola's captivity within the harem brings about a lasting separation. During this period, both are wretched, and they are constantly together in their thoughts.

Dodola repudiates the child that she has conceived with the Sultan because she compares him unfavorably to Zam: "That which came from me was not familiar like the one I'd adopted" (267).

Meanwhile, Zam, who does not know what has happened to Dodola, thinks that she has rejected him because of his impure thoughts. He is taken in, having become a walking skeleton, by a group of eunuchs known as "Hijras" who beg for a living, a small community split between those who practice asceticism and those who practice sensuality. They disguise him as a woman. After his castration he discovers that desire has still not died in him.

Once he has saved Dodola from the harem and she has regained her health, they live together as a couple—but Zam does not dare show himself naked and conceals his status as eunuch from her.[18] For Dodola, there is no further obstacle to their life together as lovers. She kisses him on the mouth (562) and tells him that she wants to have a baby with him (581). This drives Zam to despair: "I lived as a boy, then a girl, then a eunuch, but never as a man" (600). They nonetheless end up by having a family, and it would not be inaccurate to write that, as far as the two heroes are concerned, *Habibi* has a fairly conventional happy ending: love has conquered all, it has won out and their suffering is in some way redeemed. Dodola and Zam are martyrs to love just as, in a different era, were Héloïse and Abelard (the latter also condemned to castration).

Habibi is narrated in the first person by Dodola, but she is an intermittent narrator. She regularly says "I" in the first chapter, and a few more times but much less often in the two following ones (81, 90, 117, etc.). Then her voice is silenced, to be heard again much further on (441 and again on 554). Of course she cannot recount events that are experienced by Zam in her absence. In any case, a number of Biblical episodes are interspersed throughout the narrative, without it being clear whether they are among the stories that Dodola never stops telling the child in her care. And the penultimate chapter, entitled "Orphan's Prayer," consists of nine pages without images, over the course of which a text unwinds, divided up to fit into the nine compartments of the grid. It is a long monologue addressed to Allah by Zam, who is unsure whether to live or die. In this soliloquy he examines his conscience and takes possession of his own story by becoming, in his turn, its narrator.

In this way, Thompson brings the first person into his narration, but not systematically, simply as the dramatic need arises. The delegation of the narration to Dodola at the beginning, on the one hand, establishes her from the outset as a storyteller and, on the other hand, amounts to an assertion of feminism. The woman may be humiliated, denied all rights, bruised, and battered, but she has control over language and the power to speak the truth.

The page layout displays the same absence of system, the same flexibility in managing all the parameters that contribute to the progress of the narrative. The first few pages alone offer a display of the diverse models that are rotated by the artist: a regular waffle iron grid (9, 23), a jagged layout, with sharp-angled panels, to emphasize the violence of the murder of Dodola's husband (20–21), drawings that bleed off the page (22, 24–25, 30), and pages with an ornamental frame (26–27, 34). Thompson constantly reinvents the space of the page, freely and with intelligence. To borrow the categories proposed by Benoît Peeters, we might say that his general tendency is rhetorical, in that the layout is adapted to accommodate developments in the story, but that it is also, on an ad hoc basis, regular, decorative, or productive.

Finally, we would need a separate study to account for Thompson's management of narrative time. The first twenty pages seem to promise a linear narrative. They are followed by a caption that looks like a classic indicator of a flashback: "That was three years prior." Except that the second sequence, introduced by these words, seems completely unrelated to the previous one, and the reader is at this stage unable to make the link between them. And on page 54 we read the words "when I was trapped in the Sultan's harem," which evoke in the past tense a period of time that has not yet been recounted and that does not yet seem to have arrived. The first explanations appear in the flashback that begins on page 56: we learn how Dodola has saved Zam from the slave traffickers who think he has no market value by passing him off as her brother. The reader rapidly takes on board a simple code: a black background around a page always signals it as a flashback. But Dodola's pregnancy is portrayed at length in chapter 2, while her arrival at the harem—where the Sultan will impregnate her—does not happen until chapter 4. The thread of the story is constantly interrupted, the chronology of events disrupted. Page 117 picks up the thread of the story that had been interrupted on page 49 and takes us back to before the pregnancy and birth. And, leaping over almost the entirety of his plot, Thompson reintroduces us on page 609 to Dodola's husband, whose throat had been cut 600 pages earlier.

However, even if readers are sometimes disconcerted, they are never really lost, and gradually all the pieces of the jigsaw fall into place. Thompson is an audacious and highly self-confident storyteller. He and his heroine Dodola are worthy heirs of Scheherazade.

CHRIS WARE
Building Stories (2012)

BACKGROUND

Franklin Christenson Ware was born on December 28, 1967, in Omaha, Nebraska. He and his mother were abandoned by his father (who served on a US Navy submarine) before he was a year old. His mother worked as an editor on the local newspaper, the *Omaha World-Herald*. So Ware was familiar from an early age with the smell of ink and the sound of printing presses. From 1985 to 1990, he studied painting, sculpture, and printmaking at the University of Texas at Austin.

His first publication was a strip that ran in the student newspaper *The Daily Texan* from the end of 1986 until 1991, sometimes daily, sometimes weekly. It caught the eye of Art Spiegelman, and, as a result, Ware contributed to two issues of the avant-garde review *RAW*, in 1990 and in 1991.

In the same year, the young artist moved to Chicago. His work began to appear regularly in *New City*, an independent weekly magazine. In 1993, Fantagraphics published the first edition of *The Acme Novelty Library*, an auteurist review for which he had sole creative responsibility.

In 2000 he gained a worldwide reputation with the publication by Pantheon Books of the graphic novel *Jimmy Corrigan, the Smartest Kid on Earth*.[1] Its formal innovations, the scope of the story, the originality of its treatment of time and of the expression of emotion, and its emphasis on the ever-present inner world of the imagination amid everyday reality were all factors in the widespread acknowledgement of the historic significance of this outstanding book. A French version was published in November 2002 by Delcourt.

Special thanks to Chris Ware for providing the images in this chapter.

Several other books followed (*Quimby the Mouse*, the *Acme* anthology, and two volumes of notebooks[2]), while two new graphic novels, *Rusty Brown*[3] and *Building Stories*, began to be published in serial format in 2005.

Building Stories was published by Pantheon in 2012, in the unconventional format of a large box (29.5 x 42.2 x 4.7 cm). It was subsequently brought out in French by Delcourt under the same title.

As a regular contributor to the *New Yorker*, a much sought-after graphic designer, and an exhibitor at major American art galleries, Chris Ware is the most prominent contemporary American comics artist.

PLOT

Building Stories is presented as a set of fragments. The box contains fourteen printed elements very disparate in their format, scale, and appearance, not ordered chronologically, and with no instruction manual.[4] It is through this unusual and disconcerting format that we become acquainted with the story of characters who live in a Chicago apartment building, consisting of a semibasement and three other floors. The owner of the building is an elderly woman who has lived there all her life and who hates her tenants. The young woman who lives on the top floor is single and disabled (one of her legs has been amputated below the knee). She spends long empty hours with only her cat for company, and has no romantic life. She works part time in a local flower shop. Both the young woman and the elderly woman are gripped by powerful feelings of frustration. The middle floor is occupied by a childless couple, who are unable to communicate and seem to be on the verge of separating. The hundred-year-old building has retained the memory of its previous occupants, and shares its own reflections with the reader. Some sequences consist of flashbacks or flash-forwards that shed light on the fate of the characters, in particular that of the disabled young woman, who, later in life, goes on to get married and have a daughter.

THE DOUBLE MEANING OF THE TITLE HAS GENERATED MUCH COMMENT. *Building Stories* can mean "stories about a building" or "the building of stories." Note that the action of building stories applies both to the author and, in a different way, to the reader, who has to find a way through this narrative jigsaw puzzle. Access to the telling of the story depends on first building it.

But *story* also means the floor of a house.[5] So a third reading of the title would be "the floors of a building," which is far from absurd since each floor has its own narrative arc, the story of its occupant(s).

The building that serves as a backdrop, and almost as a character in its own right, is to a large extent based on the house in which the author lived from 1995 through 2001, which he has portrayed in his notebooks (see *Acme Novelty Datebook* 2, 162) and captioned "Our Apartment Building."[6] So *Building Stories* is firmly anchored in memories, not in relation to its events (although some of those obviously draw upon the author's personal experience), but in relation to place.

Moreover, architecture has long been an interest of Ware's, testified by his taste for axonometric perspectives and the long sequence in *Jimmy Corrigan* that recreates the magnificent pavilions of the 1893 World Columbian Exhibition in Chicago. In 2014 the Art Institute in that same city mounted an exhibition called "The Comic Art and Architecture of Chris Ware," in which the artist's drawings and the archival documents that he used as sources were displayed side by side.

In a page from his notebooks dated 1995, Ware copied a famous quotation from Goethe, "Architecture is frozen music," adding this comment: "This is, I think, the aesthetic key to the development of cartoons as an art form." From that moment on, he began to explore the formal analogy between the composition of a comics page and the architecture of the façade of a building.[7]

Chris Ware's project has evolved over time. As far as we know, he originally intended to tell the story of a building and its occupants, somewhat in the style of Georges Perec in *Life, a User's Manual*[8]—except that Ware's building is more modestly proportioned than the one at 11 rue Simon-Crubellier. Ware almost certainly also drew inspiration from Will Eisner, whose album *A Contract with God and Other Tenement Stories* was a collection of tales about the occupants of a Brooklyn tenement built in 1920;[9] later, *The Building*, by the same author, handed the narration over to four ghosts posted at the entrance to a brand new skyscraper, who remembered their life in the old building that had been demolished to make way for it.[10]

But Ware's narration gradually focuses on the character of the young disabled woman, whom I will henceforth refer to as "the florist," since the author does not give her a name. Eight out of the fourteen fragments that make up *Building Stories* are almost entirely devoted to her. Although the principle of a multivoiced choral narration is not abandoned, it seems to be gradually overtaken by a different priority, that of offering an intimate and comprehensive portrayal of a female character.

Toward the end of our analysis we will try once again to determine the meaning of this strange object. Before embarking on any interpretation, we can note two points of fact. First, the author has always aimed to promote the active participation of the reader. This is at the very heart of his conception of the medium. Ware has argued that "the big difference between film and comics is that the film spectator is relatively passive, while the comics reader is much more involved in the actual meaning making. When you watch a film, it's like listening to recorded music, whereas when you read a comic, it's like reading a score. It's up to us as readers to bring the music from the score alive."[11]

Is it to stimulate this emotional and intellectual participation that the author goes so far as to suggest that the reader should engage in some very practical activities? In *Jimmy Corrigan*, he had already invited us, on a number of pages, to fold, cut out, and re-glue the book, or to make toy theatres, robots, or items of furniture. It is doubtful, however, whether many people who bought the album could bring themselves to follow these instructions and cut it up. But with *Building Stories*, Ware no longer gives us the choice: physical manipulation of the book is a precondition for reading it. Not only is it up to us to define the order in which we assemble the scattered fragments inside the box, but some of them require us to carry out additional manipulations, such as opening the flaps of the fold-out board (A), turning C upside down because pages 6 and 7 are inverted, and unfolding the oblong fold-outs (J and L). (See note 4, p. 220, which lists the components denoted by each letter.)

Our second observation concerns the fact that, as the inside of the box lid makes clear, "Portions of this work originally appeared in *The New Yorker, The New York Times, McSweeney's Quarterly Concern, The Manchester Guardian, nest* and *The Chicago Reader*," a list to which can be added *The Acme Novelty Library*, the author's own review. So *Building Stories* was published as separate contributions, over a period of seven years, to press outlets of varying formats, each with its own constraints. It is obvious how difficult it would have been to homogenize all these disparate pieces and integrate them into a single work. Ware had, however, already overcome a similar difficulty in the case of *Jimmy Corrigan*, much of which had been pre-published as separate sequences in different issues of the *Acme Novelty Library*, whose varied formats were the product of his own ingenuity.

The rationale for the box did not, in fact, lie only in the solution it offered to the problem of the incompatibility of component parts that could not be brought together in book form. Ware had proposed the project to his publisher, Pantheon Books, as far back as 2006, six years before he produced the object itself. He apparently took inspiration from the boxes that had contained his childhood games, and also from Marcel Duchamp's *Box in a Suitcase*, a portable museum created in twenty near-identical copies between 1936 and 1941, that included reproductions of the artist's own major works: miniature replicas, photographs, and color reproductions numbering seventy elements in total.

It is worth noting that comics has always been characterized by a poetics of the fragment and of the discontinuous: pre-publication in the form of serialization in the press has been standard practice in the industry, and a majority of albums are themselves parts of a greater whole as volumes in a series. Everything indicates that Chris Ware had chosen to exacerbate a particularity of the medium by taking the logic of the fragment one degree further.

Furthermore, the fourteen elements that make up *Building Stories* differ from each other not only in terms of their material characteristics. From one fragment to the next, it is not just the format and the scale—both physical heft and temporal extension—that vary, but also their way of occupying space, their narrative devices (first- or third-person narration, silent sequences, and manipulations of narrative time), and even their graphic style. This latter aspect particularly applies to the playful counterpoint of parts M and N, which are set in the world of bees, drawn in a far more stylized, caricatural way than the humans, and smuggling in a few discreet borrowings: Branford, the male bee, wears white gloves like Mickey Mouse, while his wife Betty wears a pink bow on her head like Minnie Mouse. (*Quimby the Mouse* had, similarly, alluded to the early days of American animated films.)

Let us return to the main protagonist, the florist. Any attempt to work out a coherent narrative from the elements of her life that we are presented with can only be a retrospective reconstruction, given that we encounter them in random order. But discussing the text necessarily means forsaking the deliberately open-ended arrangement intended by Chris Ware, in order to make the narration intelligible.

As his readers are aware, Chris Ware is not known for having an especially light-hearted view of existence. The same feelings of unremitting solitude, the sense of being a misfit, deserted, and abandoned that were expressed in *Jimmy Corrigan* also pervade *Building Stories*.[12] The occupant of the second floor is wasting her life with a good-for-nothing husband, and spends most of her time brooding on the failure of her marriage. The owner of the apartment house (an old woman whose red telephone is a rather obvious visual echo of the one that linked Jimmy to his mother) lives only in the past. Even Branford, "the best bee in the world" (another ironical reference to Jimmy, the "smartest kid"), suffers guilt on account of his fantasies about fertilizing the queen of his hive. But it is the character of the florist who sets the tone, and most of the episodes are viewed through the prism of her depressive temperament.

During the episodes in which she lives in the building that is the main setting in *Building Stories*, the young woman spends long empty hours with only her cat for company and has no romantic life. Not only does she have a prosthetic leg but she also needs to go up two floors on foot to get to her apartment, an effort that leaves her breathless because she has a weak heart.

Through a series of flashbacks (mostly concentrated into fragment E), we are given a good deal of information about her. We learn, for example, that it was after a boating accident on a lake that she had her leg amputated.

She worked as a nanny for a wealthy family, but was sacked because the boy that she was looking after began to be attracted to her. She studied art and took courses in creative writing but has since given up any creative ambition. A man twice her age called Lance, whom she met at the art school where he worked as a model, seduced her; she fell pregnant and had an abortion and was dumped without so much as a goodbye. Even so, she has never stopped thinking about this first love affair.

Other scenes portray her life after she leaves the apartment building. The last page of fragment B manages the transition between these two periods using a device that is unexpected in Chris Ware's work, a happy ending.

We have just read an hour-by-hour chronicle of an ordinary day that interweaves the activities of the different occupants of the building. We have seen the florist dealing with plumbing problems, thinking back over her failure to fulfill her artistic ambitions, and ending her day alone again when a young man that she had invited home (after a reunion with college friends) kisses her but then leaves. The happy ending turns up in the form of an epilogue that the structure of this fragment had by no means led us to expect. And so we leave the time frame that had been established at the beginning, encompassing a single day, September 23, 2000, and find ourselves catapulted forward five years, to the year 2005. The florist drives past the house where she had once lived and which is now up for sale (presumably as a consequence of the death of the owner). She is dressed in green, a color that Ware systematically associates—even if ironically—with renewal and hope. And we realize that she has a baby with her, strapped into the back seat of the car.

And it does indeed turn out, as F, G, H, I, and J will confirm, that our antiheroine has married Phil, an architect and interior designer. They have moved to Oak Park, in the suburbs of Chicago, and they have a daughter, Lucy.

However, we should not conclude too hastily that she has at last found the happiness that she aspired to. The glimpses that we get of her new life cast some doubt on any notion that it has brought unalloyed bliss. She has been affected by the suicide of her best friend, Stephanie; she has put on weight and no longer believes herself to be attractive; her relationship with Phil has become platonic (for example, in I, "Besides, sex is **so** overrated ... Phil and I go for months and it's no problem at all"); although she seems to suspect nothing, the end of H implies that he may be having an affair with another woman; the recession has brought the value of their house down and they have money problems; she is worried about her child—who, in fragment J, is portrayed as emotionally fragile—and is unsure whether she is a good enough mother; and

The florist has become a car driver and a mother: an unexpected turn of events (B)

she finds domesticity a burden, it bores her, and she cannot stop feeling that she has made nothing of her life.

In reality, her feelings are highly changeable and volatile. In I, for example, within the space of two pages we find these two contradictory reflections: "I **relish** the time I get alone, even if it is just spent shopping. [. . .] Especially when my husband is being such a **dick**"; but, "I love my husband so much ... He's one of the smartest and most talented people I've ever met." This woman who has always dreamed of finding a partner, having a family, discovers at the very least that the attainment of these objectives is not enough to overcome her doubts and frustrations. And the phases of weariness and discouragement seem to outweigh the moments of happiness.

Has Ware read Freud? His work offers a consummate illustration of a familiar Freudian theme, that of the "harshness of life," which Paul Ricœur describes as

> another name for the helplessness of the ego in its primal situations of subjection to its three masters, the id, the superego, reality; the harshness of life is this initial primacy of fear. To this threefold fear—real fear, neurotic fear, fear of conscience—*Civilization and its Discontents* will add a further trait: man is basically a discontented being, for he cannot achieve happiness in a narcissistic manner and at the same time fulfill the historic task of culture which his aggressiveness impedes; this is the reason why man, threatened in his self-regard, is so enamored of consolation.[13]

This discontent underlies all the episodes narrated in *Building Stories*, and sets the tone.

In relation to his previous work, the most striking innovation is, clearly, Ware's decision to focus, on this occasion, on a female character, and the remarkable exercise in projection and empathy that has resulted in an introspective account of this character's inner life, her experiences, and her most intimate feelings—what we would once have dared to call her soul. As Frédéric Potet has noted, "everything that his heroine thinks, says and does is recorded in entomological detail."[14]

It is worth remembering that in *Jimmy Corrigan*, the story of the Corrigan family was extended over four generations but recounted only from the point of view of the male line. The wives and mothers were dead or had walked out. The few female characters who were included in the story were mostly out of frame, shown from the back, or framed in such a way that their features were barely visible or completely invisible.

When *Jimmy Corrigan* came out, Ware was wont to cite Flaubert and Tolstoy among his literary influences. Getting inside the skin of a woman, like Flaubert when he claimed "Madame Bovary, c'est moi," and using comics to create a study of a woman as sensitive, comprehensive, and vibrant as Tolstoy's portrayal of Anna Karenina was, it seems, the challenge that Ware set himself with *Building Stories*. He put a lot of himself into his character: "Of course, a lot of details refer to my own life. I've lived in Chicago and in Oak Park, I have a daughter, and I sometimes feel like a failed artist."[15] But the fact that he has lent his protagonist certain background elements from his own life, along with the self-deprecating tendency that comes over so clearly and so surprisingly (given his artistic accomplishments) in all the interviews with Ware, is of lesser significance than his obvious concern to enter into the intimate life of a female character, to examine her psyche and track its hidden recesses. This has been achieved through detailed attention (unusual in fiction in general and even more so in comics) to the routines of daily life: washing, personal hygiene, epilation, deciding what to wear, and child care. Ware does not shrink from recounting the most prosaic events or even the crudest: in fragment B, it is because a tampon has been flushed down it that the toilet is blocked, necessitating a visit from a plumber, who, like the florist herself, is embarrassed by the incident; even so, she goes on to make the same mistake later, in G.

The artistic challenge that Ware has set himself is not without risk: he may reinforce the usual stereotypes about "feminine" behavior, emotions, and moods. *Building Stories* offers a certain vision of what it is to be a woman; it is up to female readers to say how far they identify with it.

It is noteworthy that jealousy and romantic rivalry are not among the emotions that preoccupy Ware. On the other hand, one of the components of femininity that he dwells upon is the anxious and ever-vigilant relationship that women have with their appearance. Reacting to a remark by Phil, who calls her friend Stephanie "fat," the florist makes this reflection: "If guys would just not focus so much on what women looked like, the world would be a much better place . . . Men have absolutely **no idea** the stress women undergo every minute of their lives worrying about how they look" (G). Whether it is something forced upon them or not, this concern about their appearance is evident in the many instances of a confrontation of the female characters with their image in a mirror, which they interrogate with perplexity, avid curiosity, or disgust.

These instances are particularly numerous in fragments E and K. They lead the florist to speculate about the respective importance of the features she has inherited from each of her parents and to reflect anxiously on her age. As a child, she looked at herself in the mirror, hoping to see what her future would hold; when she thinks she is pregnant, she scrutinizes her body for confirmatory signs. Even when she is brushing her teeth or putting make up on in front of the mirror, she seems to be staring at herself with unusual attention. It was by using a mirror that she had drawn her self-portrait as a student. She can also be seen, in E, gazing at herself in her underwear, putting on different outfits, and, several pages further on, taking advantage of her employer's absence to try her dresses on. In K, clutched by her boyfriend Lance, she examines the reflection of her own genitalia. And it is worth mentioning once more the scene in J, where she looks at her own naked body and at that of her daughter Lucy—whose eyes are covered by a towel, and who is therefore denied access to this image of a woman at two stages of her life.

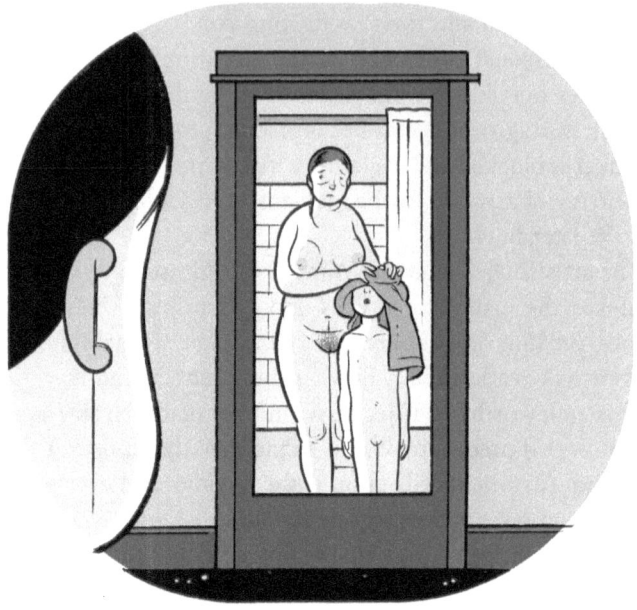

(J)

Even if the occasions where the florist comes face-to-face with herself are remarkable for their frequency, such contemplative moments are not reserved to her. In C, it is the landlady who is shown interrogating her reflection, at two different stages of her life (youthful and elderly). In D, it is the woman from the second floor who pulls a face as she looks at herself: she wonders if it is because she has become "repulsive" that her husband has lost interest in her. And this self-scrutiny is diffracted through the interaction of two variables: yesterday versus today, dressed versus undressed.

The florist seems less worried about the effect that her disability might have on other people (and on the opposite sex in particular) than about the pounds that she has put on over time. And she shares this weight complex with her downstairs neighbor, who is able-bodied. Ware thereby seems to imply that most women are subject to it.

In many respects, *Building Stories* sets up careful rhymes and correspondences between its heroine and other women. She takes exception to her friend Stephanie's assumption that she has a monopoly on depression (without realizing that it will eventually drive Stephanie to suicide). In many ways, she sees her landlady as her own double, the premonitory portrait of the embittered old woman that she risks turning into. The old lady has also felt herself to be unattractive, been conflicted about the idea of motherhood, and had "art academy dalliances" (C).

In the final analysis, it is through an innocuous-sounding sentence, buried away near the bottom of a page of this tentacular work, that Ware clarifies his project. The florist, about to go on holiday with her husband, is looking for a book to read on the journey. The ones that are on their shelves do not appeal to her: she wants to find not yet another "great book" about "criminals or perverts," but a book that is simply about "**regular** people living everyday **life**" (F). But this everyday life that preoccupies Ware—this banality, ordinariness, or even "infra-ordinariness," to cite Georges Perec's term,[16] of which the bee seems to offer an allegory—is on the one hand dissected and laid out for inspection with an attention to detail that is unprecedented in comics[17] and, on the other hand, inflected and colored by the gender of the protagonist. To portray the everyday life of a woman is, by that very token, to question the status of women.

In an incisive article, Joanna David-McElligatt has summed up the aim of *Building Stories* very accurately: "a comic about women and the private lives they lead, and it investigates more fully than any other comic [. . .] the way they age, fall in love, explore their sexuality, come to terms with compromises they've had to make as they've grown, accept their limitations, confront squandered ability, have children (or choose not to have children), marry (or stay single), and make sense of the world around them."[18]

Ware's exploration involves a use of nudity that is strikingly obtrusive. I have noted above a few instances where female characters gaze at their bodies in mirrors, but these are far from being the only occasions where the naked female body is displayed to us. Nudity is unusually frequent in *Building Stories* (appearing in almost thirty scenes), whereas it was absent from *Jimmy Corrigan*. The question could be posed as to why nudity is banished from one story whose main protagonist is male and so insistently present in another whose focal character is female. The fact that these two characters do not, as it happens, have the same issues concerning their own body constitutes only a partial answer. There is no doubt that Ware has sought to position himself in relation to the naked images that circulate in our culture, including pornographic images, and that he therefore aligns himself with a tradition, artistic as well as pornographic, that has always been strongly associated with the exhibition of the female anatomy.

In keeping with the coherence of the work, and its determined emphasis on realism and transparency, we have to suppose that Ware undresses his heroine in order to get as close as possible to her private self and her inner truth. One particularly compelling sequence, in the final pages of fragment E, can be read as an ironical *mise en abyme* of this objective. The florist is

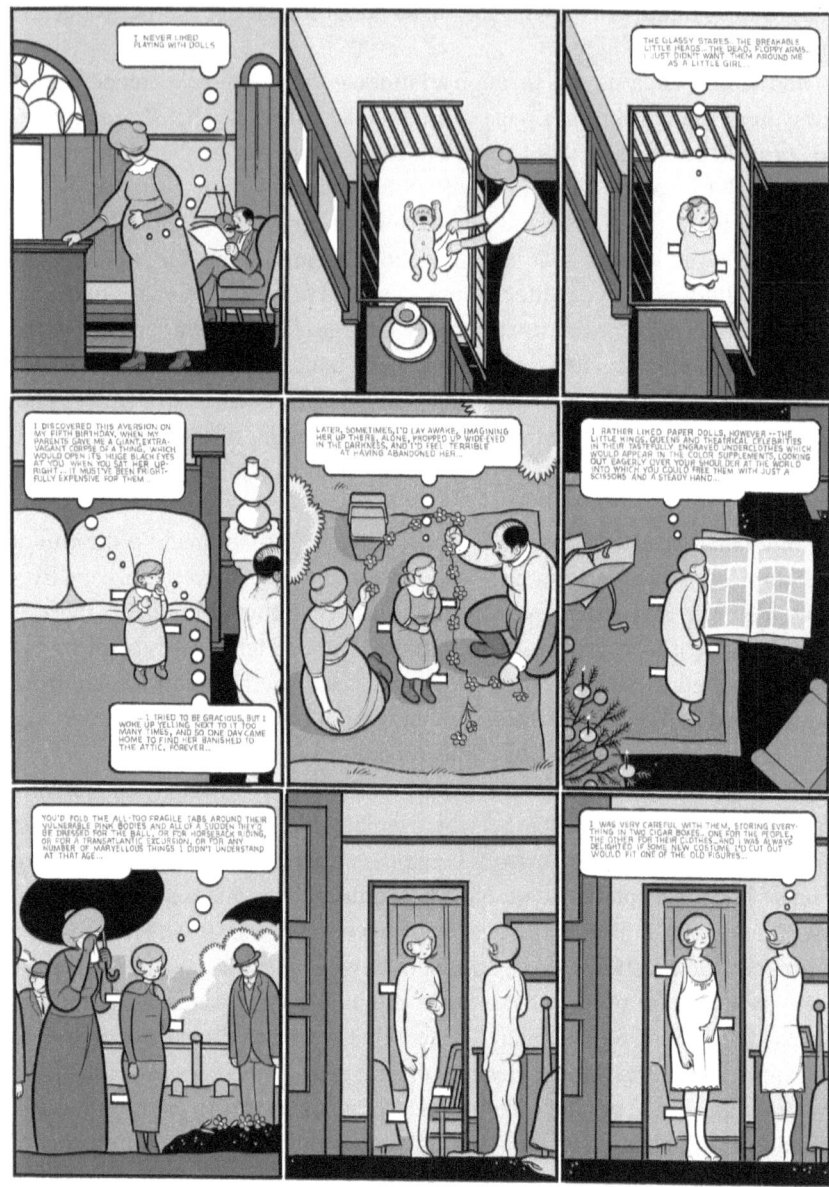

A speeded-up version of the landlady's life: face to face with herself (C)

portrayed full-length, facing the reader, on three successive recto pages, over twenty centimeters high. She is the central motif on each of these pages, out of proportion with the surrounding panels; the configuration seems to have been inspired by a technique in shojo manga to which I gave the name "catwalk effect."[19]

In the first of these instances, the young woman is dressed (and her disability is invisible); in the second, she is naked; in the third, it is her skeleton that is represented (the heart and, oddly, the intestines are the only organs included in the image; the face is flayed). There is a double reference to nudity here, both in the form of the life class model—art school features as one of the contextual elements of the sequence—and in the sex scenes that appear on the same page. The unexpected depiction of the skeleton can be linked back to a text that appears a little earlier describing an encyclopedia that she read as a child, which had "a section of acetate overlays of the human body that you could peel away, starting with the skin, all the way down to the skeleton." But this is merely an anecdotal connection, and does not account for the impact that these three pages have on the reader. It is, in fact, as if Ware were trying to make us share his sense of the impossibility of reaching the heart, the ultimate truth, of his female character. Stripping her naked is insufficient, that does not bring us close enough, we have to delve beneath the superficial appearance, open up the envelope. It is as if the artist were a cannibal symbolically nourished by the flesh of his heroine.

A similar principle is at work on the following double page, which presents along its center seam a drawing of a vulva, the lips wide apart (and pixelated, like a blurred porn image). Although it is contextualized (as we have noted, the heroine's boyfriend encourages her to gaze at her sex in a small mirror and to masturbate in front of him; and they watch X-rated films together), it also seems like another desperate attempt to attain the unattainable: through an extreme close-up on the most secret part of the body, supposed to be the locus of who knows what deeply buried truth. This image is the first of another series of three: the second is a painting (the work of one of the students in the art class) displaying the same motif without pixelation and bearing the inscription "FUCK ME HARDER," and the third is the metaphorical image of a flower, red and open.

We should not forget that our character is by profession a flower seller. Is the author discreetly suggesting an analogy between selling flowers and selling one's sex, or in other words prostituting oneself? The painting, at least, exemplifies a type of art that, under the pretext of provocation and irony, is clearly shown here to be simply a straightforward imitation of pornography, an art that Ware might, then, describe as a form of "prostitution."

In the entry "Nudity" of the *Aesthetic and Thematic Dictionary of Comics*,[20] I wrote that nudity in comics is "first and foremost a color" and that "that color is merely indicative; it is in no way carnal. It designates flesh but does not make it appear on the page." This applies particularly to those artists closely or more distantly associated with a clear line aesthetic, a group that includes Ware. However, in *Building Stories*, nudity takes on certain qualities of the filmic image: the ability to get "right up close to bodies, [to] show them in their intimacy, sometimes to the point of obscenity,"[21] as well as the weight of the real, the "this has been" that for Roland Barthes was the force of photography.[22] In fact, even though the florist is a fictional character, the author brings a documentarist's eye to his study of her. This is what a woman is, this is what it is to be a woman, and this is what this woman in particular is, he seems to keep saying to us at every moment.

It is noteworthy that on more than one occasion (in G, H, I, and K), the artist offers us close-ups of his heroine's face drawn with abundant detail, and with greater realism than his usual style. We are switched into portrait mode. (Similarly, a life-size extreme close-up of the florist's daughter—across the centerfold of the middle of fragment G—shows her teeth, her eyelashes, and her eyebrow hairs, all of which Ware's usual style leaves out: this disproportionate image is manifestly intended to create the illusion that we are looking at the child herself.) In *Jimmy Corrigan*, there was only one instance of close-ups that were large enough to call attention to themselves: the face-to-face encounter between Jimmy and his father when they had just been reunited. But the two faces remained impassive; what was noticeable was the resemblance between the two men, a generation apart; enlarging them was a way of underlining the symbolic importance of this initial confrontation.

In *Building Stories*, the close-up, with the increase in realism that it entails, sometimes serves simply to register a change of expression (for example, in H, two adjacent panels represent the opposition of closed versus open eyes), or a detail that would be imperceptible from further away (the drops of sweat on the florist's face when she is jogging). But most often it serves to create empathy or psychological depth, showing the distress of the character (after her daughter hits her), her extreme concentration in front of the computer screen where her ex-boyfriend has just appeared, her puzzlement when she runs into Cary in the street, her moments of doubt or loneliness, and her efforts to keep up appearances. From this point of view, the vulva drawn in extreme close-up has nothing to tell us (unlike the face, which is a signature, it is condemned to anonymity: we cannot say with any certainty who it belongs to), and we can again suspect Chris Ware of irony.

Returning to the images of nudity, they can be read in two very different ways: identification with the character and voyeurism, two modes of

Ware tries his hand at portraiture in a sparse number of close-ups (F)

perception with an irresolvable tension between them. Moreover, these images can be divided into three categories: the first, already commented on, consists of the woman looking in the mirror, scrutinizing herself, evaluating herself, judging herself; the second consists of the woman washing, having a bath, or bathing her child; the third consists of the woman engaged in sexual activity, losing herself in an erotic dream (B), or becoming the object of the sexual fantasies of her downstairs neighbor (A).

An infrequent instance of a whole-page image, in I, portrays the florist standing naked and uncertain before her indifferent husband (although he is himself naked), who is lying on the bed glued to his iPad. Even if the following page suggests that, taking advantage of Lucy's absence at the cinema, her parents are about to make love, this image, given prominence by its unusual size, can only be read as a stark résumé of the lack of communication between the couple and the feelings of solitude and frustration that are bred and nurtured by marital routine.

But whether the florist is naked alone or in front of someone else, in both cases the images are displayed to a reader, male or female, who should not be there. We should more properly refer to these as stolen images, an intrusion into the private life of the character—while, clearly, a literary description of these same scenes would not give the same impression of invasiveness. It is in this sense that the attempt to paint the intimate portrait of a woman in comics format is challenging. Ware uses techniques like internal monologue and stream of consciousness to give us access to the character's thoughts; in the case of her body (which is so important to her), the picture, by its very essence, condemns the artist to an insurmountably external view. *Building*

Stories is, so far, the most accomplished attempt at resolving this equation, fascinating even where it leads to a logical impasse.

Just like the nude and the portrait, the still life is one of the traditional genres in classical painting. If we are prepared to liken much of the story recounted by *Building Stories* to a series of genre scenes (in other words, representations of domestic or everyday life), and if we consider that the landscape also plays a role (on this occasion, the urban landscape), it is surely not a coincidence that Ware should have included not only the nude and the portrait but also the still life in his work. It is as if the artist had wanted to measure himself against the great genres of painting, to assess their compatibility with graphic literature as a sequential and narrative art form, and, in so doing, to disrupt conventional artistic hierarchies. (It is only history painting, ruled out by the everyday, banal setting of *Building Stories*, that has no equivalent in the comic.)

Fruit and flowers are among the most frequent motifs in still life painting. Both can be found in this book. There are flowers chanced on during a walk, flowers from which Branford gathers pollen, and of course the bouquets and arrangements that fill the shop where the protagonist works. Fruits also abound: the fruit and vegetable display in the supermarket where she shops is portrayed several times (in E, H, and I.) The artist juxtaposes images drawn from a high angle, portraying crates and stands (composing, on two occasions, a triptych), apparently relishing, like painters of old, the combinations of colors and forms that the subject permits. And this is a subject that does not lack an erotic dimension, given how closely some of the fruits resemble women's breasts.

The category of still life can be extended to other static portrayals of objects that have no narrative function, and are elevated to the status of autonomous iconic motifs: for example, the inside of the fridge, the contents of plates, dirty dishes, the linen basket, the toy basket, implements, personal objects (such as, in C, a telephone, a coat, and a camera), and architectural details (a picture window). These images that are not connected to the action are introduced into the narrative flow when in fact they are a matter of pure monstration—graphic narration.[23] While they form part of the author's documentary project and seem to be sampled from the physical reality of the world, they also have the effect of intensifying the "purely contemplative potential" of comics, as Fabrice Leroy has noted.[24]

There is another type of image that figures prominently in *Building Stories*, as it also did in *Jimmy Corrigan*: I am referring to photographic images. Each of the occupants of the building has a relationship with photographs. The landlady, who virtually never leaves her armchair, lives in the past. As a young woman, she possessed an oval-shaped image of herself with her parents that

(E)

hung on the wall opposite her, to the left of the picture window. This photo has subsequently been replaced by a different frame. Elsewhere (in fragment C), there appear six black and white photos, again portraits of her and her parents. These snapshots bring out the very strong resemblance between her as a young woman and her mother. "Why did she have to bob her hair like mine, anyway? Trying to look young." The father himself said that "in our big coats he could hardly tell us apart."[25] In fact, in one of the photos, only the color of the coat indicates that it is the mother, and not the daughter, that the father is carrying on his shoulders.

These photographs are not shown in their materiality as objects: we do not know if they have been kept, and we do not see the old woman reading them or handling them. They appear in the middle of other images that are themselves from the past (memory images), but do not take the form of material objects. In other words, the photos are integrated into the landlady's stream of consciousness, among other elements of her past life; they are images upon which associations and daydreams can be hung, images that facilitate the resurfacing of emotions felt long ago, rather like a Proustian madeleine or paving stone. Only the fact that they are in black and white, along with their outer frame, marks them out as photographs.

The portrait of the landlady's mother appears next to the account of her death, which happened after a long illness that had lasted several decades. During this period she had been unable to leave her bed, and her daughter had had to look after her, sacrificing any chance of a life of her own.

On the second floor, the young couple have hung six photographs of themselves on the wall (C). One, in black and white, shows the young woman as a

The theme of the stolen image in "Those People" (E)

child next to her mother (and provokes the inevitable reflection: "I'm looking more and more like my mom"); the others, in color, evoke happy times for the couple and show him as a young musician. In fragment A (fourth flap of the board), the woman can be seen hanging up a seventh photo, a souvenir of their holiday two years previously, but on the second flap the husband can be seen hurling it angrily to the floor and smashing the frame.

In fragment B, he shouts at his wife over the phone, venting his grievances against the landlady and against her. During this conversation, he is standing in front of the photos on the wall, and these images spark memories of their first meeting; immediately moved by this reminiscence, he apologizes to her. A few hours (pages) later, after another argument, he stands outside the closed bedroom door and says that he is sorry: "You know I don't **hate** you" and we see him glancing at the photographs again, as if he found in them the encouragement that he needed to make the effort to save his marriage, as if contemplating lost happiness led him to believe that it could return.

The story of the disabled florist also involves photographs. Ware shows us in particular a snapshot of her standing next to her former boyfriend (K), as well as her official wedding photo (G). The period during which she had been employed as a nanny in a wealthy but far from united family is evoked over nine pages in fragment E. The four double pages that open this sequence all include a photograph centrally positioned across the seam. These four photos make up a sequence of their own that runs through the story and offers what amounts to a synthesis of it. They recount, in four stages, the progressive integration of the young woman into the family life of her employers: absent from the first image, she features next to the parents and their son in the three others, the informality of the poses revealing their increasing closeness. Significantly, the sequence ends on a ninth page, does not continue onto the facing page, and does not include a photo. The page marks the breakdown of the relationship between the florist and the family after she has called the father "a real **asshole**."

This same fragment contains other references to photography, however: we later see, in passing, four photographs of her from childhood to adulthood, and, crucially, the page headed "Those people" shows her turning her head away to ensure that her face does not appear in snapshots being taken not far away from her, where she is accidentally present in the frame. The young woman reflects on the number of snapshots that have been taken over the years without her consent that must include her in the background. This thought leads on to another more profoundly existential question. She wonders whether in her life she is destined always to be just an extra, or whether she could ever play a starring role. She is particularly preoccupied with her romantic prospects and dares to imagine that maybe, one day, someone will notice her in one of these photos and will find her interesting or even attractive. A forlorn hope: no one would spot her unless they had a magnifying glass, and she keeps turning her head away, voluntarily making herself invisible.

Other scenes portray the young woman looking through an old photo album in an antique shop and looking at family photographs.

The adventures of Branford offer a kind of parodic counterpoint to the pursuits of the main protagonists. He may be a bee, but that does not stop Branford from having a bourgeois home life with wife and children. His wife Betty, left alone during the day while "the master of the house" goes about his business, can gaze at the portrait of him that hangs on the wall. And Branford himself has a locket in which he keeps a photo of his wife and children, whom he loves desperately.

In Chris Ware's work, photographs are inseparable from the life of each protagonist, human or bee. They may convey information or be imbued with emotion, and they can set off nostalgia, disillusion, or the revival of long-buried feelings, serving as mirrors that crystallize a series of questions around identity, heredity, marriage, and happiness. It is through them that links with the past and relationships to others are established; everyday life is doubled by a life that is dreamt, fantasized, conjured up again.

The photograph, then, is an essential element in Ware's pursuit of his goal: "to succeed in putting my finger on the way in which human beings meet, discover, and 'assemble' each other's personal histories and lives but also the

182　CHRIS WARE, *BUILDING STORIES*

The landlady turns around and the story leaps back into the past (C)

way in which we recall and reconstruct the memories that we have of our own lives."[26]

It is worth noting, incidentally, that photographs are—along with two or three paintings produced by the florist or her art school contemporaries—the only images that Chris Ware "quotes." No billboards are visible in his urban landscapes, and all the other frames or screens (cinema, television, or computer) that are supposed to display something or other are systematically monochrome or blank, emptied out and cleansed of their content.

I have alluded to the four photos that, in E, straddle the centerfold. I will now move on to consider at greater length the very unusual way in which Ware organizes the space of the page. Two major principles alternate.

The first one is the familiar division of the page into an orthogonal multiframe, which may be a "waffle iron," as regular as can be (see for example the first and last pages of the giant fragment F, four instances in B, and two instances in I), or a more personal style of composition displaying the features that were already in evidence in *Jimmy Corrigan*: blocks of panels differently shaped but standardized in that they are perfect multiples of each other (one average-sized panel equates to four small ones, a large one equals two medium-sized ones, etc.). Average-sized panels tend to be less common than large ones that draw attention to themselves or very small ones in which the same motif undergoes a series of inflections. In addition, Ware tends to favor symmetry and likes to counteract the left-to-right directionality of reading by the inclusion of vertical series (small images stacked one above another, "bracketed" together). The division into strips is not particularly visually distinct, and the pages are subject to a constant tension between the horizontal and vertical axes; they often resemble a piece of marquetry through which the eye has to find a path.

The other principle of page design that is often to be found in *Building Stories*, and that seems to me to be used by the author for the first time here, works on the higher-level unit constituted by the double page. In order to make this new practice conspicuous, Ware almost always positions an image, usually a fairly large and significant one, so that it straddles the central seam, which becomes a privileged *site* and even a *place*.[27] As well as the four family photos and the "pornographic" miniseries already mentioned, among other images placed across the centerfold, around which the whole double page is organized, are close-ups on faces (C, D, and K), a flower, another photo (C), a banknote, a plastic mask, a pack of pills (I), a notebook (E), a huge portrait of Lucy as a little girl (G), and a life-sized sleeping baby (F). Around this focal point, the remaining panels, which make up what Benoît Peeters has called the *perifield*, are quite freely distributed, without covering the available space (although we can still call it a hyperframe, it is systematically interrupted by gaps here): areas of whiteness flow around the page, with blocks of text fitted in among images grouped into irregular-shaped clusters. The double page looks like a collection of semi-autonomous mini-sequences.

It could be argued that the deconstruction of the book as object is matched by the deconstruction of the space of the page, which no longer lends itself to a linear decoding. The reading difficulty is real—and sometimes accentuated by the giant format that makes it difficult to handle (F, G, and K)—and one can imagine that the effort demanded will put off quite a few readers, while sharpening the curiosity of others.

On closer inspection, the alternation between the two principles of page composition that I have just identified (between which can also be found some intermediate models) is not determined by the whim of the author, but is motivated by, and correlates with, the mode of enunciation. The "classic" layout corresponds to a narration devolved entirely onto dialogue, with no intervention from the narrator: the story seems to unfold before our eyes, bearing the stamp of objectivity. The "deconstructed" layout corresponds to a first-person narration. The enunciator is most often the florist, but not always. The images work to reinforce a subjective discourse, made up of memories, daydreams, fantasies, and speculations riven with doubts and interwoven with multiple emotions—which outweigh the facts.[28] The text and images taken together compose a kind of internal monologue, or stream of consciousness. By deploying the blank space on the page and building in gaps, Ware emphasizes the disorderly and incomplete nature of a narration that makes no claim to linearity or control. In so doing, he exacerbates what he believes to be an intrinsic property of the medium: "Comics, through their combination of images, words, gestures, colors, motifs, and silent music, allow for an approach to consciousness and memory that works both simultaneously and by layers, very much like the way in which our consciousness both communicates and interrupts our experiences of the present."[29]

If *Building Stories* stands out by its highly innovative management of space, its management of time is no less sophisticated. It should be remembered that the fourteen fragments are not tied down to a chronology. There is no doubt that some postdate others, but not all can be situated within a precise time frame. To cite but one example, fragment L is set *at some point* during the interval of several years between the florist's break-up with Lance and her meeting with Phil, as can be deduced from the sentence: "I almost had everything . . . almost had . . . a family of my own." Moreover, most of the fragments span long periods, insofar as the present of the action includes retrospective passages (flashbacks, reminiscences, accounts of events in the past, etc.) or, less often, anticipatory sections. The transitions from one time frame to another are not always clearly indicated; it can happen that it is only the cars or the clothes that alert the reader to the fact that the cursor has moved backwards in time. And the succession of verbal utterances can remain continuous, extended over the whole of a sequence (usually in the form of an internal monologue) while the images reveal, in contrast, the discontinuity of time periods that jolt up against each other beneath the smooth coating of the text. An example of this technique can be found on the first double page of fragment C, in which the leap backward in time that occurs between the left-hand and right-hand pages is disguised by the impression of continuity of the décor and the symmetry of the composition, which lures the reader into assuming a straightforward progression. Three double pages further on, Ware employs more or less the same subterfuges, and it is the fact that the character of the landlady is shown (from the back) as elderly and then, two panels later, turns round and appears (in front view) as several decades younger that signals to the reader the switch from one period to another.

Ware is extremely inventive in this respect and deploys multiple techniques for embedding time frames within each other (see in particular C, G, and K) or for indicating the passage of time—but the limits of the present study do not allow us to offer a detailed account. Sometimes he relies on the changing seasons (as in fragment A, but although each flap corresponds to a season, they are not set out in the usual order), sometimes a twenty-four-hour day is cut up into hourly blocks (B), sometimes sequences are assembled in no chronological order (H), and at other times he has recourse to the memory of the building itself (B) presented as a set of statistics. Everything that has taken place under its roof is enumerated: 106,323 breakfasts, 21,779 toenail clippings, 231 drain clogs, 17 changed locks, 296 birthday parties, etc. The result is both comical and dizzying.

Furthermore, as one reads *Building Stories*, or *Jimmy Corrigan* before it, there emanates from it a sense of a cyclical time, a reiterative time, made up of incidents that will inevitably be reenacted. This impression is partly due to the repetition of the same events and to visual rhymes contrived by the author. The florist loses two cats (E and G); she blocks the toilets twice, in the same way; the beginning and end of fragment E are very similar to the beginning and end of fragment H (apart from one detail: in the former she is sleeping beside Lance and in the latter beside Phil); and so on.

The most substantial rhyme—which involves twenty-five panels, repeated three times—is also, paradoxically, relatively discreet. Unless, by chance, one reads them one after another, one would not necessarily notice that the succession of images that makes up fragment L is rigorously identical to the three main strips on the center pages of fragment C, but also to the three main strips on the center pages of fragment D. In each case, a woman comes out of the building, goes down the stoop, takes a few steps in the street, stands still on the sidewalk facing the intersection, becomes lost in thought for a while, and then goes back inside. The route, the breakdown, the framing—everything is alike. What changes is first the identity of the protagonist: the landlady, the florist, and the woman from the second floor in succession. And also the weather and the season: a clear summer sky, a gray winter sky, a snowy day. But for the florist and her downstairs neighbor, this sequence corresponds to a moment of profound distress: the latter would like to leave her husband and never go back home, the former would like to keep walking until she falls down into the snow and puts an end to everything.

Chris Ware is, to be sure, not the merriest of fellows, and reading his books is not an experience from which one emerges reinvigorated and filled with

186 CHRIS WARE, *BUILDING STORIES*

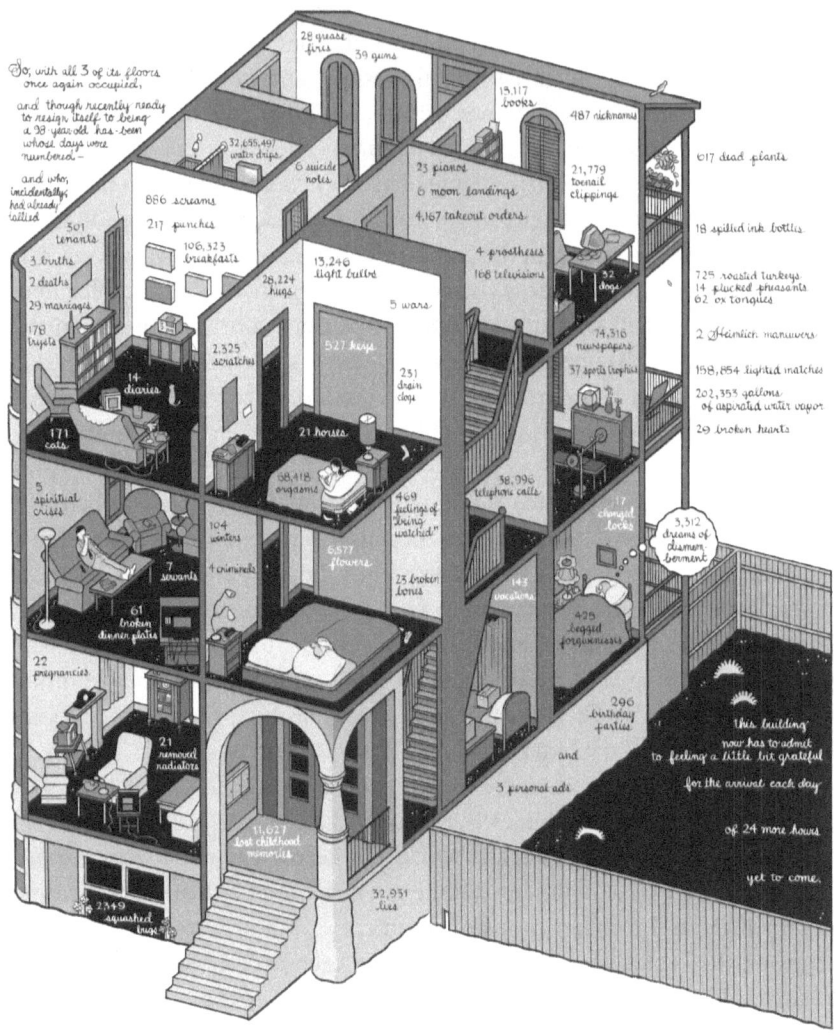

(B)

high spirits. However, the overall depressive tonality of *Building Stories* does not exclude humorous touches. For example, the repeated gag whereby the florist is interrupted by a phone call from her mother as she is about to make love with someone. I am also thinking of the scene (in I) where Lucy is making fake banknotes so that she can play store with her toy cash register at the precise moment when her parents are struggling with a pile of invoices. The personality that is attributed to the anthropomorphized building is droll in its archness, and its flirtatiousness toward the women lodgers for whom it does not hide its preference. It mentally addresses the florist in these terms: "You shoulda seen me in my heyday, honey" (B). And the adventures of Branford the bee are a fantasy in which Ware parodies his own work, while having fun by satirizing domestic life and ideals of virility.

Finally, an aspect of the work that needs to be emphasized: its metanarrative elements. In the first instance, there is a *mise en abyme* of drawing itself: as the florist speaks on the phone, she draws the building opposite and then, unhappy with her drawing, scribbles it out (B); elsewhere, she draws her dying father, but this time we are not shown the result (G); then there is the self-portrait that she does at art school, criticized for its "romanticism" because it is supposedly too flattering, and so fails the test of "truth telling" (K); in the family where she works as a nanny, she realizes the attraction that Jeffrey has toward her when she finds the nude drawings that he has done of her (E); her daughter Lucy draws herself an imaginary friend on a plate (G); the little girl's best drawings are exhibited in the "art gallery" in the house (I); and the composite sketch of a thief is published in the newspaper (I). In at least three of these examples, drawing is called upon to give flesh to the wishes of the characters, to materialize their desire. This is drawing that serves the absence of realism, the opposite of Ware's own project as an artist.

And then there is that emblematic object, the Sunday comics supplement of a daily newspaper. It appears several times, at different periods: the landlady read one as a child (probably around 1930) (C), there is another one on the strip of wasteland next to the building (it can be spotted in B), and the bees use it as a shelter (M; the design of this fragment is itself reminiscent of the comics supplements).

But reflexivity concerns above all the act of recounting the lives of the protagonists of *Building Stories*. This act is self-referentially alluded to in three different ways. First, the building includes the key events of their lives in its statistics. Second, the final page of fragment I features this superb example of metalepsis: the florist tells her daughter Lucy that she has dreamt about a book in which someone had recounted their life story in pictures. The book was unusual in its conception: "it wasn't really a **book**, either ... it was in **pieces**, like books falling apart out of a carton, maybe ... but it was ... **beautiful** ... it made **sense** ..." The character is imagining the very work that has brought her into being, and outside of which she would not exist. Third, fragment D contains a proleptic flash-forward, a scene that transports us to 2156: a graduate student from the future decides to study, using techniques as yet unknown to us, the memory of a woman who lived 150 years earlier (in fact, the woman from the second floor).

This futuristic episode is probably an implied homage to Richard McGuire, the author of *Here*.[30] A first version of this radical work had appeared in *RAW* in 1989. Ware had been deeply marked by it. For him, these few pages had

(I)

"revolutionized comics forever."[31] *Here* recounted the story of a small corner of rural America from prehistoric times up to 2033. That is where the idea of extending the time frame of *Building Stories* beyond the present of narration comes from. The homage is confirmed by the images in fragments E and G, which, on the model of the first panel of *Here*, frame just an angle of empty floor or ceiling.

Here epitomizes the deconstruction of narration in comics. McGuire "grabs hold of time, cuts it up into images, and then deals it out, shuffling the cards—past, present, future—as deadpan as a poker player."[32] It is also in this respect that McGuire's work was a source of inspiration for the fragmented form of *Building Stories*.

Chris Ware wanted, without any doubt, to reaffirm his faith in print by deliberately conceiving a work that would be impossible to exploit in an electronic format. But, beyond the commitment to a certain idea of comics, *Building Stories* materializes above all the fact that human life does not fit into a grand, unified, and coherent narrative, and that its course cannot be represented in linear fashion as a long quiet river. Our life is not neatly packaged up, it is made up of blocks of experiences and memories, recurring fantasies, projections into the future, hopes, and regrets. The control that we think we exert over it is mostly illusory, for we are at the mercy of chance meetings, accidental happenings, coincidences. What we take to be reality is merely our subjective perception; faced with the same events, others would see them very differently. All of these considerations are given clear expression by one or another episode of Ware's work, and they are given metaphorical incarnation by its form, a narrative jigsaw puzzle.

In a letter to his mistress Louise Colet, Flaubert set out his ambition as "writing well about mediocrity." What his descendent Chris Ware wants to achieve "above all" is, he says, "to leave a trace for people not yet born of what 'ordinary life' could be at the beginning of the 21st century."[33] He depicts this ordinary life, in keeping with his temperament, as doomed to failure and dissatisfaction. Any one of his characters could cry out the words pronounced by a vindictive little middle-aged man in a Sempé cartoon: "Who are you? Where are you? Forces of darkness, you've stopped me becoming what I could have been." But the characters in *Building Stories* are less subject to vindictiveness than to resignation and frustration. The limitation of this masterful comic is perhaps its failure to interrogate social structures and relationships of power and domination. Rather than a political reading of the world, Ware prefers to portray our subjective experience of it. *Building Stories* remains an extraordinary lesson about life, the constraints it imposes, the opportunities it offers, all its settings, and its rituals—an inexhaustible book that never ceases to amaze, whichever way you approach it.

JENS HARDER
The Grand Narrative: Alpha, Beta (2009, 2014)

BACKGROUND

Jens Harder was born in 1970 in Weisswasser, in the former German Democratic Republic. He studied graphic art in Berlin. Since 1999 he has been working with Monogatari, a collective of artists of which he is a founding member. Rejecting fiction, he first made his name as one of the pioneers of comics journalism through his investigative reporting. His reportages, in comics format, were featured in several journals and collections. A three-month residency in Marseilles, in 2000, led to the five-chapter *Marseilles Electricity*. After falling Obélix-like into the cauldron of the Parc Saint-Jacob Football Club in Basel, he produced *Quick, Shoot!*, an X-ray examination of the footballing milieu (in the collectively authored *Operation Gingerbread*). A period spent in Jerusalem was the basis of *Ticket to God* (in the collective volume *Cargo* and in an extended version under the title *The City of God*).[1]

His first two books were published by Éditions de l'An 2: Leviathan and The City of God.[2] He then embarked upon a twenty-year project to recount in images the story of life on Earth from the most distant past through to the future. The first part, Alpha . . . directions, was published simultaneously by Actes Sud (French edition) and Carlsen (German edition) in 2009. The book won the Prix de l'Audace [Prize for artistic innovation] at the Angoulême comics festival and the Max-und-Moritz prize at the Erlangen festival. In 2014, the French edition went into its fifth reprint, which included so many amendments that it was effectively a new edition.

Because of the breadth of his subject matter, Harder decided to split the sequel, *Beta . . . civilizations*, into two volumes, the first of which was published in January 2014. The four-volume trilogy that was given the generic title *The Grand Narrative* [*Le Grand récit*] once it was in progress will culminate with *Gamma . . . visions*. To give himself some breathing space in the middle of this lengthy undertaking, Harder has turned his attention to an adaptation of the *Epic of Gilgamesh*.

A monograph about his work, which included much unpublished material, has been published under the title *MIKROmakro*.[3]

PLOT

Alpha condenses fourteen billion years of life on Earth, from the Big Bang to the emergence of the first humans, and borrows from astronomy, physics, chemistry, biology, and paleontology, with the aim of "bringing together all the visual representations" available, according to its afterword (339). The book displays all the operations and strategies of evolution: variation, mutation, symbiosis, combination, convergence, adaptation, and so on.

Beta continues by tracing the evolution of hominids over four million years, and zooms in on 30,000 years of the history of human civilization up to the beginning of the Christian era.

In *Beta I*, Harder, drawing more than ever on a massive archive, tackles topics like the development of primates, the invention of fire, the origins of language, the shift from nomadism to settlement, architecture, livestock farming, the establishment of cities, and the emergence and uses made of different art forms.

Volume 2 will bring us up to the present. Then *Gamma* will go into futuristic mode with some potential evolutionary scenarios.

UNLIKE THE OTHER WORKS ANALYZED IN THIS BOOK, this one is still unfinished, with only two of the four promised volumes currently available. However, the incredible scale of the ambition that underlies them, the originality of the form, the heft of the two books so far available (*Alpha* is 356 pages long and volume 1 of *Beta* has 368 pages), and the enthusiastic critical reception and commercial success with which they have been met combine to consecrate Jens Harder's "great work" as one of the most significant achievements of the beginning of this millennium.

The artist's early output was based on documentary observation and investigative reporting. After *Leviathan*, his work noticeably changed direction: he started to come to grips with treasures to be found in libraries, the archives of humanity, whether myths from the past or present-day scientific accomplishments.

Leviathan was enriched by Harder's reading of Milton, Hobbes, sacred texts, and, of course, Melville's *Moby Dick*. Indeed, he acknowledges his sources in the form of quotations placed at the head of each section, the only texts to be found in the book. The heroine of this album is a whale of monstrous proportions—the fabled, invincible, and mythological great white whale—depicted over five chapters grappling with other sea creatures but also with oil rigs and ships like the *Santa Maria*, Noah's Ark, and the *Titanic*. Leviathan prefigures the later books in that Harder reveals in it his passion for natural history and mythology, and, already, a maelstrom of images swirls over the reader who is carried along, stirred up, and sent reeling, but never drowned. And the author succeeds in making us identify with the giant cachalot: it is with this proud and solitary creature that we empathize, even though it attacks those humans who dare to contest its supremacy over the oceans; it is this creature that is the object of our compassion when it succumbs to the destructive power of the elements.

With the trilogy that he subsequently conceived, Harder considerably broadened the range of his sources, which gave his work an encyclopedic dimension. *Alpha* seems to have been created in response to these words of Michel Serres:

> We are now familiar with the broad outline of our biological history. We know how humans spread over the Earth and how cultures came into being. Better still, we can connect this history to a narrative much wider in scope—that I am calling the Grand Narrative—that retraces the development of the Universe, from its genesis to the formation of the solar system and our planet.

And Serres marvels at the fact that "we can henceforth look back at a chronological horizon of tens of billions of years, much further than the horizon that was visible when I was a student, which was limited to a few thousand years."[4] *The Grand Narrative* is the generic title that Jens Harder decided on at the end of 2013, with reference to Serres, to designate the whole of the cycle still in progress.

Harder's chosen method consists of creating as few original images as possible. Ninety-five per cent of the panels are from existing visual sources, eclectic borrowings from across the cultural spectrum: cave paintings, old masters, illustrations, comics panels, maps, diagrams, photographs, film stills, digital animations, etc. However, the images are not reproduced in their original state: the artist redraws them, adding the imprint of his personal style. Each volume contains over two thousand drawings in an ordered flow, a kaleidoscope of pictures, and meets the challenge of recapitulating all the visual images that the history of the world has inspired humans to create, from the most realist to the most symbolic. A journalist from *Chronic'art* called it "the imaginary catalogue of a wildly unrealizable exhibition"; *Philosophie magazine* called it "a fascinating synthesis of the pictorial memory of humanity."

Harder's subject matter, we will argue, is exactly what the historian Jacques Le Goff defines as the "imaginary":

> What is the imaginary? We now know that individual human lives and the collective life of society are not limited to what is material and tangible. The life of a society includes, and so also can be explained by, the representations that its members have created of their own history, the role of their society and their own place in it. [...] But over and above the objectivized image, the drawn image, the painted image, and the sculpted image—the vast territory of the image that lies beyond the boundaries of the history of art—there are also mental images, mental representations in the shape of images. In their abstract form, they belong to the general history of representations.[5]

By articulating images together, and thereby "objectivizing" them, Harder summons up, and calls into question, our mental representations. The author of *The Grand Narrative* situates himself less as a creator of images than in the dual role of creator of meaning and graphic designer.

In other words, although he declines to deploy the demiurgic power of drawing, refusing to create original forms or fictional worlds, Harder nonetheless proves himself to be a comics author in the full sense of the word. In fact, this is the very basis of the art of comics: the linking and sequencing of multiple images that work together to produce meaning. Furthermore, to the temporal linear dimension of the text or the reel of film, comics adds a spatial dimension: its unit of narration is the page, and the images are arranged on it not only in a given order but in a particular spatial configuration, which is orchestrated according to various criteria: position, shape, and size. These are the two axes that structure Jens Harder's work: bringing images into collision with each other, exploiting all possible modes of relationship between adjacent panels (complementarity, serial variation, metaphor, antithesis, the anachronistic telescoping of time frames, and dazzling ellipsis), and playing, like a virtuoso, upon the spatial organization of the page.

The originality of his project is particularly noticeable in relation to the first of these axes. In place of the principle of breakdown, the fragmentation of a continuous narrative, a plot, into discrete images corresponding to key moments of the action, Harder substitutes a different principle, that of montage or collage. In this case, the images already exist but meaning arises when they are brought into contiguity.

Since the language of comics has the peculiarity of being discontinuous, it forces the reader to make inferences in order to interpret each new image appropriately, or in other words to understand how it correlates with the previous one and with the whole of the work of which it forms a part. In a classic comic, what has to be read is usually a matter of what has *intervened*: a temporal interval separates each image from the preceding one, and, in this interval, something has happened, the situation has evolved. But panels do not have to be articulated according to a causal chain. Frequently, the juxtapositions in Jens Harder's comic are nothing to do with what has intervened and can only be understood in terms of what is *signified*. It is incumbent upon the reader to infer what meaning may arise out of these juxtapositions, to identify or perform the ideational leap that justifies them.

This is truer of *Beta* than of *Alpha*, and we must now move on from general observations to consider the differences between the first two volumes of the cycle. These differences reside, on the one hand, in the disparity between the temporal range of the two periods covered and, on the other hand, in the fact that *history* does not mean the same thing in each case.

In the afterword to volume 1 of *Beta*, the author himself makes the point:

> If we do the sums, this time there is one image for every two thousand years. The main narrative covers a period of four million years starting from the emergence of the Australopithecus, which we can divide by the two thousand images in the book. In *Alpha*, statistically, there was seven million years between each image, so that we could insert the whole of this book between two pages of *Alpha* (350).

Alpha, indeed, "represents more than 14 billion years in just 350 pages," which, says Harder, "is something of a joke" (*Alpha* 340). The book, then, covers an exceptionally long period. In this respect, it may be illuminating to compare it to other famous comics narratives that, in a more condensed format, are similarly ambitious in terms of the length of time that they encompass. I am thinking of Richard McGuire's *Here* and Robert Crumb's *A Short History of America*.

Here consists of six pages and appeared in Art Spiegelman and Françoise Mouly's magazine *RAW* in 1989 (2.1). The principle is well-known: to convey, in a "static shot," the history of a small corner of America, from the most distant past (five billion years BC) to the near future (the year 2033). The story includes eighty-five images, of which about fifty are inserted within other images. The chronology is disrupted, with different periods clashing up against each other. However, the narration is particularly focused on the story of a house built in 1902 and destroyed by fire in 2029, and on its occupants, most notably a certain William, known as Billy, born in 1957 like McGuire himself, whose life seems to hold no interest whatsoever. What can the pathetic life of a man represent or be worth from the perspective of the passing centuries and millennia? That is the question that the author seems to pose.[6]

Crumb's *A Short History of America*[7] includes, in its original (and most widely circulated) version, twelve panels of equal size. It consists, again, of a "static shot," framing a landscape whose location is not made clear. The first image shows unspoiled nature, where only animals tread. Then the artist "records" the construction of a railroad, then a first log cabin, then a village, and finally an urban center entirely concreted over, crisscrossed by electric power cables and automobiles. Crumb does not directly show humans acting upon the landscape, only the result of their action: the gradual devastation, the methodical destruction of nature. The first panel condenses the entire period preceding civilization—the existence of Native Americans is completely erased—and therefore corresponds to the entirety of *Alpha*. The arrival of the train must date from between 1850 and 1860 at the earliest. The remaining panels seem to be broken down, more or less, into decades.

In these two comics, by McGuire and Crumb, what clearly interests the artists is human time, the time of recent history, mainly because the changes are more rapid and more marked. And the static shot seems like an obvious device for observing what has changed over time, as if an unvarying viewpoint, an intangible frame were necessary in order to make visible the dynamic of History.

In both these respects, Jens Harder breaks with the conventions observed by his predecessors. He invites us to roam the entire surface of the Earth. And the prehuman period is accorded as much attention as the period since humans appeared. For it is not the story of humanity that Harder is setting out to recount, but that of life, in all its manifestations.

With *Alpha*, comics perhaps returns to its own ontological foundations. The Belgian philosopher and semiotician Henri Van Lier described the comics multiframe as an ideal site for the study of forms, their deformations and their catastrophic mutations, and maintained that the title of D'Arcy Thompson's 1917 treatise on topological mutation, *On Growth and Form*, would make an excellent subtitle for "any discerning study of comics."[8] It is indeed growth and the increasing complexity of forms that are the subject matter of *Alpha*, whose "protagonists" are particles, amoebae, bacteria, trilobites, shellfish, insects, dinosaurs, continents, oceans, and galaxies. And the author is passionate about the mutation of life forms.[9]

This passion has its roots in his childhood, as he explains in the afterword to the opening volume: "My parents took me to palaeontological oriented exhibitions, where we would join the long lines in front of the Natural History

Museum in Berlin and we went on trips to the ever-growing dinosaur theme park at Kleinwelka in Bautzen ..." (*Alpha* 338).

Books about prehistoric animals illustrated by the Czech painter Zdeněk Burian (1905–81), extensively quoted from in *Alpha*, were also a determining influence.

By chance, the book came out in 2009, the bicentenary of Darwin's birth. *Alpha* is, manifestly, a Darwinist book, a veritable ode to Evolution. As well as offering an artist's vision, it can be considered a popularizing scientific work, and, moreover, serves to demonstrate the extraordinary educational value of comics.

Undoubtedly, a book like this is all the more timely given the spread of a new obscurantist fundamentalism under the name of "creationism" or "intelligent design," which purports to cast doubt on Darwinian theories. Although Francophone countries have been relatively unscathed, the same cannot be said of other regions of the world. For example, the New York–based Pantheon Books seriously considered publishing the book, but pulled out for fear of provoking controversy.

Because *Alpha* focuses on the prehuman period (not to be confused with prehistory, which designates the period between the appearance of humans and the earliest written documents), the evolutionary processes that are recounted and illustrated are extremely slow, taking tens or hundreds of thousands of years. We are struck, on reading the book, by the cyclic nature of the major events that marked the Cryptozoic and then the Paleozoic and Mesozoic eras: periods of glaciation alternating with periods of global warming and successive waves of extinction of a large proportion of living species.

The prehuman period predates History. It is measured out by natural processes, not by states of affairs resulting from decisions taken by human agents. Harder therefore cannot, in *Alpha*, adopt the practice that he uses intensively in the next book, that of tracking variations on a theme through different civilizations, or following the development of an invention or of some instance of human progress from its beginnings to its furthest and most unpredictable consequences. His story in the first book stays linear, and is less dense, in the sense that readers are not yet, as they will be in *Beta*, bombarded by disparate references and a patchwork of images.

However, the technique of visual collage, with citation effects, is already present.

From the opening pages, exploiting the fact that the circular form is common both to planets and to the conventional representation of atoms, Harder embarks on a series of variations on the motif of the circle, bringing in billiard balls, Newton's pendulum, Foucault's pendulum and the Brussels

Atomium—which represents an iron crystal whose nine constituent atoms have been magnified 165 billion times.

Further on, after having recounted the formation of the sun, he portrays the forms taken by the cult dedicated to the centermost star of our solar system in different civilizations (Egyptian, Celtic, Indian, Maya) and it takes him just one page to convey the universality of the phenomenon (57). In the case of the moon, he juxtaposes its representation through art (Magritte) and its conquest, both as imagined by nineteenth-century science fiction (Verne) and as actually carried out by NASA in the twentieth century (76).

Thus, the two main principles of montage that operate in *Alpha* are, first, formal analogy, either illustrative or metaphorical, which uses the multiframe like an echo chamber as the container for a series of visual rhymes; and, second, a series of variations on a theme or phenomenon in time or space.

The analogies serve an educational purpose: they make certain mechanisms more visible and comprehensible by juxtaposing them with more familiar examples. Continental drift and the collision of tectonic plates are portrayed alongside an image of a mechanical excavator moving earth (125); the development of exoskeletons is likened to architectural design (176–77). Some of these analogies are dubious from a scientific point of view (the human eye is not exactly a camera lens as suggested on page 171), but all are clear enough for the analogies to make sense and to be, if not enlightening, at least evocative.

The technique does not always avoid the pitfall of anthropomorphic or anthropological projection. When the author refers to the defense mechanisms adopted by living organisms ("armor and spines against claws and teeth"), he describes them as an "arms race" (173) and immediately devotes a double page to the weapons developed by humans and the wars and conflicts that divide them (174–75). The reader may feel that this extrapolation is far-fetched. It does, however, encourage reflection, and implicitly raises genuine questions: Is it the fact that humans have no natural defenses that has driven them to invent more and more sophisticated weapons? If other living beings engage in interspecies struggles over territory, food, and survival, why do humans, who form a single species, engage in fratricidal, intraspecies wars? Jens Harder leaves it up to the reader to formulate these questions. But it is his aesthetic of montage/collage that invites reflection. He has molded his *Grand Narrative* into a powerful "dream machine" (to quote the former subtitle of *Métal hurlant*), as well as a "thought machine."

Furthermore, through these visionary flash-forwards, Harder involves humans in the prehuman period, and he thereby suggests that this distant history already concerns us, that we result from it, and that it is the source of

Alpha, page 76. Courtesy of Tony Bennett, Knockabout Ltd.

our collective destiny. In addition, it points, in a number of sequences, to the impact that human action will subsequently have on nature and on animals that were long protected from our intervention. The elephant appears in the Cenozoic era, its size "respectably gigantic." But a discreet panel reminds us that this giant will one day be exhibited as circus animal (322).

When Harder embarks on a series of thematic variations, he traces out a symbolic trajectory, turning into a sociologist, a comparatist, and a historian of civilizations. And the range of references upon which he draws is dazzling, from the most respected "high art" (Bosch, Botticelli, Brueghel, Cranach, Dürer, Michelangelo, and Leonardo, to name but a few) to the most familiar works of contemporary popular culture. For example, the portrayal of carnivorous fish and the first sharks provides an opportunity to allude to *Red Rackham's Treasure* and to *Jaws* (209). A few quotations, however, evoke less well-known works, and it is as a professional comics artist that Harder demonstrates a fraternal complicity with other artists that he admires (for example, when, on the subject of dinosaurs, he invokes Winsor McCay's *Gertie*) (264–265). This postmodern intermingling does not hierarchize but neither does it level down: it suspends all judgments about the "quality" of the images quoted. It does not matter whether they belong to a major or minor art form, whether they are the work of an acknowledged genius or the product of an anonymous process. Their individual, empirical properties are not relevant here, they function as documents. And it is this suspension of judgment that, in some way, enables them to be available for new combinations and original configurations that make us see them differently.

Beta is something else altogether. This second volume follows the more densely woven thread of human history. In his afterword, the author explains:

> In the development of our cultures and civilizations, I am less interested by the factual aspect, the succession of kingdoms and dynasties (a conception of history teaching that has tortured several generations of pupils by making them learn dates off by heart, thereby discouraging them from taking more of an interest in certain periods), than in the processes, the unfolding of events, the different contexts and interactions (*Beta*, vol. 1, 351).

The time frame of this second volume, that of the history taught in schools, is, in principle, much better known to readers than the period covered by *Alpha*. And the profusion of information is so dense that the poet-chronicler has had to be rigorously selective. The choices that he makes, among all the images in the world, are all the more significant (and will no doubt be even more so in volume 2 of *Beta*, which will concern modern history). They are also more controversial.

Alpha, page 265. Courtesy of Tony Bennett, Knockabout Ltd.

The subjects dealt with in volume 1 of *Beta* include, most notably, the evolution of primates, the discovery of fire, the advent of language, the shift from nomadism to settlement, architecture, livestock farming, the development of cities, and the emergence and spread of different art forms.

Anachronism, prefiguration, the collapsing of time frames—these now become the rule, the basis of the narrative technique in this volume. Moreover, certain subjects are raised and then lost from view before reappearing several dozen pages further on, which confers a musical dimension upon the book, with the presentation of themes, reprises and variations. We can take the example of the hand: the subject is introduced on pages 26 and 27, where the author duly celebrates the arrival of the great apes with opposable thumbs. A selection of images shows how this prehensile organ will allow for precise and efficient gestures that act upon the animal's environment, how humans, who are descended from primates, will use it for boxing as well as for greeting, or for sealing a deal (by shaking hands), and how it will also transform sexual behavior. Hands later reappear on pages 82 and 83, wielding tools, drawing, praying, blessing, miming, and performing other symbolic gestures. Still further on, tributes are paid to the hands of painters and sculptors. Themes already touched upon in *Alpha*, like invocations to the sun, return to appear on pages 248 and 249.

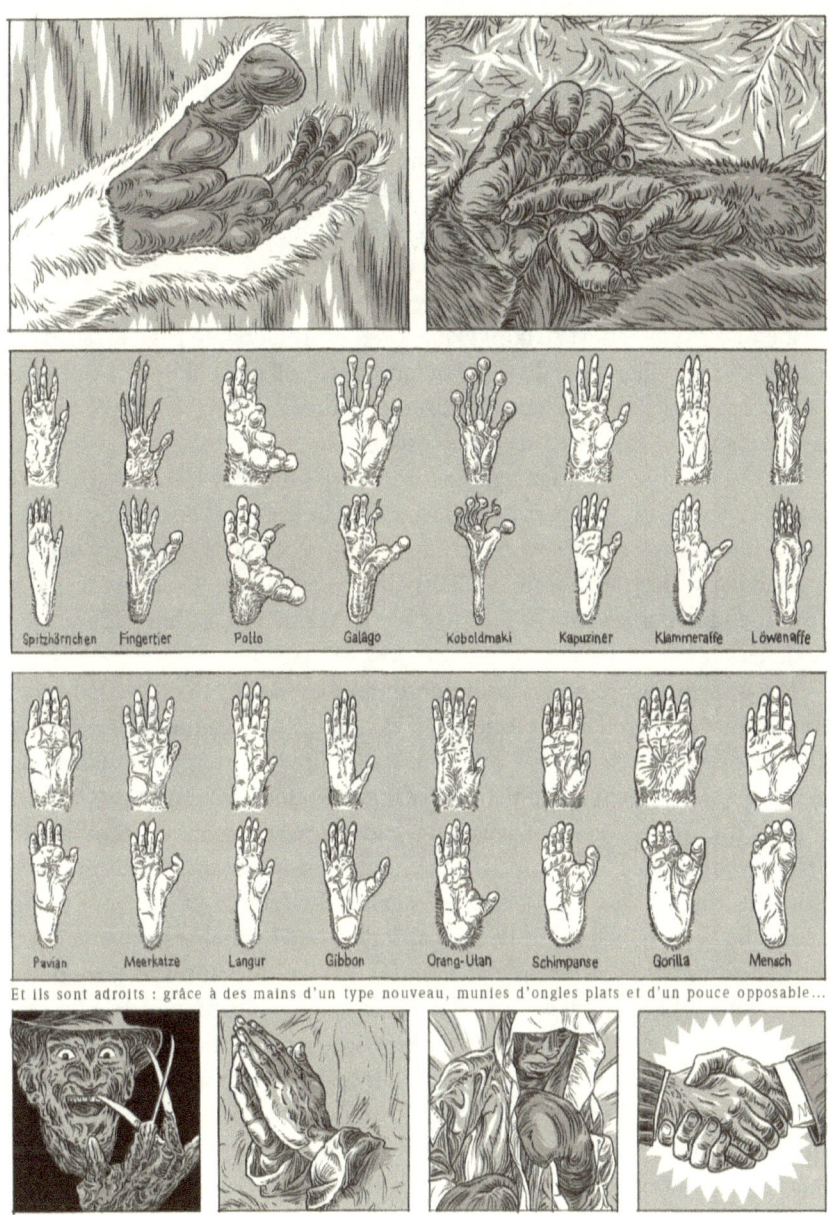

Beta, vol. 1, page 26

Although volume 1 of *Beta* ends, officially, at the beginning of our era, reserving the two millennia of recent history for the next volume, the modern period is in fact omnipresent in the first part, because the author constantly makes links between past and present. The sequence on architecture, and more precisely on monumental buildings, takes us without transition from the Tower of Babel and the Pyramids to twentieth- and even twenty-first-century skyscrapers (*Beta*, vol. 1, 298–301). Similarly, the sequence on the domestication of fire opens with a kind of chain reaction that leads, via the Olympic flame and church candles, to electricity and atomic energy (100–107). And the theme of writing—most strikingly explored over "a double page that anyone who loves the calligraphic diversity of languages will find sublime"[10]—plunges us forward to the giant neon advertisements in the streets of Tokyo, and the digital display of stock market prices (290–93).

This becomes a systematic procedure: every time that Harder arrives at a major invention, he explores its logical consequences, and does so by drilling through time frames. The overreaching ambition of hubris has rarely been so spectacularly illustrated. And, implicitly, the reader detects Charles Alexandre de Calon's famous maxim: "If it is possible, it is done; if it is impossible, it shall be done."

The transitions are more abrupt and more audacious than in *Alpha*, as if Harder, more assured of his technique, were pushing it to the limit. It is startling to see, on page 21, Jesus Christ, Superman, Elvis Presley, and Adolf Hitler in four panels aligned along the same strip. The close proximity between the Son of God (in the view of Christians) and the most appalling criminal ever to have walked the Earth is provocative, and some would find it blasphemous. However, the justification for this collage is to be found in a sentence higher up on the page, which reminds us that "primates," by their very name (from the Latin *primas, primatis*, "the one who occupies the first place"), are designated "lords of the animals" (21). The four disparate human figures who then come into view suggest—although the text does not specify this and it is up to the reader to work it out—that humans, in turn, have constantly proclaimed themselves lords of creation and have distinguished within their own ranks, and worshipped, beings reputed to be superior and designated as such by their names—King, or indeed *Führer*. And the comparison ends there.

The presence of Superman and Elvis in this foursome shows that, for Harder, art has a role to play in history. The place taken up in his project by the products of the imagination testifies to his conviction that works of art express, transmit, symbolize, and perpetuate human history by exploring its meaning. However, art is also involved in *Beta* as a subject in its own right, since the book refers to the discovery by humans of various means of artistic expression and the subsequent development of techniques. As an artist,

Beta, vol. 1, page 301

Leurs descendants se qualifieront de primates, « seigneurs des animaux » dans le système des êtres vivants.

Beta, vol. 1, page 21

Harder has a particular interest in the "need to produce images," and the progression of figurative art across all media (195–206). He sets out from the Lascaux caves and arrives at the ceiling of the Sistine Chapel, the Mona Lisa, Dada, and then contemporary and abstract art. If the representation of the human figure quite naturally attracts his attention, it is also noticeable that he particularly focuses on animal art in cave paintings and engravings, which, of course, he associates with the work of Jeff Koons and Louise Bourgeois (205–6). As someone who is passionate about natural history and who has drawn so many animals in *Alpha*, Holder is able on these pages to take up his place in an artistic lineage, and to give way to his fascination for the mystery of the graphic line. In fact, a number of comics albums have demonstrated the shared understanding among comics artists that they belong to the same community as their "prehistoric colleagues."[11]

Alpha and *Beta* could form the basis of a valid theory of montage. Numerous theoreticians have reflected on the way in which the juxtaposition of images generates ideas. "There is no such thing as an image, there are only relationships between images," Jean-Luc Godard has said.[12]

In this respect, Jens Harder's undertaking follows on, perhaps unconsciously, from the *Mnémosyne Atlas* by the German art historian Aby Warburg (1868–1929). This great compendium of images, created between 1921 and 1929, was conceived with the aim of making visible the traces of antiquity in Western culture by mapping out a history of artistic production without texts. Warburg had begun by creating about forty wooden boards covered with black cloth, onto which were pinned almost a thousand reproductions of works of art, press cuttings, and advertisements originating from different cultures and periods and with contrasting aesthetics juxtaposed. As Georges Didi-Huberman's analysis has shown, Warburg wanted to found an "iconology of the interval," in which the gap between the images would be a *Denkenraum* (thinking space).[13]

This way of thinking about montage—or about intervals—is endlessly fascinating, and one critic has noted that "there is, therefore, a risk that admiration for Harder's spiritual enterprise takes precedence over contemplation of the book that we have before us. Here, it is the thought that controls the image, whose evocative power is sacrificed to the idea that underpins it."[14] In other words, the reader may forget to look at the images for themselves, distracted by the effort to put them in perspective, to reflect upon them, and to interpret them.

In certain digitally generated comics that are highly interactive, it seems to me that the pleasure of manipulating the screen content can outweigh the pleasure of the fiction, which becomes secondary. The experience that is offered is less like reading and more like gaming—two fundamentally different modes of attention that are in competition. A similar difficulty may arise in the case of certain sequences of Jens Harder's work: it is possible that, absorbed by our thoughts on the intervals between the images—our rumination on whatever is evoked by the sequencing of disparate images from heterogeneous sources—we allow the reading process to stall, to seize up, and we lose the narrative thread. But what surely distinguishes great innovative works—as we have seen with Chris Ware in the previous chapter—is that they change the nature of the reading experience and therefore have to, in some sense, invent a new reader.

In this case, the persistent and highly dynamic visual intertextuality, or inter-iconicity, that pervades the text activates another process that slows down reading and informs reflection: the game of identifying the source images and, where relevant, attributing them to an artist. Each panel prompts not one but several questions: what civilization and what period does this image refer to? Can the people and places depicted in it be identified? And in the case of a work of art, is there a named artist? Who created it? Readers have to dredge up memories from schooldays and draw on their general knowledge and on their encyclopedia, in the sense that Umberto Eco gives to the word. In some cases identification is immediate and unambiguous, in other cases it remains vague and uncertain, and of course there are a number of instances where the reference remains elusive.

Some will find this game intimidating and exhausting; others will find it stimulating and thrilling. But, crucially, not having an answer to certain questions or failing to find the source of certain images never poses an insurmountable problem: the reader can be carried away by the evocative power of the sequential flow without stumbling over every unknown quantity in the equation, and it is perhaps this way of approaching the text—we can call it naïve—that, initially, is the most pleasurable.

It is, of course, not insignificant that the quoted images are never reproduced in their original format but systematically redrawn. "Pictorial quotation cannot be literal in the same way as literary quotation, because it is mediated by the hand and style of the person who quotes," as Jacques Derrida wrote.[15] Harder's approach is the opposite of Goblet's; the Belgian artist creates original images in several different styles, while her German colleague samples from heterogeneous images and minimizes the jarring effect of their visual coexistence by redrawing them in his own style. The immediate consequence of this procedure is to achieve compatibility between aesthetics and media that are initially very disparate.

Rather than referring to quotations, it would be more accurate to call these borrowings "evocations." The decision to use duotone effaces one obvious difference: black and white documents can no longer be distinguished from those that were originally in color: both undergo chromatic modification.

Every twenty-four pages there is a random change of color, not correlated with the division into chapters and sequences. In *Alpha*, seven Pantone colors are used in succession and each has a range of different intensities; in *Beta*, the number of colors is reduced to three: gold, silver, and bronze. Sometimes Harder uses the chosen color over flat surfaces to make them stand out and to contrast different planes; sometimes he uses it to enrich his drawings, shaping and molding them, adding shading and highlighting, and accentuating details. Similarly, the background of the panel is sometimes colored in and sometimes left blank.

The images most resistant to reinterpretation are those taken from humorous comics or animations. When he borrows from Barks, Hergé, Uderzo, Trondheim, Blain, or Ware, Harder remains very faithful to their respective styles. If he pushed them further toward realism, he would render them unrecognizable and would destroy all the pleasure to be had from these playful allusions. The cartoon-style or clear-line images always look like inserts from other comics. By keeping their speech balloons, the author deliberately signals, in fact, that that is their provenance.

In spite of their differences, all the other images more or less merge into a single flow, onto which "the hand and the style of the person who quotes" confer a superficial homogeneity. Even though he creates (almost) no original images, Harder nonetheless manifests a very personal graphic handwriting: his images are dense, his line meticulous, descriptive, sensuous, and, when appropriate to the subject matter, a little quivering or even spiky.

He is not at all dogmatic about layout. He has no basic template, no matrix with a few predetermined variations. Most of his pages include between two and four strips of differing heights. Some are arranged around a large central image, and others form a mosaic with smaller panels imbricated in larger ones in constantly renewed configurations. Sometimes the layout takes account of the double page.

While *Alpha* was subtitled *directions*, *Beta* has *civilizations*, in the plural, added to its title. This is an interesting choice, in that German researchers—in conformity with French archeologists and anthropologists—usually prefer the term *Kultur* to that of *Zivilisation*. Civilizations can be defined as the set of characteristics of the collective life of an identifiable group or period, in a designated geographical area, within a certain climate range. Henri Van Lier, whose *Anthropogenics* lists nine great "planetary civilizations," observes that their internal coherence "confers upon them a certain hermetic quality." He concludes that "all things considered, nothing in one civilization is identical to what happens in another, although it may appear so at a superficial glance."[16]

The artist who concerns us here does not go in for superficial glances; Harder does not claim that civilizations are identical. But, aware that everywhere humans "have to reproduce themselves, eat, clothe themselves, speak, and prepare food,"[17] he shows how their ways of fulfilling these needs have changed across space and, above all, over time. "*Beta* is an action comic whose main character is time; it shows the effects of the actions of time on humans, how it has transformed their way of life and relationship to the world," observes Sébastien Charbonnier.[18]

This is why we may judge that the plural ending given to *Beta . . . civilizations* may prove to be ultimately deceptive. Admittedly, *Beta* concerns the historical period in the course of which the great human civilizations emerged and established their distinctive characteristics, but what the reader retains above all is the dynamic that persists through evolutions and revolutions: the "process of civilization," in essence, to quote the title of a work by the German sociologist Norbert Elias.

This is not the place to attribute to Jens Harder any particular conception of progress or historical determinism: I leave that to others better qualified than myself. But it is certain that this book can spark off sociological, anthropological, historical, and even metaphysical debates around different cosmological interpretations of the universe. It will continue, well into the future, to provoke controversy and to give rise to interpretations and attempts at refutation of one point or another.

An inexhaustible and substantial work, Jens Harder's *Grand Narrative* is an exhilarating journey through time and through images, a treatise and a fresco, an epic and a poem.

NOTES

TRANSLATOR'S FOREWORD

1. Originally published as *Système de la bande dessinée* (Paris: Presses Universitaires de France, 1999). English translation by Bart Beaty and Nick Nguyen (Jackson: University Press of Mississippi, 2006).

2. Originally published as *Bande dessinée et narration* (Paris: Presses Universitaires de France, 2011). English translation by Ann Miller (Jackson: University Press of Mississippi, 2013).

3. Charles Hatfield, *Hand of Fire: The Comics Art of Jack Kirby* (Jackson: University Press of Mississippi, 2012), 110.

INTRODUCTION

1. I do not particularly like this term. It may have had historical importance, and tactical effectiveness, but it introduces a blurred categorization into the field of comics creation, which is not, in my view, useful. I therefore use it sparingly, and only for convenience. For a discussion of the concept of the graphic novel, I refer readers to my article on the subject: "Roman graphique" [Graphic novel], *Dictionnaire esthétique et thématique de la bande dessinée* [Aesthetic and thematic dictionary of comics], *Neuvième Art 2.0*, http://neuviemeart.citebd.org/spip.php?rubrique77.

2. I retraced them myself in *La Bande dessinée, son histoire et ses maîtres* [Comics, its history and its masters] (Paris: Skira Flammarion; Angoulême: Cité internationale de la bande dessinée et de l'image, 2009).

3. Blutch, *Péplum* in *(A Suivre)*, 1996. English translation, *Peplum*, by Edward Gauvin (New York: New York Review Comics, 2016).

4. Hugo Pratt, *Fort Wheeling* in *Misterix* (1962).

5. Gilles Ciment and Jean-Pierre Mercier, "Entretien avec Blutch" [Interview with Blutch], *Neuvième Art* [Ninth Art] 14 (January 2008), 112–25.

CHAPTER 1: HUGO PRATT, *BALLAD OF THE SALT SEA*

Originally published as *Una Ballata del Mare Salato* in the magazine *Sgt. Kirk* (1967–69). English translation by Ian Monk (New York: NBM, 1996) (7 vols.). Page references are given in the form of volume number: page number. Ellipses in quotations are original unless they are enclosed in square brackets. —Trans.

1. Hugo Pratt, *Gli scorpioni del deserto*, 5 vols., 1969–92. First volume published in *Sgt. Kirk* and successive volumes in *Linus* and *Alter Alter*.

2. In the Italian editions of *Ballad of the Salt Sea*, these cannibals express themselves, oddly, in Venetian dialect.

3. He meets Death, and speaks with her, in a later album, *Le Elvetiche* [The Helvetics] (1987).

4. Hugo Pratt, *Le Désir d'être inutile* [The desire to be useless], conversations with Dominique Petitfaux (Paris: Robert Laffont, 1991), 202.

5. The English-language edition published by Harvill Press also features only Corto Maltese. Of the seven volumes published by NBM, four show Corto alone, one shows Corto and the Monk, one shows the Monk alone, and one shows Pandora alone. —Trans.

6. Hugo Pratt, *De l'autre côté de Corto* [On the other side of Corto], conversations with Dominique Petitfaux (Tournai: Casterman, 1990), 58. In Greek mythology, Pandora is the first woman. Created on the orders of Zeus to exact revenge on men for the theft of fire by Prometheus, she punishes them for their pretentions.

7. Jean Van Hamme and Dany, *Histoire sans héros* (Brussels: Lombard, 1977).

8. Pratt, *De l'autre côté de Corto*, 57.

9. Florian Rubis lists the borrowings from cinema in *Hugo Pratt ou le sens de la fable* [Hugo Pratt or the feeling for a story] (Paris: Belin, 2009).

10. Pratt, *De l'autre côté de Corto*, 154.

11. Hugo Pratt, *Conversation avec Eddy Devolder* [Conversation with Eddy Devolder] (Gerpinnes: Tandem, 1990), 27.

12. Alain Hervé, in a special edition of *Géo: Le Monde extraordinaire de Corto Maltese* [The extraordinary world of Corto Maltese] (Nov. 2001), 28.

13. Quoted in Vincenzo Mollica and Mauro Paganelli, *Pratt* (Hounoux: SEDLI-Jacky Goupil, 1984), 13.

14. This map does not appear in the NBM version of the book. —Trans.

15. Pratt, quoted in Mollica and Paganelli, *Pratt*, 13.

16. Pratt, *De l'autre côté de Corto*, 144.

17. The future Communist militant and author of *Ten Days that Shook the World* was then aged twenty-three.

18. Juan Antonio de Blas, preface to the deluxe edition of the album *Corto Maltese—la jeunesse* [Corto Maltese—his youth] (Tournai: Casterman, 1985).

19. *Corto Maltese: Mémoires* [Corto Maltese: Memoirs], text by Michel Pierre, water colors and drawings by Hugo Pratt (Tournai: Casterman, 1988).

20. Hugo Pratt, *La Jeunesse de Corto Maltese*, in *Le Matin de Paris* (1981).

21. Jean-Michel Charlier and Jean Giraud, *Ballade pour un cercueil* (Paris: Dargaud, 1974).

22. In *The Youth of Corto Maltese*, Rasputin shouts, after having killed officers in the two opposing camps: "I've decided to do whatever I like. A man like me can't be the plaything of fate."

23. Nor in the NBM edition. —Trans.

24. Hugo Pratt and Michel Pierre, *Les Femmes de Corto Maltese* [Corto Maltese's women] (Tournai: Casterman, 1994).

25. Hugo Pratt, "Burlesque entre Zuydcoote et Bray-Dunes," in *Les Celtiques* (Tournai: Casterman, 1980).

26. *Corto Maltese en Sibérie* [*Corto Maltese in Siberia*] (1979) contains this dialogue between Rasputin (who wants to get rich through arms dealing and transporting mercenaries) and Corto: "Don't be a hypocrite, Corto. You too are a gentleman of fortune." "That's just it. A gentleman of fortune, not a mercenary like you."

27. Hugo Pratt, "Entretien avec Hugo Pratt" [Conversation with Hugo Pratt], in *À la rencontre de . . . Hugo Pratt* [A meeting with Hugo Pratt], originally published in the fanzine *Fumo di China* 14 (May 1982).

28. Pratt, *De l'autre côté de Corto*, 58.

29. Pratt, *Le Désir d'être inutile*, 195.

30. In France, it appeared only in the paperback version, in the "J'ai lu BD" collection in 1987. [It is not included in the NBM version. —Trans.]

31. See my article "La Conquête du silence" [The conquest of silence], *Art Press*, special edition 26 (2005): 68–73.

32. Jean Arrouye, "Images aveugles chez Pratt" [Blind images in Pratt], in *À la rencontre de ... Hugo Pratt*, 73–77.

33. Rubis, *Hugo Pratt ou le sens de la fable*. Emphasis in original.

34. Not entirely unprecedented, to be precise. Jacobs's *Le Secret de l'Espadon* [The secret of the Swordfish], which was serialized in *Tintin* magazine over a period of four years, amounted to 142 pages (collected in two volumes); *Fils de Chine* [Son of China], the epic tale by Gillon and Lécureux that appeared in *Vaillant*, amounted to 150 pages. But these were isolated cases, and it was ten years before *Fils de Chine* was published in album format.

35. Platteau, quoted in Nicolas Finet, *(À suivre), 1978–1997: Une aventure en bandes dessinées* [*(À suivre)*, 1978–1997: An adventure in comics] (Tournai: Casterman, 2004), 15.

CHAPTER 2: MŒBIUS, *AIRTIGHT GARAGE*

The publication history of the original French version is complicated, as the introduction to this chapter makes clear. English translation *Airtight Garage*, by Randy and Jean-Marc Lofficier (New York: Epic Comics, 1993) (4 vols.). Each episode is headed, *The Garage Hermetic of Lewis Carnelian*. Mœbius had taken the name "Jerry Cornelius" from Michael Moorcock (see discussion later in this chapter), and Marvel Comics (the parent company) insisted that the name should be changed in the English version. Page references are given in the form of volume number: page number. —Trans.

1. Mœbius, *La Déviation*, *Pilote* 688 (1973).

2. Mœbius, Jean-Marc Lofficier, Eric Shanower (vols. 1–3), and Jerry Bingham (vols. 4–5), *Le Monde du garage hermétique*, 5 vols. (Paris: Les Humanoïdes associés, 1990–1992).

3. Mœbius, *L'Homme du Ciguri* (Paris: Les Humanoïdes associés, 1995).

4. Mœbius, *Le Chasseur déprime* (a play on words with "Le chasseur de primes") [The bounty hunter] (Paris: Stardom, 2008).

5. Mœbius, *Le Monde d'Edena*, 5 vols. (Paris: Les Humanoïdes associés, 1983 [vol. 1]; Tournai: Casterman, 1988–2001 [vols. 2–5]).

6. Mœbius, "Avant-propos" [Foreword], in *Major fatal* (Paris: Les Humanoïdes associés, 1979). [The English translation by Randy and Jean-Marc Lofficier does not include this foreword. —Trans.]

7. Daniel Pizzoli rightly states that in *The Deviation*, Mœbius "watches himself drawing, as if dazzled by his own virtuosity." *Mœbius ou les errances du trait* [Mœbius or the wandering line] (Paris: PLG, 2013), 25.

8. François Boudet, "Entretien avec Thierry Smolderen," [Conversation with Thierry Smolderen] (1998), http://frboudet.pagesperso-orange.fr/Smoldint1.html.

9. This long-unobtainable work, "Les Carnets volés du Major, ou les aventures de Hergé et Mœbius, feuilletonistes," is now available on the website of the journal *Neuvième Art 2.0*, http://neuviemeart.citebd.org/spip.php?article765.

10. Hergé, *Les Cigares du Pharaon* (Tournai: Casterman, 1934).

11. Allow me to quote from my own article, "Improvisation," *Dictionnaire esthétique et thématique de la bande dessinée* [Aesthetic and thematic dictionary of comics], *Neuvième Art 2.0* (March 2014), http://neuviemeart.citebd.org/spip.php?article751.

12. Mœbius, *40 days dans le Désert B* (Paris: Stardom, 1999).

13. Mœbius, interview by Charles-Louis Detournay, actuabd.com (May 14, 2008).

14. Groensteen's discussion obviously refers to the original French title, to which we have therefore temporarily reverted here, since the English title avoided using the name of Moorcock's protagonist. —Trans.

15. Michael Moorcock, *The Final Programme* (London: Allison and Busby, 1969), 7.

16. Ibid., 34.

17. Ibid., 10.

18. Ibid., 40.

19. Ibid., 24.

20. In *The Man from the Ciguri*, Grubert enters the bedroom where his double is lying thanks to a sliding painting that shows "the soul and its god."

21. Interview in *Tao* 4 (January 1998), 10.

22. Mœbius, "Mœbius: J'ai très tôt été attiré par l'envers du décor" [Mœbius: I was attracted at a young age by what went on behind the scenes], interview by Stéphane Jarno, *Télérama* 3168 (October 2010).

23. Raymond Roussel, *Impressions d'Afrique* (1909); *Comment j'ai écrit certains de mes livres* [How I wrote some of my books] (1935).

24. Concerning this period of his life, see Mœbius, *Entretiens avec Numa Sadoul* [Conversations with Numa Sadoul] (Tournai: Casterman, 1991), 48–62.

25. See in particular the album *Sur l'étoile—une croisière Citroën* [On the star—a Citroën cruise], 1983.

26. Umberto Eco, *L'Œuvre ouverte* [The open work] (Paris: Seuil, 1979 [1965]), 10.

27. Alain Robbe-Grillet, *Un roman qui s'invente lui-même* [A novel that invents itself], 1954. This study of the novels of Robert Pinget is included in *Pour un nouveau roman* [For a New Novel] (Paris: Minuit, 1963).

28. Jean-Michel Charlier and Jean Giraud, *Angel Face* (Paris: Dargaud, 1975); *Nez cassé* (Paris: Dargaud, 1980).

29. Another text (1:20) implies that this world does not really exist but is a mere illusion.

30. In the English version this has been changed to "May-Pole leaf" (1:20). —Trans.

31. Mœbius, *Cauchemar blanc*, in *La Citadelle aveugle* (Paris: Les Humanoïdes Associés, 1974).

32. Mœbius, interview by Stéphane Jarno, *Télérama* 3168 (October 2, 2010). "Jean Giraud is my Cartesian, diligent, perfectionist side. [. . .] Mœbius is a jazz solo, total improvisation, the freedom to draw a panel without knowing what is coming next. Giraud needs a frame, Mœbius works hand in hand with his unconscious."

33. Jean-Didier Urbain, *Secrets de voyage* [Travel secrets] (Paris: Payot et rivages, 1998), 75.

34. Smolderen, *Les Carnets volés*, 25.

35. Thierry Smolderen, "Le 'Scanning' autobiographique" [Autobiographical scanning], *Les Cahiers de la bande dessinée* 73 (Jan–Feb 1987), 80–82.

36. He specifically makes reference to *La Gnose de Princeton* [The Gnosis of Princeton] (Raymond Ruyer, 1974), a mixture of science, philosophy, and religion about which Mœbius speaks at length in his conversations with Numa Sadoul, and which apparently inspired the first and fourth episodes of *Garage*.

37. Jean Giraud, *Mœbius/Giraud: Histoire de mon double* (Paris: Éditions°1, 1999), 166.

38. Mœbius, *Entretiens avec Numa Sadoul*, 182.

39. Andrea Pazienza, *Le straordinarie avventure di Penthotal* (Milan: Baldini and Castoldi, 1977).

40. Jean Giraud, *Mœbius/Giraud: Histoire de mon double*, 113.

41. Alejandro Jodorowsky and Mœbius, *L'Incal*, 5 vols. (Paris: Les Humanoïdes associés, 1981–1988).

42. Ibid., 167.
43. Ibid., 130.
44. Mœbius, interview by Jarno.
45. Giraud, *Mœbius/Giraud: Histoire de mon double*, 173.
46. Ibid., 174.

CHAPTER 3: ALAN MOORE AND DAVE GIBBONS, *WATCHMEN*

1. Divided up into twelve chapters of twenty-eight pages each, except for the first, which is slightly shorter (twenty-six pages) and the last, which is slightly longer (thirty-two pages). References are given here in the form volume: page number. panel number.

2. The publication history of these works is complex, so here we simply cite artists and dates of publication of the first versions. Alan Moore and Eddie Campbell, *From Hell* (1989–96); Alan Moore and Kevin O'Neill, *The League of Extraordinary Gentlemen* (1999–2007); Alan Moore, J. H. Williams III, and Mick Gray, *Promethea* (1999–2005); Alan Moore and Melinda Gebbie, *Lost Girls* (1991–2006). —Trans.

3. This edition is undoubtedly the finest. Contributing factors are the exceptional quality of the translation, the large format and the previously unpublished cover design by Dave Gibbons.

4. The authors, tongue in cheek, go so far as to show him walking on water (12:25.6).

5. Since the September 11 attacks, this finale has taken on resonances that the authors could not have anticipated.

6. On the role played by extreme violence in *Watchmen*, see for example Aaron A. Cloyd, "Voices from the Margins: The Place of Wildness in *Watchmen*," *International Journal of Comic Art* 16.1 (Spring 2014), 223–43.

7. The pirate story, *Tales of the Black Freighter*, extracts of which, read over the shoulder of a young black boy, are interpolated into *Watchmen* at regular intervals, is similarly over the top in its macabre details. In my view, this story is largely superfluous, and pointlessly overloads a narrative that is already dense and complex.

8. Alan Moore, Dave Gibbons, and Neil Gaiman, "A Portal to Another Dimension," *The Comics Journal* 116 (July 1987), http://www.tcj.com/a-portal-to-another-dimension-alan-moore-dave-gibbons-and-neil-gaiman/. At the end of *Watchmen*, another actor who has the same initials as Reagan runs for president: Robert Redford.

9. It should be recalled that, although most superheroes are defined by their superpowers, this is not true of all of them. For example, Batman does not have any; he is a highly trained athlete who depends on a whole battery of gadgets, a tradition borrowed from Doc Savage (the hero created by the novelist Kenneth Robeson six years previously) and subsequently upheld by James Bond.

10. "Super-héros" [Superhero], *Dictionnaire esthétique et thématique de la bande dessinée* [Aesthetic and thematic dictionary of comics] (November 2012), *Neuvième Art 2.0*, http://neuviemeart.citebd.org/spip.php?article479.

11. Stuart Kelly, "Alan Moore: 'Why shouldn't you have a bit of fun while dealing with the deepest issues of the mind?'" *The Guardian* (November 22, 2013), http://www.theguardian.com/books/2013/nov/22/alan-moore-comic-books-interview.

12. Pádraig Ó Méaloid, "Last Alan Moore Interview?," *Slovobooks* (January 9, 2014), https://slovobooks.wordpress.com/2014/01/09/last-alan-moore-interview/#comments.

13. "We had worms in the apple, eating it from the inside," as Hollis Mason, the first "Nite Owl," writes in his memoirs (appendix to chapter 2).

14. Paul Gravett, *Graphic Novels: Stories to Change Your Life* (London: Aurum Press, 2005), 82.

15. Alan Moore, untitled article, *Urban Comics* (January 1988), http://www.urban-comics.com/sur-la-creation-de-watchmen-alan-moore/. [Translation mine. —Trans.]

16. Objectivism is a philosophical theory developed by Ayn Rand whose ethical principles involve the rejection of altruism.

17. For more details on these sources, see Gary Spencer Millidge, *Alan Moore, Storyteller* (London: Ilex Press, 2011).

18. Hatfield, *Hand of Fire*, 110.

19. This is the origin of his borrowed name, Rorschach, which refers to a famous projective test that involves the interpretation of symmetrical inkblots. Rorschach will himself take the test in chapter 6.

20. He shows pity on a single occasion (10:6.6–8), because he identifies with the child who clings to his abusive mother.

21. Alan Moore's working notes mention Michelangelo's David, the English actor Barry Foster and the singer Julio Iglesias as models.

22. History deviated from its course on the day in March 1960 when the world learned that "the Superman **exists** and he is **American**" (4:13.1). The existence of a being with almost unlimited powers, Dr. Manhattan, has affected the unfolding of events, and changed the balance of power. Although the story is dated 1985, the world that it describes does not correspond to the world as it really was at that date.

23. DC Comics, the publisher of *Watchmen*, was still submitting part of its output for the approval of the Comics Code Authority up until 2001. This code of conduct for comics publishers, adopted in 1954, insisted particularly on decency.

24. See, most notably, Dali's famous melting clocks, visible in the background of one panel (4:18.2) and the damaged pocket watch, stopped forever, on the cover of the issue of *Time* magazine commemorating Hiroshima week (4:24.7). The moon itself is assimilated to a clock face when Daniel superimposes a minute hand onto it, by drawing with his finger on the condensation on the window (7:8.3).

25. For more details, see "Doomsday Clock," *Bulletin of the Atomic Scientists*, http://thebulletin.org/overview.

26. Groensteen, *Comics and Narration*, 138.

27. Alan Moore, untitled article (January 1988).

28. The title is borrowed from William Blake's poem "The Tyger." The words "fearful symmetry" have also been used as the title for at least two novels, several music albums, and episodes of television series. The celebrated literary theoretician Northrop Frye published an essay, *Fearful Symmetry: A Study of William Blake*, in 1947. Alan Moore was influenced by its analyses.

29. The shadow of a soldier was indeed imprinted onto a wall by a flash from the explosion. The artist Ernest Pignon-Ernest was struck by this and reproduced it. The shadow of a disintegrated *couple* is of Moore and Gibbons's own invention.

30. The mask became world famous after being adopted in 2008 by the network of hackers called "Anonymous" and then by other groups of protesters.

31. The authors themselves were conscious of this expansion of the scope and ambition of the work as the creative process progressed. Moore writes, for example, "So, having begun with a relatively conventional nuclear-powered superhero, we found ourselves getting caught up in quantum-theoretical post-Einsteinian reflections on time." Alan Moore, untitled article (January 1988).

32. See "La construction de *La Cage*: Autopsie d'un roman visuel" [The construction of *The Cage*: Autopsy of a visual novel], in M. Vaughn-James, *La Cage* (Brussels: Les Impressions nouvelles, 2010 [1986]).

33. Gary Spencer Millidge has noted that this is analogous with Dr. Manhattan's perception, which brings together the past, present, and future. According to Millidge, "the reader is encouraged to flip forwards and backwards through the narrative to appreciate the hidden connections that lay within." *Alan Moore, Storyteller*, 127.

34. Matthew J. Pustz, *Comic Book Culture: Fanboys and True Believers* (Jackson: University of Mississippi Press, 1999), 138.

35. Jean-Patrick Manchette, interview by Thierry Groensteen, *Les Cahiers de la bande dessinée* 79 (Jan 1988), 21.

36. Concerning these references, see Elizabeth Strobel, "Watchmen as a Work of Literature" (PhD dissertation, Oregon State University, 2008), http://ir.library.oregonstate.edu/xmlui/handle/1957/8111.

CHAPTER 4: DAVID B., *EPILEPTIC*

Originally published as *L'Ascension du haut mal*, 6 vols. (Paris: L'Association, 1996–2003). English translation *Epileptic*, by Kim Thompson (New York: Pantheon, 2005). Since Groensteen's analysis asserts the significance of the division into volumes, references here are given first to the French volume number and page, and then to the English page number. (Page numbers are identical in the first volume.) —Trans.

1. David B. and Olivier Legan, *Pas de samba pour Capitaine Tonnerre* (Grenoble: Glénat, 1985).

2. David B., *Le Timbre maudit* (Montrouge: Bayard Press, 1986).

3. David B., *Le Nain jaune*, 5 vols. (Paris: Cornélius, 1993–94); *Les Quatre Savants*, 3 vols. (Paris: Cornélius, 1996–98).

4. David B., *Le Cheval blême* (Paris: L'Association, 1992).

5. David B., *Le Tengû carré* (Paris: Dargaud, 1997); *La Lecture des ruines* (Marcinelle: Dupuis, 2001); *Par les chemins noirs* (Paris: Futuropolis, 2007); *Les Incidents de la nuit*, 3 vols. (Paris: L'Association, 1999–2002).

6. David B. and Jean-Pierre Filiu, *Best of Enemies: A History of US and Middle East Relations*, 3 vols. (London: SelfMadeHero, 2012).

7. A composition that is repeated inside the first volume, on pages 19 and 35, and then, in parodic mode, on page 50.

8. David B., "Entretien avec David B." [Conversation with David B.], by Gilles Ciment and Thierry Groensteen, *Neuvième Art* 11 (October 2004): 58.

9. Two years after the publication of the first volume of *Epileptic*, Edmond Baudoin recounted a similar experience in *Piero* (Paris: Seuil, 1997), the album dedicated to his brother.

10. David B. and Christophe Blain, *Hiram Lowitt et Placido*, 2 vols. (Paris: Dargaud, 1997 and 2000).

11. David B. and Emmanuel Guibert, *Le Capitaine Écarlate* (Marcinelle: Dupuis, 2010).

12. David B., *Le Prophète voilé*, in *Le Jardin armé et autres histoires* [The armed garden and other stories] (Paris: Futuropolis, 2009).

13. David B., *Entretien*, 60.

14. Ibid., 61.

15. Ibid., 60.

16. David B., interview by Thierry Bellefroid, *BD Paradisio* (2000), www.bdparadisio.com/intervw/davidb/intdavid.htm.

17. Catherine Mao, "La Bande dessinée autobiographique francophone (1982–2013): transgression, hybridation, lyrisme" [French-language autobiographical comics (1982–2013): transgression, hybridization, lyricism] (PhD dissertation, Université de Paris-Sorbonne, 2014), 188.

18. Renaud Pasquier, "David B., le sommeil de la raison" [David B., the sleep of reason], *Labyrinthe* 25 (2006): 107–17.

19. David B., *Entretien*, 58.

20. Tardi and Forest, *Ici Même* (Tournai: Casterman, 1979).

21. This is the title of an essay by the philosopher René Girard, *Des choses cachées depuis la fondation du monde* (Paris: Grasset, 1978). —Trans.

22. Éric Flux, interview with David B., *Tao* 5 (January 2000), 42.

23. Ibid., 43.

24. Fabrice Neaud, *Journal*, 4 vols. (Angoulême: ego comme x, 1996–2002); Xavier Mussat, *Carnation* (Brussels: Casterman, 2014).

25. Sylvianne Rémi-Giraud, "Métaphore et métonymie dans le *Journal* de Fabrice Neaud" [Metaphor and metonymy in Fabrice Neaud's *Journal*], *Neuvième Art* 9 (October 2003): 85–89.

26. David B., "Entretien avec David B." [Interview with David B.], by Thierry Groensteen, in *Nocturnes: Le Rêve dans la bande dessinée* [Night scenes: Dreams in comics] (Angoulême: CIBDI; Paris: Citadelles & Mazenod, 2013), 173–80.

27. David B., *Les Complots nocturnes* (Paris: Futuropolis, 2005).

28. David B., *Babel*, 2 vols. (Bologna: Coconino Press, 2004 and 2006).

29. David B. and Joann Sfar, *La Ville des mauvais rêves* [The city of bad dreams], vol. 1, *Urani* (Paris: Dargaud, 2000).

30. "La Langue idiote des songes. Notes sur David B." [The idiotic language of dreams: Notes on David B.] *Neuvième Art 2.0* (November 2014), http://neuviemeart.citebd.org/spip.php?article855. Laurent Gerbier has written three other texts on this topic: "La Bataille des rêves: *Babel* de David B." [The battle of dreams: David B.'s *Babel*], *Neuvième Art* 13 (2007): 278; "La Force des images: David B. et la bataille des rêves" [The power of images: David B. and the battle of dreams], *Papiers Nickelés: La Revue de l'image populaire* [Disreputable papers: Journal of popular imagery] 34.3 (2012): 10–11; and "L'Ordre des rêves, des images aux récits" [The order of dreams, from images to narratives], in *Nocturnes*, ed. Groensteen, 183–96.

31. *Jeux d'influences: 30 auteurs de BD parlent de leurs livres fétiches* [The play of influence: 30 comics authors talk about their favorite books] (Montrouge: PLG, 2001), 19.

32. Éric Flux, interview, 19.

33. Ann Miller, *Reading bande dessinée: Critical Approaches to French-language Comic Strip* (Bristol: Intellect, 2007), 62.

CHAPTER 5: ALISON BECHDEL, *FUN HOME*

1. Alison Bechdel, *Are You My Mother? A Comic Drama* (Boston: Houghton Mifflin, 2012).

2. Hillary Chute, *Graphic Women: Life Narrative and Contemporary Comics* (New York: Columbia University Press, 2010), 256n33.

3. See my entry "Corps" [Body], *Dictionnaire esthétique et thématique de la bande dessinée* [Aesthetic and thematic dictionary of comics], *Neuvième Art 2.0*, http://neuviemeart.citebd.org/spip.php?article814.

4. Alison Bechdel, interview by François Peneaud, actuabd.com (14 November 2006), http://www.actuabd.com/Fun-home-une-autobiographie-a-la-structure-narrative-complexe.

5. Jacques Dürrenmatt, *Bande dessinée et littérature* [Comics and literature] (Paris: Garnier, 2013), 197.

6. Chute, *Graphic Women*, 180.

7. This ambivalent title may have been inspired by the similarly ambivalent title of Wilde's comedy *The Importance of Being Earnest*, to which she refers throughout chapter 6.

8. Dürrenmatt, *Bande dessinée et littérature*, 198.

9. Hillary Chute, "Gothic Revival," *Village Voice*, July 4, 2006.

10. Bechdel, Interview by Peneaud.

11. Chute, "Gothic Revival."

12. For a more detailed discussion of these points, see Deviant, "Power Confusions and the Daedalus-Icarus Story in *Fun Home*," *Literature and Transgression* (June 3, 2014), http://transgresslit.wordpress.com/2014/06/03/power-confusions-and-the-daedalus-icarus-story-in-fun-home/.

13. Cf. Chute, *Graphic Women*, 207.

14. The *Addams Family* cartoons (34) are an exception, mechanically reproduced but blurred.

15. In a promotional video for *Fun Home*, the author is shown taking photographs of herself with a digital camera, and then immediately reproducing the posture on the page. Alison Bechdel, "Fun Home: A Family Tragicomic," accessed December 8, 2014, https://www.youtube.com/watch?v=MScwlAQYVuA.

16. Hillary Chute, Interview, 2008, qtd. in Chute, *Graphic Women*, 186.

17. Ibid., 179.

18. For Bechdel, the decision to become an artist rather than a writer was a way of marking out her distance from both her parents.

19. Alison Bechdel, "What the Little Old Ladies Feel," *Slate*, March 2007, http://www.slate.com/articles/news_and_politics/memoir_week/2007/03/what_the_little_old_ladies_feel.html.

CHAPTER 6: DOMINIQUE GOBLET, *PRETENDING IS LYING*

Originally published as *Faire semblant c'est mentir* (Paris: L'Association, 2007). English translation by Sophie Yanow (New York: New York Review Comics, 2016). The book is unpaginated. —Trans.

1. Dominique Goblet, *Portraits crachés* (Brussels: Fréon, 1997); *Souvenir d'une journée parfaite* (Brussels: Fréon, 2000).

2. Dominique Goblet, Thomas Ott, Caroline Sury, and Vincent Vanoli, *L'Association au Mexique* (Paris: L'Association, 2000).

3. Adolpho Avril, Olivier Deprez et al., *Match de catch à Vielsalm* (Brussels: Frémok, 2012).

4. Dominique Goblet and Nikita Fossoul, *Chronographie* (Paris: L'Association, 2010).

5. Dominique Goblet, *Plus si entente* (Brussels: Frémok; Arles: Actes Sud, 2014).

6. Dominique Goblet, interview by Xavier Guilbert, *du9*, April 2, 2011 (July 2011) www.du9.org/entretien/dominique-goblet.

7. Ibid.

8. Dominique Goblet, email to author, May 16, 2007.

9. Blandine's faceless face can also be likened to Breccia's portrayal in *Perramus* of the henchmen belonging to the death squads that were the armed wing of the Argentine military dictatorship. Their cadaverous faces proclaimed their mission: to administer and deal out death. See Alberto Breccia and Juan Sasturain, *Perramus*, in *Fierro* (1985).

10. Edmond Baudoin had already supplied analogous examples of current events breaking into the work as it was being produced: the beginning of the first Gulf War is reported in *Couma Aco* [Like that] (Paris: Futuropolis, 1991) and the suicide of Guy Debord is mentioned in *Éloge de la poussière* [In praise of dust] (Paris: L'Association, 1995).

11. Goblet, interview by Guilbert.

12. Catherine Mao, "L'œil et l'oreille dans *Faire semblant c'est mentir* de Dominique Goblet: D'un faire semblant sonore à une esthétique sonore" [The eye and the ear in *Pretending Is Lying* by Dominique Goblet: From sonic pretense to a sonic aesthetic], *Images Re-vues* (July 2009), http://imagesrevues.revues.org/434.

13. Ibid.

14. Catalogue from the exhibition *Regards croisés de la bande dessinée belge* [Divergent views on Belgian comics] (Ghent: Snoeck Editions, 2009), texts by Didier Pasamonik, with Eric Verhoest. Pages 210 to 219 are devoted to Dominique Goblet.

15. Pratt, *De l'autre côté*, 166–67.
16. For an explanation of the term "reciter" see Groensteen, *Comics and Narration*, 88–97.
17. Gustave Doré, *Histoire pittoresque, dramatique et picturale de la Sainte Russie* (1854), http://gallica.bnf.fr/ark:/12148/bpt6k1044804x/f13.image.r=Histoire+pittoresque+dramatique+et+caricaturale+de+la+Sainte+Russie.langEN.
18. Guillaume Dégé, "Jusqu'au bout de la plume" [Right to the tip of the pen], *Gustave Doré ogre et génie* [Gustave Doré ogre and genius] (Strasbourg: Éditions des Musées de Strasbourg, 2014), 23–29.
19. Goblet, interview by Guilbert.
20. Mao, "L'œil et l'oreille."
21. Simone de Beauvoir, *Memoirs of a Dutiful Daughter*, trans. James Kirkup (Harmondsworth: Penguin, 1958), 169.
22. André Gide, *If It Die*, trans. Dorothy Bussy (New York: Vintage Books, 1935), 250.
23. Dominique Goblet, email to author, May 16, 2007.

CHAPTER 7: SHAUN TAN, *THE ARRIVAL*

This book is unpaginated.
1. Moebius, *Arzach* (Paris: Les Humanoïdes associés, 1976); Guido Crepax, *La lanterna magica* (Milan: Edizioni d'arte Angolare, 1979); Peter Kyper, *The System* (New York: Vertigo, 1997); Alberto Breccia, *Dracula Dracul, Vlad?, Bah . . .* (Madrid: Sinsentido, 1984); Jim Woodring, *Frank* (Seattle: Fantagraphics, 1996–2001); Blanquet, *La Nouvelle au pis* (Paris: Cornélius, 2001); Nicolas de Crécy, *Prosopopus* (Marcinelle: Dupuis, 2009); Eric Drooker, *Flood! A Novel in Pictures* (New York: Four Walls Eight Windows, 1992); Benoît Jacques, *L* (Paris: L'Association, 2010); Nicolas Presl, *Heureux qui comme* (Geneva: Atrabile, 2012).
2. Shaun Tan, *Sketches from a Nameless Land: The Art of The Arrival* (Sydney: Hachette Australia, 2010), 5.
3. Ibid., 20.
4. Shaun Tan, interview with Nicolas Verstappen, *du9* (January 2008), http://www.du9.org/en/entretien/shaun-tan922/.
5. See the catalogue, Vincent Marie, and Gilles Ollivier, eds., *Albums, des histoires dessinées entre ici et ailleurs: Bande dessinée et immigration 1913–2013* [Albums, immigration stories between here and elsewhere: comics and immigration 1913–2013] (Paris: Futuropolis / Musée de l'histoire de l'immigration, 2013).
6. Henry Yoshitaka Kiyama, *The Four Immigrants Manga* (San Francisco, 1931); Muñoz and Sampayo, *Sudor Sudaca*, in *Fierro*, 1983–85; Yvan Alagbé, *Nègres jaunes* (Paris: Amok, 1995); Farid Boudjellal, *Petit Polio*, 2 vols. (Toulon: Soleil, 1998–2000); Cyril Pedrosa, *Portugal* (Marcinelle: Dupuis, 2011); Marjane Satrapi, *Persepolis*, 4 vols. (Paris: L'Association, 2001–2003).
7. Tan, *Sketches*, 6.
8. Ibid., 35.
9. Ibid., 9.
10. Ibid., 39.
11. Raymond Briggs, *The Snowman* (London: Hamish Hamilton, 1978).
12. Tan, *Sketches*, 29.
13. Hergé, *Les Bijoux de la Castafiore* (Tournai: Casterman, 1963).
14. Benoît Peeters, *Lire Tintin: Les Bijoux ravis* [Reading Tintin: The purloined jewels] (Brussels: Les Impressions Nouvelles, 2007), 131.
15. Shaun Tan, interview with Verstappen.
16. Ibid.
17. Which also inspired James Gray's film *The Immigrant* (2013).

18. Sophie Van der Linden, *Lire l'album* [Reading albums] (Le Puy-en-Velay: L'Atelier du poisson soluble, 2006), 83.

CHAPTER 8: CRAIG THOMPSON, *HABIBI*

1. Craig Thompson, *Goodbye Chunky Rice* (Marietta, GA: Top Shelf Productions, 1999).
2. Craig Thompson, *Blankets* (Marietta, GA: Top Shelf Productions, 2003).
3. Edmond Baudoin, *Piero* (Paris: Seuil, 1997).
4. Craig Thompson, *Carnet de Voyage* (Marietta, GA: Top Shelf Productions, 2004).
5. Craig Thompson, interview with Nicolas Verstappen, *Xeroxed 3* (March 2004): 5, http://goldenchronicles.blogspot.co.uk/2005/12/xeroxed-iii-craig-thompson.html.
6. This is not a completely unprecedented exercise. I am thinking in particular of the comic books of Patrick Atangan devoted to Chinese folk tales in *Silk Tapestry* (New York: NBM, 2004) or Japanese legends in *The Yellow Jar* (New York: NBM, 2002). The neutral, "clear-line" style of the author harmonized in the case of the first with the aesthetic of classical Chinese scroll paintings and watercolors and in the case of the second with the *ukiyo-e* (Japanese woodblock prints).
7. Craig Thompson, interview by Olivier le Bussy, *La Libre Belgique* (December 31, 2011), http://www.lalibre.be/archive/un-monde-sans-pitie-mais-pas-sans-amour-51b8ddaee4bode6db9c3dfd6.
8. See Constant Hamès, "Problématiques de la magie-sorcellerie en islam et perspectives africaines" [Issues arising from magic and witchcraft in Islam, and African perspectives], *Cahiers d'études africaines*, 189–90 (2008): 81–99, http://etudesafricaines.revues.org/9842.
9. Thompson, interview with Verstappen, 5.
10. Our discovery of Wanatolia takes us first to the Sultan's palace, then the capital city. Some of the action is also situated in a large village just across the border, in the middle of the desert, in a country that is never named.
11. Craig Thompson, Casterman press pack (2011).
12. On page 343, Thompson portrays the finding of Moses by quoting a painting by the English artist Edwin Long.
13. Kathleen Gros, "Orientalism, Harems, and Craig Thompson's *Habibi*," *The Art of Orientalis: A Digital Archive*, accessed March 3, 2015, https://orientalisms.wordpress.com/the-harem/kathleen-gros/. For similar reservations, see also Faterneh Fakhraie, "I'm Not Your Habibi: Thoughts on Craig Thompson's Graphic Novel," http://www.racialicious.com/2011/11/03/i'm-not-your-habibi-thoughts-on-craig-thompson's-graphic-novel/.
14. *Castermag* 30 (April 2011). The episode involving the babysitter is referred to in the opening pages of *Blankets*.
15. Casterman press pack.
16. Vandana Shiva and Maria Mies, *Écoféminisme* (Paris: L'Harmattan, 1999, first published 1993).
17. *Castermag* 36, (October 2011).
18. The scar that Dodola will ask to see is also hidden from the reader's view. It is, oddly, the only time when Thompson is overcome by modesty, when elsewhere he is so willing to show the body and the assaults of all kinds that it undergoes.

CHAPTER 9: CHRIS WARE, *BUILDING STORIES*

1. Chris Ware, *Jimmy Corrigan, the Smartest Kid on Earth* (New York: Pantheon, 2000).
2. Chris Ware, *Quimby the Mouse* (Seattle: Fantagraphics, 2003); *Acme Novelty Datebook*, 2 vols. (1986–95 and 1995–99) (Montreal: Drawn and Quarterly; Amsterdam: Oog & Blik, 2003 and 2007).

3. *Rusty Brown* in *Acme Novelty Library* 16 (self-published, distributed by Seattle: Fantagraphics, 2005), *Acme Novelty Library* 17 and 19 (Montreal: Drawn and Quarterly, 2006 and 2008).

4. In order to facilitate understanding of the remainder of this text, it seems useful to agree on a code enabling the rapid identification of the fourteen documents contained in the box. Since they are not numbered, I propose to attribute a letter to each of them, although the alphabetical order does not imply any particular order of reading, as follows:

> A. The stiff four-panel fold-out board
> B. The thirty-page hardback album, 21.5 x 24 cm, with a gold-colored spine and a cover showing the florist writing in her diary and a title page headed "September 23rd, 2000"
> C. The sixteen-page stapled booklet, 21 x 28 cm, whose first panel features a telephone
> D. The sixteen-page stapled booklet, 21 x 28 cm, whose first panel shows the couple from the second floor sitting on the steps
> E. The hardback book with a canvas spine, 23.5 x 31 cm, with a plain green cover
> F. The four-page broadsheet, unstapled, with a regular twenty-panel grid on the cover and life-sized baby across the centerfold
> G. The twenty-page broadsheet, unstapled, opening with a huge square panel and the word "god"
> H. The thick landscape-format booklet, stapled, 7.6 x 24.8 cm, showing the florist and her cat at night
> I. The twenty-page stapled booklet, 23 x 30.5 cm, whose opening page bears the title "Disconnect"
> J. The landscape fold-out featuring the little girl with the pink hood
> K. The 33 x 45.8 cm page folded in half and opening on "Recently"
> L. The landscape fold-out featuring a snow scene
> M. The edition of the *Daily Bee* newspaper consisting of four tabloid pages folded in half
> N. The booklet with a red cover called "BRANFORD," 13.6 x 19.7 cm

5. Not in British English, where it is spelled *storey*. —Trans.

6. Chris Ware explained to me in an email exchange that he did not copy his former home in exact detail: "the house where we lived was bigger, deeper, built out of different materials and inhabited by completely different people."

7. See Daniel Raeburn, *Chris Ware* (New Haven: Yale University Press, 2004), 25–26.

8. Georges Perec, *La Vie mode d'emploi* (Paris: Hachette, 1978).

9. Will Eisner, *A Contract with God and Other Tenement Stories* (New York: Baronet Books, 1978).

10. Will Eisner, *The Building* (Northampton, MA: Kitchen Sink Press, 1987).

11. Contribution to debate transcribed in "Table ronde" [Round table], *Humoresques* 10 (1999), 123–26.

12. With his habitual self-deprecation, the author writes on one of the sides of the box: "Whether you're feeling alone by yourself or alone with someone else, this book is sure to sympathize with the crushing sense of life wasted, opportunities missed and creative dreams dashed which afflict the middle- and upper-class literary public."

13. Paul Ricœur, *Freud and Philosophy: An Essay on Interpretation*, trans. Denis Savage (New Delhi: Motilal Banarsidass, 2008), 250.

14. Frédéric Potet, "Les Histoires gigognes de Chris Ware" [The nested stories of Chris Ware], *Le Monde* (November 11, 2014).

15. Frédéric Potet, "Chris Ware, 'Toute autobiographie est une fiction'" [Chris Ware, "Any autobiography is a work of fiction"], *Le Monde*, November 20, 2014, http://bandedessinee.blog.lemonde.fr/2014/11/20/chris-ware-toute-autobiographie-est-une-fiction/

16. Georges Perec, *L'Infra-ordinaire* (Paris: Seuil, 1989).

17. It is worth bearing in mind a sentence that appears on the dust jacket of *Jimmy Corrigan*: each page has been "scientifically engineered to contrive the most natural forgery of ordered human experience that contemporary pictographic strategy will yield."

18. Joanna Davis-McElligatt, "Body Schemas," *Comics Journal* (October 24, 2012), http://www.tcj.com/body-schemas/.

19. See Thierry Groensteen, *Comics and Narration*, 57.

20. Groensteen, "Nu" [Nudity], *Dictionnaire esthétique et thématique de la bande dessinée, Neuvième Art 2.0* (October 2012), http://neuviemeart.citebd.org/spip.php?article465.

21. Ibid.

22. Roland Barthes, *Camera Lucida*, trans. Richard Howard (London: Jonathan Cape, 1982), 107.

23. See Groensteen, *Comics and Narration*, 84–86. —Trans.

24. Fabrice Leroy, "Une tragédie de détails: L'Architecture de l'infra-ordinaire dans les *Building Stories* de Chris Ware" [A tragedy of details: The architecture of the infra-ordinary in Chris Ware's *Building Stories*], in Livio Belloi and Maud Hagelstein, eds., *La Mécanique du détail: Approches transversales* [The mechanics of detail: Transversal approaches] (Lyon: ENS éditions, 2013), 229–46.

25. I have shown elsewhere the importance of the theme of resemblance in Chris Ware's work. See Thierry Groensteen, "Transmission, ressemblances, impermanence," *Neuvième Art 2.0* (January 2010), http://neuviemeart.citebd.org/spip.php?article17.

26. Frédéric Potet, "Chris Ware, 'Toute autobiographie est une fiction.'"

27. I am using "site" and "place" here in the technical sense that I defined in *The System of Comics*, 147–49.

28. Ware illustrates the unreliability of memory with a precise example. In fragment E, the florist thinks back twice to a couple that she had seen in the L train. The first time, she visualizes the scene at night (page headed "My Life"), and the second time in daylight ("Her Leg").

29. Frédéric Potet, "Chris Ware, 'Toute autobiographie est une fiction.'"

30. Richard McGuire, *Here* (New York: Pantheon Books, 2014).

31. Chris Ware, "Une appréciation reconnaissante" [A grateful appreciation], *Neuvième Art* 12 (January 2006): 48.

32. Ibid. To celebrate the publication of the new version of *Here*, extended to full-length book-size, Ware wrote an article for the *Guardian*, "Chris Ware on *Here* by Richard McGuire—a game-changing graphic novel," December 17, 2014, http://www.theguardian.com/books/2014/dec/17/chris-ware-here-richard-mcguire-review-graphic-novel.

33. Frédéric Potet, "Chris Ware, 'Toute autobiographie est une fiction.'"

CHAPTER 10: JENS HARDER, *THE GRAND NARRATIVE: ALPHA, BETA*

Originally published as *Alpha . . . directions* and *Beta . . . civilisations*, vol. 1 (Arles: Actes Sud—l'An 2, 2014). English translation, *Alpha . . . directions* and *Beta . . . civilizations*, vol. 1, by Nora Goldberg (London: Knockabout Comics, 2015 and 2016). Only *Alpha* was available at the time of writing, so translations from *Beta* are my own. —Trans.

1. Jens Harder, *Électricité Marseille* (Berlin: Monogatari, 2000); *Schnell, Schuss!* in Ulli Lust, Kai Pfeiffer et al., *Operation Läckerli* (Berlin: Monogatari, 2004); *Ticket to God*, in Tim Dinter, Jan Ferndt, Jens Harder, Rutu Modan, Guy Morad, and Yirimi Pinkus, *Cargo* (Berlin: Avant-Verlag, 2005); *La Cité de Dieu* (Angoulême: Éditions de l'an 2, 2006).

2. Jens Harder, *Leviathan* (Angoulême: Éditions de l'an 2, 2003, second edition 2005); *La Cité de Dieu* (Angoulême: Éditions de l'an 2, 2006).

3. Jens Harder, *MIKROmakro* (Nuremberg: Verlag für moderne Kunst, 2007).

4. Michel Serres, interview in *Télérama* 2989 (20 April 2007).

5. Jacques Le Goff, interview with Illel Kieser 'l Baz, *Conscience de* 17 (November 1990), www.hommes-et-faits.com/Histoire/LeGoff_01.htm.

6. For more details, I refer readers to my article "Les lieux superposés de Richard McGuire" [The superimposed places of Richard McGuire], *Urgences* (May 1991), 95–103. Since the present chapter was written, the album *Here* (New York: Pantheon, 2014) has been published, which extends the concept over 304 pages.

7. Robert Crumb, *A Short History of America*, in *Co-Evolutionary Quarterly* (1979).

8. Henri Van Lier, "La bande dessinée, une cosmogonie dure" [Comics, a hard cosmogony], in *Bande dessinée, récit et modernité* [Comics, narrative and modernity], ed. Thierry Groensteen (Paris: Futuropolis; Angoulême: CNBDI, 1985), 9.

9. The artist Frederik Peeters takes on the same challenge, but in fictional mode, in his science-fiction series *Aâma*, 4 vols. (London: SelfMadeHero 2014–2015), when he depicts the emergence of life on the planet Ona(ji) and the swarm of more and more complex organisms.

10. Sébastien Charbonnier, "*Beta*: Première approche d'un chef-d'œuvre" [*Beta*: a first approach toward a masterpiece], *Neuvième Art 2.0* (March 19, 2014), http://neuviemeart.citebd.org/spip.php?page=blog_neuviemeart&id_article=755

11. See in particular the album *Rupestres* [Cave paintings] (Paris: Futuropolis, 2011), by Étienne Davodeau, Emmanuel Guibert, Marc-Antoine Mathieu, David Prudhomme, and Pascal Rabaté et Troubs, from which I took this expression.

12. Interview with Régis Debray, reprinted in *Jean-Luc Godard par Jean-Luc Godard*, [Jean-Luc Godard by Jean-Luc Godard], vol. 2 (Paris: Cahiers du cinéma, 1998), 430.

13. Georges Didi-Huberman, *Histoire de l'art et temps des fantômes selon Aby Warburg* [History of art and the time of ghosts according to Aby Warburg] (Paris: Éditions de Minuit, 2002).

14. Vincent Jung, review of *Beta . . . civilisations*, vol. 1 (April 26, 2014), www.chronicart.com.

15. Quoted in Colette Deblé, *Lumière de l'air* [Light of the air] (Creil: Bernard Dumerchez; Paris: L'Arbre Voyageur, 1993), 14.

16. Henri Van Lier, *Anthropogénie* (Brussels: Les Impressions Nouvelles, 2010), 890.

17. Ibid.

18. Charbonnier, "*Beta*: Première approche d'un chef-d'œuvre."

SOURCES

CHAPTER 1
Hugo Pratt and Ian Monk. *Ballad of the Salt Sea*. New York: NBM, 1996.

CHAPTER 2
Moebius and Randy and Jean-Marc Lofficier. *Airtight Garage*. New York: Epic Comics, 1993.

CHAPTER 3
Alan Moore and Dave Gibbons. *Watchmen*. New York: DC Comics, 1987.

CHAPTER 4
David B. and Kim Thompson. *Epileptic*. New York: Pantheon, 2005.

CHAPTER 5
Alison Bechdel. *Fun Home: A Family Tragicomic*. Boston: Houghton Mifflin, 2006.

CHAPTER 6
Dominique Goblet and Sophie Yanow. *Pretending Is Lying*. New York: New York Review Comics, 2016.

CHAPTER 7
Shaun Tan. *The Arrival*. New York: Arthur A. Levine, 2007.

CHAPTER 8
Craig Thompson. *Habibi*. New York: Pantheon, 2011.

CHAPTER 9
Chris Ware. *Building Stories*. New York: Pantheon, 2012.

CHAPTER 10
Jens Harder. *Alpha . . . directions*. Trans. Nora Goldberg. London: Knockabout Comics, 2015.
———. *Beta . . . civilizations*, vol. 1. Trans. Nora Goldberg. London: Knockabout Comics, 2016.

INDEX

Page numbers in *italics* refer to images.

Aâma (Peeters), 222n9
Abellio, Raymond, 92
abstraction: in *Ballad of the Salt Sea*, 23, 24; in *The Grand Narrative*, 193; in *Pretending Is Lying*, 120, *121–22*, *123*; in *Watchmen*, 57
Abu Dhabi, 152
Accursed Stamp, The (David B.), 73
Ache, Caran d', 127
Acme Novelty Library, The, 163
Actes Sud, 190
adolescence: in *Epileptic*, 74, 78–79, 80, 82; in *Fun Home*, 101–2, *102*; in *Habibi*, 154, 160
adulthood. *See* maturity
adventure comics: *Airtight Garage* and, 30, 36–40; *Ballad of the Salt Sea* and, 7, 11, 19, 21; Mœbius's early work in, 28; *Watchmen* and, 50, 52–53, 58
age. *See* adolescence; childhood; maturity; time
Airtight Garage (Lofficier, Shanower, and Bingham), 27
Airtight Garage (Mœbius), 3, 26–47; adventure comics and, 30, 36–40; beginning of, 26, 31, 33, *34–35*; characters in, 38–39, 42, 44, 45, 212n36 (*see also individual character names*); clothing in, 32, 33, 40, 41, 42, 44; comics medium and, 41, 47; decorations and paraphernalia in, 33, 36, 38, 41; drawing style in, 28, 42, 44, 45, 121; dreams in, 27–28, 30, 32, 41, 45; ending of, 33, 40–41, *46*; enigmas in, 40, 41, 47; genre and, 28, 29, 37, 41; innovations of, viii, 26, 28, 29, 44–45; readers of, 28, 29, 31, 40–41, 44; serialization of, 26, 28, 30–31, 36–40; sources and allusions of, 29–30, 31–32, 38; title of, 26, 31, 38, 39, 211n (chap. 2)

Airtight Garage, form and narration in: braiding effects, viii, 33; circularity, 33, 36, 40; improvisation and, 26, 30–31, 33, 36–37; layout, 44; metanarrative, 40–41; metaphors for, 28–29, 32–33; serialization, 26, 36, 37, 38, 42
alcoholism, 83
Alexander the Great, 55
Allah, 157
allegory: in *The Arrival*, 137–38; in *Epileptic*, 81, 88
allusions. *See* sources and allusions
alternative medicine, 74, 80
ambiguity: in *Epileptic*, 91; in *Pretending Is Lying*, 120, 121
ambivalence: of *Are You My Mother?*, 103; in *Ballad of the Salt Sea*, 10, *15*; in *Pretending Is Lying*, 114
analepses: in *The Arrival*, 136; in *Building Stories*, 164, *182–83*, 184; in *Epileptic*, 82–83
anger, 78–80, *79*
Angoulême comics festival: *The Arrival* at, 126; *Ballad of the Salt Sea* at, 8; *Epileptic* at, 73; *Grand Narrative* at, 190; *Pretending Is Lying* at, 111; *Watchmen* at, 48
animals: in *Aâma* (Peeters), 222n9; in *The Arrival*, 131–33, *131*, *132*, *134–35*, 143; in *Building Stories*, 181; in *Epileptic*, 87, 90–91; in *The Grand Narrative*, 195–96, *197*, *199*, *200*, *205*; in *Leviathan*, 191–92. *See also* dragons; environment; monsters
Anna Karenina (Tolstoy), 99, 101, 170
Ann of the Jungle (Pratt), 7
Anthropogenics (Van Lier), 207
Anthroposophy, 89, 90
Anubis, 90–91
apocalypse, 49, 61, 67
Arabic calligraphy, x, 147–49, *148*, *149*, 150, 160

224

Arab Muslim world, 151–52
Archer, 33, 39, 42
archetypes, 53. *See also* myths
architecture: in *Airtight Garage*, 38; in *The Arrival*, 128, *132*, 133, *134–35*, *140*, 141; in *Building Stories*, 164, *169*; in *The Grand Narrative*, 202, *203*; in *A Short History of America*, 195
Are You My Mother? (Bechdel), 97–98, 103, 108
Aristotle, 152
Arrival, The (Tan), 4, 126–44; animals in, 131–33, *131*, *132*, *134–35*, *143*; architecture in, 128, *132*, 133, *134–35*, *140*, 141; beginning of, 130, 142, *142*, 144; braiding effects in, *142*, 143–44, *143*; circularity in, 130–31, *142*, 143–44, *143*; comics medium and, 127, 128, 138; decorations and paraphernalia in, 128, 130, *134–35*, 139, *142–43*, 143–44; drawing style in, x, 138–39; ending of, 133, *142*, *143*, 144; family in, *142*, 143–44, *143*; immigration in, 126–31, 133, *134–35*, 136, *137*; innovations of, 129–30, 141–42; photographic images in, x, 130, 136, *137*, 138–39; silence in, ix, 127, 128, 141; symmetry in, *142*, 143–44, *143*; universality in, 129, *129*, 130, 136–38; writing in, 129, *129*, 133
Arrival, The, characters in: creature, 131–32; development of, 130; family and, *142*, 143–44, *143*; girl, 130–31, 139, *143*, 144; individuality of, 130; photographs and, 139; universality of, 127, 137–38; woman, 139, *142*, 143–44, *143*; wordless narrative and, 128–29
Arrival, The, form and narration in: circularity, *142*, 143–44, *143*; immigration and, 136; lack of text, 127–29, *134–35*; layout, 141–43; photographic images and, *137*, 138; realism and documentarism, 128, 130, *137*, 138–39; sections, 130
Arrival, The, sources and allusions of: *Bicycle Thieves*, 133; comics, 127; New York, *134–35*, *140*, 141; photographs, 139, 141; teepees, 136
Arrouye, Jean, 23
Art Institute of Chicago, 165
Arzach (Mœbius), 26, 29, 41, 42
astrology, 147
(À suivre) [To be continued], 8, 25, 73
Atangan, Patrick, 219n6
audience. *See* readers

autobiography: in *Airtight Garage*, 41–42; in *Building Stories*, 165, 170, 220n6; Craig Thompson and, 145; in *Epileptic*, 77–78, 82–84, 85–86, 90; in *Fun Home*, ix, 98, 103, 108, 110; in *Pretending Is Lying*, ix, 114, 124–25

B., David (Pierre-François Beauchard): artistic development of, 82; background, 73; dream transcription by, 91; *Epileptic* (see *Epileptic*); imaginary of, 74, 76, 80–81, 82, *89*, 90; on marginalization, 94; mother of, 83, 92; other works by, 73, 91; on seizures of brother, 88; on symbols, 90; university education, 73, 82, 92. *See also* Beauchard, Pierre-François (character)
background and foreground: in *Airtight Garage*, 38; in *The Arrival*, 128; in *Ballad of the Salt Sea*, 11–13, 22–23; in *Building Stories*, 165; in *Epileptic*, 75–76, *75*, 92, *93*, 94; in *Habibi*, 162; in *Pretending Is Lying*, 116, 117, 121; in *Watchmen*, 61. *See also* decorations and paraphernalia
Bahia Palace, 151
Bain turc (Ingres), 151
"ballad," 9
Ballad for a Coffin (Charlier), 15
Ballad of the Salt Sea (Pratt), 3, 7–25; adventure comics and, 7, 11, 19, 21; characters in, 10, 13–15, 17–19, 21 (*see also individual character names*); clothing in, 18, *20*, 22–23; comics medium and, 10–11, 22, 24–25; drawing style in, viii, 19, 21, 22–23; enigmas in, 8, 15, 21, 22–23; genre and, viii, 7, 10, 11; history in, 10, 13, 22; innovations of, 5, 22, 23–24; plot of, 8–9, 15–17, 19, 21; readers of, 19, 22, 23; sources and allusions of, 9, 11–12, 21–22, 107; symbolism in, 18, 23, 24
Ballad of the Salt Sea, form and narration in: characters and, viii, 10, 15, 17–19; faults of, 19, 21; genre and, 9, 10; length and scope, 24; ocean and, 11–13, *12*; silent panels, 22–23
banality. *See* everyday life
Barnier, Engineer: circularity and, 33; creation of, 32; feminine transformation of, 42, *43*; Major Grubert and, 40; plot and, 27
Barthes, Roland, 176

Batman, 57, 213n9
Baudoin, Edmond, 145, 149, 215n9, 217n10
Bayard Presse, 73
Beauchard, Jean-Christophe: death and, 88; deterioration of, 74–75, *75*, 77; gigantism of, 86–87; portraits of, 74–75, *75*, 77; seizures of, 84–86, *84*, *85*
Beauchard, Pierre-François (artist). *See* B., David
Beauchard, Pierre-François (character): anger of, 78–80, *79*; books and, *93*; on covers, 74–75, *75*; drawings by, 78–79, *80*; dreams of, 90–91; imaginary of, 80–81, *81*; perspective and, 86–87; plot and, 74; portraits of, 74–75, *75*, 77. *See also* B., David
Beauvoir, Simone de, 124
Bechdel, Alison (artist): background, 97–98; *Fun Home* (see *Fun Home*); other works by, 97, 103, 108; working methods of, 108, 139, 217n14, 217n15
Bechdel, Alison (character): contrasted to father, *100*; growth of, 101–2, *102*; plot and, 98
Bechdel, Bruce: as character, 98–99, *99*, 106–7; contrasted to daughter, *100*; death, 102–3, *104*; decorative talents of, 101; distance from Alison, 109–10, *109*, 217n18; plot and, 98; youth, 102, *107*
Bechdel, Helen, 110, 217n18
Before Watchmen (DC Comics), 48
beginnings: of *Airtight Garage*, 26, 31, 33, 34–35; of *The Arrival*, 130, 142, *142*, 144; of *Ballad of the Salt Sea*, 11, 13, 14; of *Building Stories*, 164; of *Epileptic*, 83; of *Fun Home*, 98–99, *99*; of *Pretending Is Lying*, 113; of *Watchmen*, 67, 69, 70
Bergier, Jacques, 80
Bertieri, Claudio, 7
Best of Enemies (David B. and Filiu), 73
Bible, 145, 147, 159
Bicycle Thieves (De Sica), 133
Bildungsroman, 102
Billiard, Star, 42, *44*, 47
Bilqis, 159
Bingham, Jerry, 27
biography. *See* autobiography
birds, 131–32, *132*
black and white. *See* colors and values
Blake, Edward. *See* Comedian

Blake, William, 214n28
Blandine, 113–14, *115*, 118, 122, 217n9
Blankets (Thompson), 145, 146–47, 152, 155, 219n14
blind images, 23
Blueberry, 15, 28
Blueberry (Mœbius), 37
Blue Lagoon, The (Stacpoole), 11
Blue Sky, 126
Blutch (Christian Hincker), 5
bodies: in *Building Stories*, 168, 171–73, *172*, *174*, 175–78; in *Epileptic*, 77, 85, 88, 92; in *Fun Home*, ix, *100*, 101, 102, *102*; in *The Grand Narrative*, 200, *201*; in *Habibi*, 154–55, 219n18
Boilet, Frédéric, 139
Bond, James, 31, 213n9
books: in *Epileptic*, 92, *93*, 94; in *Fun Home*, 99, *99*, *100*, 101; in *Habibi*, 147
Borges, Jorge Luis, 10
borrowings. *See* sources and allusions
Bosch, Hieronymous, 85
Bougainville, Lewis de, 21
boundaries and borders, 12, 32
Bourgeois, Louise, 205
Box in a Suitcase (Duchamp), 166
braiding effects: in *Airtight Garage*, viii, 33; in *The Arrival*, 142, 143–44, *143*; in *Building Stories*, 172, 185, 221n25; in *The Grand Narrative*, 196–97; in *Habibi*, 157, 159–60; in *Watchmen*, 70, 214n33. *See also* circularity; symmetry
Branford, 167, 181
Breccia, Alberto, 217n9
Briggs, Raymond, 136
British empire, 8–9
Bruce. *See* Bechdel, Bruce
Brussels, 113
Building, The (Eisner), 165
Building Stories (Ware), 4, 163–89; analepses in, 164, *182*–*83*, 184; autobiography in, 165, 170, 220n6; bodies in, 168, 171–73, *172*, *174*, 175–78; braiding effects in, 172, 185, 221n25; clothing in, 171–72, 179, 184; colors and values in, 176, 178, 179; comics medium and, 165–66, 176, 177–78, 184; decorations and paraphernalia in, 175, 178–80, 182, 184; drawing style in, 167, 176; everyday life in, 171, 173, 178, 181, 189, 221n17; gender in,

x, 165, 168–69, 170–73, 175–77; innovations of, 170–71, 173, 188–89; love affairs in, 167, 168, 175, 177, 179–80; memory in, 165, 179–82, 184–85, 187, 221n28; nudity in, 171–72, *172*, 173, *174*, 175–78; photographic images in, x, 176, 178–82, *180*; portraits in, 176, *177*, 178–79; sexuality in, 168, 172–73, 175, 176–77, 178; sources and allusions of, 164–65, 170, 175, 182, 187–88

Building Stories, florist in: being a woman and, 170–71; body and appearance of, 171–73, *172*, 175–77, *176*; Chris Ware's object and, 165–66, 173; narration of life of, 164, 165, 167–70, *169*; photographs and, 180–81; time and, 184

Building Stories, form and narration in: architecture and, 164–65, *169*, *186*; box form, x, 164–66, 187, 188; characters and, 167–70, 172–73; invasiveness and, 177–78; layout of, x–xi, 164–65, 166–67, 182–84, *182–83*; reader participation and, 164, 165–66, 220n4; realism and documentarism, 170–71, 173, 175–76, 178; space and, 164, 165, 167, 182–84, *182–83*; stolen images, 177–78, *180*, 181; time and, 164, 167–68, 184–85, *186*, 188

Building Stories, other characters in: Betty and Branford, 167, 181; development of, 170–71; landlady, 172–73, *174*, 178–79, 184–85; photographs and, 178–82; plot and, 164; realism and, 165, 167–68; woman from second floor, 172, 179–80, 187

Building Stories, readers of: florist (character) and, 171; as intrusive, 177–78; page design and, 183–84; participation of, x, 164, 165–66; tone and, 220n12

Burgess, Anthony, 50
Burian, Zdeněk, 196

Cage, The (Vaughn-James), 70
Cain, 8–9, 17, 19
calligraphy. *See* Arabic calligraphy
Calon, Charles Alexandre de, 202
"camera" position. *See* perspective
Camus, Albert, 105
capitalism, 155, 157
Caprioli, Franco, 12
caricature, 150, *150*
Carlsen, 190

Carnelian, Lewis. *See* Cornelius, Jerry
Carnet de Voyage (Thompson), 151
Castafiore Emerald, The (Hergé), 138
Casterman, 8, 10, 25, 148
Cervantes, Miguel de, 22
Cham, 157
characters. *See under individual works and individual character names*
Charbonnier, Sébastien, 208
Charlier, Jean-Michel, 15, 28
Charlton Press, 48, 55
Chic, 73
Chicago, 164, 165, 168
childhood: in *Building Stories*, 166, *172*; in *Epileptic*, 74–75, 78, 82; in *Fun Home*, 99, *100*, 101–2, *102*; in *Habibi*, 160; in *Pretending Is Lying*, 114, *115*, *116*, 117. *See also* father-daughter relationship; mother-daughter relationship
children's literature, 3, 7, 53, 126, 141
Christ, 13–14, 31, 202, *204*
Christianity, 145
Chronic'art, 192–93
Chronography (Goblet and Fossoul), 111, 125
Chute, Hillary, 101, 103, 106
Cigars of the Pharaoh (Hergé), 29–30
cinema. *See* film
circularity: in *Airtight Garage*, 33, 36, 40; in *The Arrival*, 130–31, 142, 143–44, *143*; in *Building Stories*, 185; in *Epileptic*, 82; in *The Grand Narrative*, 196–97; in *Watchmen*, viii, 61, 66–67, 69–70, 214n24, 214n33
City of God, The (Harder), 190
Clark, Kenneth, *100*, 101
clocks, 61, 67, 214n24
Clockwork Orange, A (Burgess), 50
close-ups. *See* perspective
clothing: in *Airtight Garage*, 32, 33, 40, 41, 42, 44; in *The Arrival*, 127, 133; in *Ballad of the Salt Sea*, 18, 20, 22–23; in *Building Stories*, 171–72, 179, 184; in *Epileptic*, 74–75, *75*; in *Fun Home*, *100*, 102, *102*; in *Habibi*, 154, *154*; in *Watchmen*, 52, 56–57, 60, 66, 69
Clowes, Daniel, 127
codes, 41, *89*, 90
Cold War, 49, 61, 66, 67
Coleridge, Samuel T., 9, 22, 50
Colette (Sidonie-Gabrielle Colette), 106

collage and montage: in *The Grand Narrative*, xi, 193–94, 196, *198*, 205; in *Pretending Is Lying*, 121–22
colors and values: in *The Arrival*, 130, 139; in *Ballad of the Salt Sea*, 23; in *Building Stories*, 176, 178, 179; in *Epileptic*, 80, 94–95; in *Fun Home*, 108; in *The Grand Narrative*, 206–7; in *Habibi*, 149, *149*; in *Pretending Is Lying*, 119, 121; in *Watchmen*, 60
Comedian (Edward Blake): allegiance of, 56; on cover, *51*; plot and, 49; smiley face and, 66–67; violence of, 50, 57, 63
comedy, 103, 186–87
comics medium: *Airtight Garage* and, 41, 47; *The Arrival* and, 127, 128, 138; *Ballad of the Salt Sea* and, 10–11, 22, 24–25; *Building Stories* and, 165–66, 176, 177–78, 184; evolution of, 3, 4–5; *The Grand Narrative* and, 193, 195, 196, 199, 207; *Habibi* and, 149–50; *Pretending Is Lying* and, 112; study of, vii, xi, 5; *Watchmen* and, 53, 57
concealed identity, 52, 55, 56–57
concept images, ix, 88, *89*, 90
Contract with God and other Tenement Stories, A (Eisner), 165
Cornelius, Jerry (Lewis Carnelian), 26, 27, 31–32, 211n (chap. 2)
Corto magazine, 8, 94. *See also* Maltese, Corto
costumes. *See* clothing
covers and title pages: of *Ballad of the Salt Sea*, 10, *11*; of *Epileptic*, ix, 74–75, *75*; of *Fun Home*, 108; of *Habibi*, 147; of *Pretending Is Lying*, 122, 124; of *Watchmen*, *51*, *54*, *59*, *62*, *65*, *68*. *See also* titles
Cranio, 9, 17, 18
creative process. *See* working methods
creatures. *See* animals; dragons; monsters
Creswell, Robyn, 150
critical reception. *See* reception
crucifixion, 12, 14
Crumb, Robert, 127, 194–95
crystals, 33, 36

Daedalus, 106–7
daily life. *See* everyday life
Daily Texan, 163
Dali, Salvador, 214n24
Dalxtrey, Lark, 27, 37, 38
Dan Dare (Hampson), 139

Dany (Daniel Henrotin), 10–11
Dargaud, 126
Darwin, Charles, 196
David (Michelangelo), 101, 214n21
David B. *See* B., David
David-McElligatt, Joanna, 173
DC Comics, 48, 214n23
death: in *Building Stories*, 179; in *Epileptic*, 78, *78*, 79, 87–88, 90–91; in *Fun Home*, 98, 101, 102–3, *104*; in *Habibi*, 146; in *Pretending Is Lying*, 114. *See also* violence
Death (character), 9, 210n3
de Blas, Juan Antonio, 14
decorations and paraphernalia: in *Airtight Garage*, 33, 36, 38, 41; in *The Arrival*, 128, 130, *134–35*, 139, *142–43*, 143–44; in *Building Stories*, 175, 178–80, 182, 184; in *Epileptic*, 75–76, *75*, 92, *93*, 94; in *Fun Home*, 100, *101*; in *Habibi*, 147, 148–49, 159; in *Pretending Is Lying*, 121; in *Watchmen*, 61, 64, 66–67, 69–70, 72
Defoe, Daniel, 12–13, 21
Dégé, Guillaume, 120–21
Delcourt, 145, 163, 164
Derrida, Jacques, 206
Dèsert B (Mœbius), 42, 45
De Sica, Vittorio, 133
Deviation, The (Mœbius), 28–29
Dick, Philip K., 72
Dickens, Charles, 145, 160
Didi-Huberman, Georges, 205
Dionnet, Jean-Pierre, 26
disability, 167–68, 172. *See also* epilepsy
disguises, 52, 55, 56–57
Ditko, Steve, 55
documentarism. *See* realism and documentarism
Dodola: body of, 154–55; education of, 147, *149*; growth of, 154; in harem, 152; narration and, 161–62; plot and, 146; pollution and, 155; sexual violence and, 152, 154; storytelling by, 159; water and, 157; Zam and, *156*, 159, 160–61, 219n18
Don Quixote (Cervantes), 22
Doom, Doctor, 21
Doré, Gustave, 120–21
dragons, 84–85, *84*, 87–88
Dramatic, Picturesque and Caricatural History of Holy Russia (Doré), 120–21

INDEX 229

dramatic tension: in *Airtight Garage*, 38; in *The Arrival*, 128; in *Ballad of the Salt Sea*, 21; in *Pretending Is Lying*, 116, 117; in *Watchmen*, 61, 63–64

drawing: in *The Arrival*, 129, *129*; in *Building Stories*, 187; comics medium and, 5–6; in *Epileptic*, 78–79, 92, 93; in *Habibi*, 147–49; in *Pretending Is Lying*, 115

drawing style: in *Airtight Garage*, 28, 42, 44, 45, 121; in *The Arrival*, x, 138–39; in *Ballad of the Salt Sea*, viii, 19, 21, 22–23; in *Building Stories*, 167, 176; in *Epileptic*, ix, 80, 90, 94; in *Fun Home*, *107*, 108; in *The Grand Narrative*, xi, 192, *193*, 206–7; in *Habibi*, 148–49; in *Pretending Is Lying*, 112, *115*, 118–19, *120*–21. *See also* colors and values

"drawn literature," 22

dreams: in *Airtight Garage*, 27–28, 30, 32, 41, 45; in *The Arrival*, 128; in *Building Stories*, 181; in *Epileptic*, 82, 90–92

Dreiburg, Daniel, 57–58, 64, 72. *See also* Nite Owl

dress. *See* clothing

Dubai, 152

Duchamp, Marcel, 166

Dürrenmatt, Jacques, 103

Dykes to Watch Out For (Bechdel), 97, 108

EC Comics, 61

Eco, Umberto, 36, 206

ecofeminism, 155

École Duperré, 73, 82, 92

ecology. *See* environment

Éditions de l'An 2, 190

Egyptian mythology, 90–91

Eisner, Will, 5, 38, 56, 165

Elias, Norbert, 208

Elle magazine, 145

Ellis Island, 133, *134*–*35*, *140*, 141

Empire of Light (Magritte), 95, *95*

endings: of *Airtight Garage*, 33, 40–41, 46; of *The Arrival*, 133, 142, *143*, 144; of *Ballad of the Salt Sea*, 13, 17; of *Building Stories*, 168; of *Epileptic*, 78; of *Fun Home*, 99, *99*; of *Pretending Is Lying*, 121–22; of *Watchmen*, 61, 67, 69, 70

Engineer Barnier. *See* Barnier, Engineer

"engraved literature," 22

enigmas: in *Airtight Garage*, 40, 41, 47; in *The Arrival*, 136–37; in *Ballad of the Salt Sea*, 8, 15, 21, 22–23; in *Fun Home*, 98–99; in *Watchmen*, 56–57

environment: in *The Arrival*, 131–33; in *The Grand Narrative*, 195–96; in *Habibi*, 146, 151, 155, 157, *157*; in *A Short History of America*, 195

Epic of Gilgamesh, 191

Epileptic (David B.), 3–4, 73–96; autobiography in, 74, 77–78, 82–84, 85–86, 90; background in, 75–76, *75*, 92, *93*, 94; bodies in, 77, 85, 88, 92; books in, 92, *93*, 94; characters in, 80–82, 86–87 (*see also individual character names*); childhood in, 74–75, 78, 82; concept images in, ix, 88, *89*, 90; covers and title pages, ix, 74–75, *75*; death in, 78, *78*, 79, 87–88, 90–91; decorations and paraphernalia in, 75–76, *75*, 92, *93*, 94; dragons in, 84–85, *84*, 87–88; drawing in, 78–79, 92, *93*; drawing style in, ix, 80, 90, 94; dreams in, 82, 90–92; esotericism in, 74, 80, 88, *89*, 90, 92; faces in, ix, 76, 77, 88; family in, 77–78, 80, 82–83, 94; genre and, 79, 85–86; gigantism in, 86–87, *86*, *87*; innovations of, 88, 90, 94; maturity in, 74, 80, 82; monsters and monstrosity in, 75–76, *75*, 84–85, *84*, *85*; perspective in, 86–87, *86*, *87*, 94; readers of, 77, 88, 91; silhouettes in, 75–76, *75*, 81–82, 94; sources and allusions of, 91, 92, 94; symbolism in, 84–88, *89*, 90–92, 94; time in, 75, *75*, 82–83; writing in, 92, *93*, 94

Epileptic, epilepsy in: anger of Pierre-François and, 79–80; autobiography and, 74, 83; death and, 88; as dragon, 84–85, *84*, *85*; gigantism and, 86–87, *86*, *87*; in portraits, 75. *See also* Beauchard, Jean-Christophe

Epileptic, form and narration in: basis of, 95–96; covers and, 74–77, *75*; dragons and, 85; dreams and, 91; perspective and, 86–87; portraits, 74–75, *75*, 215n7; time and, 82–83; volume division, 76–77

Erlangen comics festival, 190

Ernie Pike (Pratt), 7

eroticism. *See* sexuality

Escondida, 8–9, 10, 11, 12–13

esotericism: in *Epileptic*, 74, 80, 88, *89*, 90, 92; in *Habibi*, 147; in Hugo Pratt's work, 24

ethics, 52, 70–71
ethnicity and race, 126, 127
Euripides, 22
everyday life, 171, 173, 178, 181, 189, 221n17
evil. *See* good and evil
exorcism, 74
exoticism, 151–52
expressionism, 80

fables, 151–52
faces: in *Building Stories*, 176, *177*; in *Epileptic*, ix, *76*, 77, 88; in *Pretending Is Lying*, 113–14, 120, 217n9; in *Watchmen*, 66–67, 69. *See also* bodies; portraits
fact vs. fiction: in *Fun Home*, 103, 110; in *The Grand Narrative*, 193; in *Habibi*, 151; in *Pretending Is Lying*, 124–25. *See also* history; realism and documentarism
Falk, Lee, 21
family: in *The Arrival*, 142, 143–44, *143*; in *Building Stories*, 168–69, 179; in *Epileptic*, 77–78, 80, 82–83, 94; in *Fun Home*, 98–99, 101, 106, 109–10; in *Pretending Is Lying*, 112–13
Fantagraphics, 163
Fantastic Four, The, 21
"fantastique," 85, 90
fantasy literature, 81, 85–86
father-daughter relationship: in *Fun Home*, 98–99, 109–10; in *Pretending Is Lying*, 114, 116, 117, *118*, 121, *123*
Fawkes, Guy, 66, 214n30
femininity: in *Airtight Garage*, 42; in *Ballad of the Salt Sea*, 10, 23; in *Building Stories*, 170–71, 175; in *Watchmen*, 57
feminism: in *Fun Home*, 106; in *Habibi*, 155, 162; and response to *Habibi*, 151–52
Fez, 151
fiction. *See* fact vs. fiction
Filiu, Jean-Pierre, 73
film: *Ballad of the Salt Sea* and, viii, 12; *Building Stories* and, 166, 176; *The Grand Narrative* and, 193; *Watchmen* and, 57
Final Programme, The (Moorcock), 31–32
firefighting, 116, 117
flamboyance, 56–57
flashbacks. *See* analepses
flash-forwards. *See* prolepses
Flaubert, Gustave, 170, 189

Flesh Color (Mussat), 90
Forest, Jean-Claude, 88, 92
form. *See under individual comic titles*
Formula One, 117
Fossoul, Nikita, 111, 114, *115*, 119
Foster, Barry, 214n21
Four Wise Men, The (David B.), 73
France Soir, 7
Franquin, André, 61
Frémok (Fréon), 111
Freud, Sigmund, 30, 170
Frye, Northrop, 214n28
Fun Home (Bechdel), 4, 97–110; adolescence in, 101–2, *102*; autobiography in, ix, 98, 103, 108, 110; bodies in, ix, *100*, 101, 102, *102*; books in, 99, *99*, *100*, 101; characters in, 106 (*see also individual character names*); childhood in, 99, *100*, 101–2, *102*; clothing in, *100*, 102, *102*; death in, 98, 101, 102–3, *104*; decorations and paraphernalia in, *100*, 101; drawing style in, *107*, 108; family in, 98–99, 101, 106, 109–10; genre and, 102; innovations of, 105, 107; literariness of, 99, *99*, *100*, 101, 103, 105–6; nudity in, *100*, 101; photographic images in, *107*, 108, 217n14, 217n15; sexuality in, 98, *100*, 101, 102, 109–10; sources and allusions of, 99, 101, 105–7
Fun Home, form and narration in: literary allusions and, 105–6; photographs and, 108; realism and documentarism, 103, *107*, 108, 110; structure of, ix, 98–99, *99*, 102, 108; text and, 103, 105, 108

Gabriel, 81, *81*, 83
Garage (fictional place), 27
Garage, The Extraordinary Adventures of Penthotal (Pazienza), 44
gay life, 98, *100*, 101, 102, 109–10
gender: in *Airtight Garage*, 42; in *Ballad of the Salt Sea*, 10, 23; in *Building Stories*, x, 165, 168–69, 170–73, 175–77; in *Habibi*, 151–52, 154–55, *154*; in *Pretending Is Lying*, 113, 114; in study of comics, vii; in *Watchmen*, 53, 55, 57
genre: *Airtight Garage* and, 28, 29, 37, 41; *The Arrival* and, 127; *Ballad of the Salt Sea* and, viii, 7, 10, 11; *Building Stories* and, 176, 178; comics medium and, 3; *Epileptic* and, 79,

85–86; *Fun Home* and, 102; *Habibi* and, 151, 152; *Watchmen* and, viii, 50, 53, 58. *See also* adventure comics; autobiography
geopolitics. *See* politics
George, Saint, 84
Gerbier, Laurent, 92, 216n30
Gérôme, 151
ghosts and spectral images, 113–14, 122, *124*. *See also* spiritualism
Gibbons, Dave, 48, 57, 60; *Watchmen* (see *Watchmen*)
Gide, André, 124
gigantism, 86–87, *86*, *87*
Giordano, Dick, 48
Girard, René, 216n21
Giraud, Jean. *See* Mœbius
Glénat, 73
globalization: *The Arrival* and, 128; in *Habibi*, 151, 155, 157
Goblet, Dominique (artist): background, 111; estrangement from family, 113; Mœbius's style and, 44–45; other works by, 111, 113, 125; *Pretending Is Lying* (see *Pretending Is Lying*); working methods of, 120–21, 125
Goblet, Dominique (character): in attic scene, *116*, 117, 120; mother relationship and, 114; narrative detail and, 120; plot and, 112
Goblet, Dominique, father of: Dominique and, 112, 113, 117, *123*; iconography and, 121, *123*; portrait of, 114, *118*; voice of, 118–19, *118*
Goblet, Dominique, mother of, 112, 113, 114, 117
God, 157
Goethe, Johann Wolfgang von, 165
good and evil, 53, 66, 67, 213n13
Good-bye, Chunky Rice (Thompson), 145
Goode, Matthew, 57
Gordon, Irving, 58
Gotlib, 74
Graad, 27, 36
Grand Narrative, The (Harder), 4, 190–208; animals in, 195–96, 197, 199, *200*, 205; comics medium and, 193, 195, 196, 199, 207; drawing style in, xi, 192, 193, 206–7; innovations of, 192–94, 195, 207–8; readers of, xi, 194, 205, 206; reception of, 191, 192–93, 208; symbolism in, 192–93, 199, 200, *201*
Grand Narrative, The, form and narration in: analogy, 196–97, *198*; braiding effects, 196–97; collage and montage, xi, 193–94, 196, *198*, 205; formal innovation, xi, 193–94, 205–6; human history and, 199–200, *201*, 202; image reproduction, 206–7; layout, 193, 207; prehuman period and, 196–97; prolepses, 197, *198*, 199, *200*, *204*; variations on a theme, 200, *201*
Grand Narrative, The, history and time in: early human history, 199–200, 202, *203*; form and, 193, 194; as main character, 208; plot and, 191; prehuman period, 194, 196–97; premise and title, 191, 192, 207–8
Grand Narrative, The, sources and allusions of: human history, 199–200, 202, 205; paleontology, 195–96; plot and, 191; prehuman period, 196–97, *200*; reader and, 206–7; symbols, 199; working method and, 192–93
graphic novel: *The Arrival* and, 127; *Ballad of the Salt Sea* and, 24–25; critique of term, 209n1 (intro.); *Habibi* and, 160
graphic style. *See* drawing style
gravity of tone, 103, 150
Gray, James, 218n17
Greenaway, Peter, 155
Groovesnore, Thomas. *See* Monk
Gros, Kathleen, 151–52
Gross, Milt, 127
grotesque, 150, *150*
Grubert, Major: appearance of, 33, 36, 44; boundary crossing and, 32; as Mœbius, 26, 27, 29, 40–41, 47; origins of, 37, 40; psychoanalysis of, 30
Guilbert, Xavier, 117

Habibi (Thompson), 4, 145–62; Arabic calligraphy in, x, 147–49, *148*, *149*, 150, 160; bodies in, 154–55, 219n18; characters in, 160–61 (*see also individual character names*); decorations and paraphernalia in, 147, 148–49, 159; environment in, 146, 151, 155, 157, *157*; feminist response to, 151–52; gender in, 151–52, 154, 154–55; globalization in, 151, 155, 157; Islam in, 147, 148, 150, 151, 152; love affairs in, 152, 159, 160–61; myths in, x, 150–51, 152; nudity in, 152, *153*, 154; politics in, 150 51, 155, 157; sexuality in, 151–52, 154–55, 160–61; sources and allusions of, 148–49, 150, 151, 159, 219n12; time in, 151–52, 154, 160, 162; violence

in, 146, 152, 154, 160, 219n18; writing in, 147–49, *148*, *149*, 150, 155, 160
Habibi, form and narration in: braiding effects, 157, *158*, 159–60; foregrounded, 159; layout, 162; length, 5; polyphony, 149–50, *150*, 161–62; realism and documentarism, 150, *150*, 155; representational mode, x, 151–52; time and, 162
Ham, 157
Hampson, Frank, 139
Happy Death, A (Camus), 105
happy faces, 66–67, 69
Harder, Jens: background, 190–91; childhood, 195–96; *The Grand Narrative* (see *Grand Narrative, The*); other works by, 190–91; on time and history, 194; working methods of, 192–93, 206–7
harems, 146, *150*, 151–52, *153*, 161
Haskin, Byron, 12
Hatfield, Charles, viii, 55–56, 57
He Done Her Wrong (Gross), 127
Hegel, G. W. F., 36
Helen. *See* Bechdel, Helen
Henrotin, Daniel, 10–11
Here (McGuire), 187–88, 194, 221n32, 222n6
Hergé (Georges Prosper Remi), 29–30, 138, 199
hermeneutics, 103
heroes, 10–11, 13–14. *See also* superheroes
hidden identity, 52, 55, 56–57
Higgins, John, 48
Hinant, Guy Marc (author), 112, 124, 125
Hinant, Guy Marc (character): development of, 119; gender roles and, 114; ghostly presences and, 122, *124*; inability to commit, 113; plot and, 112; time and, 120
Hiroshima bombing, 64, 214n24, 214n29
His Majesty O'Keefe (Haskin), 12
history: in *The Arrival*, 130; in *Ballad of the Salt Sea*, 10, 13, 22; of comics medium, 4–5; in *The Grand Narrative* (see *Grand Narrative, The*); in *Habibi*, 146, 151; in *Here*, 194–95; in *Leviathan*, 192; in *A Short History of America*, 195. *See also* realism; time
Hitler, Adolf: in *Epileptic*, 77, 86, 94; in *The Grand Narrative*, 202, 204
Hobbes, Thomas, 191
Holocaust, 82, 88
homosexuality, 98, *100*, 101, 102, 109–10
horses, 91

Houghton Mifflin, 97
Hugo Award, 48
humor, 103, 186–87

Ibn Hayyan, Jabir, 152
Icarus, 106–7
iconography: in *The Grand Narrative*, 205, 206; in *Pretending Is Lying*, 121, *123*
If It Die (Gide), 124–25
Iglesias, Julio, 214n21
illness. *See Epileptic* (David B.): epilepsy in
imaginary, 192–93
Immigrant, The (Gray), 218n17
immigration, 126–31, 133, *134–35*, 136, *137*
Importance of Being Earnest, The (Wilde), 102, 106, 216n7
Impressions of Africa (Roussel), 33
improvisation: *Airtight Garage* and, 26, 30–31, 33, 36–37; Mœbius's other comics and, 28–29, 211n7
indigenous peoples: Melanesian, 8, 13, 15, 210n2; Native American, 136, 195
Indochina wars, 83
influences. *See* sources and allusions
Ingres, Jean-Auguste-Dominique, 151
innovations: of *Airtight Garage*, viii, 26, 28, 29, 44–45; of *The Arrival*, 129–30, 141–42; of *Ballad of the Salt Sea*, 5, 22, 23–24; of *Building Stories*, 170–71, 173, 188–89; of comics medium, 3–5; of comics studies, vii; of *Epileptic*, 88, 90, 94; of *Fun Home*, 105, 107; of *The Grand Narrative*, 192–94, 195, 207–8; of *Watchmen*, 50, 52, 53, 58, 60
Institut Saint-Luc, 111
intellectualism, 92, 98, 107
interpellation, 77
intertextuality. *See* sources and allusions
Islam, 147, *148*, 150, 151, 152
island archetype, 12–13
Ivaldi, Florenzo, 7

Jean-Christophe. *See* Beauchard, Jean-Christophe
Jemaa el-Fnaa square, 151
Jesus Christ, 13–14, 31, 202, *204*
Jimmy Corrigan (Ware), 163, 166, 167, 170, 176, 221n17
Jolly Roger, 64
Journal (Neaud), 90

Joyce, James, 103, 105, *105*, 106, 122
Juspeczyk, Laurel (Laurie) Jane, 57–58, 63, 64, 65, 72. *See also* Silk Spectre
Juvenal, 52

Kafka, Franz, 67
Kent, Clark, 57
Khan, Genghis, 76
Kochalka, James, 145
Koons, Jeff, 205
Koran, 147, 148, 159
Kovacs, Walter. *See* Rorschach
Kubrick, Stanley, 50

Lacan, Jacques, 30, 124
landscapes, 30, 32, 121, 195
Langsdorf, Martyl, 61
language, x, 38, 113, 129, 210n2
Lapin, 73
L'Association, 73, 82, 111
Last Canterbury Tales, The (Ray), 81, 87
Laurie. *See* Juspeczyk, Laurel
law, 52, 55–56
layout: of *Airtight Garage*, 44; of *The Arrival*, 141–43; of *Building Stories*, x–xi, 164–65, 166–67, 182–84, *182–83*; of *The Grand Narrative*, 193, 207; of *Habibi*, 162; of *Watchmen*, 61, 63
League of Extraordinary Gentlemen (Moore and Gibbons), 55
Legan, Olivier, 73
legends. *See* myths
Le Goff, Jacques, 193
Leroy, Fabrice, 178
Leviathan (Harder), 191–92
Libération, 97
Life, a User's Manual (Perec), 165
L'Isola Giovedi (Caprioli), 12
literariness: in *Ballad of the Salt Sea*, 21, 22; of comics medium, 3, 5–6; in *Epileptic*, 92; in *Fun Home*, 99, *99*, *100*, 101, 103, 105–6; in *Watchmen*, 71, 72. *See also* sources and allusions; writing
Lloyd, Frank, 12
Lofficier, Jean-Marc, 27
Lohlé, Dominique, 112
Long, Edwin, 219n12
looping. *See* braiding effects; circularity; symmetry

Losfeld, Éric, 24
love affairs: in *Building Stories*, 167, 168, 175, 177, 179–80; in *Habibi*, 152, 159, 160–61; in *Pretending Is Lying*, 119, 122, 124, 125; in *Watchmen*, 57–58, 64
Ludwig, Edward, 12

machismo, 53, 55, 57
macrobiotics, 86, 87, 88
Madame Bovary (Flaubert), 170
magic, 48
Magritte, René, 95, *95*
Malta, 14
Maltese, Corto: Cain and, 17, 19; Cranio and, 18; function of, 9, 18, 19, 210n26; indigenous people and, 18–19; as main character, 10, 15, 17; the Monk and, 18, *19*; mystery of, 13; name of, 14; Pandora and, 16, 17, 18; piracy of, 14; plot and, 8–9; Rasputin and, 15, *15*, 17; tied to raft, *12*, 13–14
Manchette, Jean-Patrick, 49, 71
Man from the Ciguri, The (Mœbius), 30
manga, 4
Manhattan, Dr. (Jon Osterman): allegiance of, 55–56; circles and, 66; on cover, *54*; at end, 58; faults of, 52–53; genesis of, 64; plot and, 49; quasi-divinity of, 60, 213n4; on responsibility, 71; smiley face and, 67; superhero myth and, 50; time and, 60, 61
Manish, Hira, 72
Mao, Catherine, 84, 118, 121–22
maps, 13
marijuana, 45
Marrakech, 151
Mars, 60, 66, 67
Marseilles Electricity (Harder), 190
masculinity, 53, 55, 57
Masereel, Frans, 95, 127
masks, 21, 52, 56, 66–67, 214n30. *See also* clothing
mathematics, 147
maturity: in *Ballad of the Salt Sea*, 19; in *Building Stories*, 171, 172; of comics medium, 3, 4–5; in *Epileptic*, 74, 80, 82; in *Habibi*, 154, 160; in *Watchmen*, 47, 53, 57. *See also* adolescence; children's literature
Maus (Spiegelman), 84, 109, 114
Max-und-Moritz prize, 190

McGuire, Richard, 187–88, 194–95, 221n32, 222n6
Mein Kampf (Hitler), 94
Melanesia, 8–9, 13; indigenous peoples, 8, 13, 15, 210n2
Melville, Herman, 11, 13, 21, 191–92
Même, Arthur, 88
Memoirs of a Dutiful Daughter (Beauvoir), 124
Memories of a Perfect Day (Goblet), 113
memory, 165, 179–82, 184–85, 187, 221n28
Métal hurlant, 26, 37
metamorphosis: in *Epileptic*, 87, 90; in *Habibi*, 154
metanarrative: in *Airtight Garage*, viii, 40–41; in *Building Stories*, 187; in *Habibi*, 159; in *Watchmen*, 69, 72
metaphor: in *Airtight Garage*, 32–33; in *The Arrival*, 128, 131–32; in *Building Stories*, 188–89; in *Epileptic*, 84–85, 88
metaphysics, 46
Michael, Saint, 84
Michelangelo, 101, 214n21
Mickey Mouse, 167
migration. *See* immigration
MIKROmakro (Harder), 191
Miller, Ann, 94
Millidge, Gary Spencer, 214n33
Milton, John, 191
Minnie Mouse, 167
Mnémosyne Atlas (Warburg), 205
Moby Dick (Melville), 13, 21, 191–92
modernization. *See* globalization; time
Mœbius (Jean Giraud): adventure comics and, 28; *Airtight Garage* (see *Airtight Garage*); background, 26–27, 28, 32, 47; Jean Giraud vs. Mœbius, 41, 42, 212n32; Major Grubert and, 26, 27, 29, 40–41, 47; other works, 26, 28–29, 31, 37, 41, 42; penchant for wordplay, 33; working methods of, 30–31, 36–37, 44–46
Monk, the (Thomas Groovesnore): appearance of, *20, 22–23*; Corto Maltese and, *18, 19*; Escondida and, 13; faults in, 21; plot and, 8–9, 15, 17–18
Monogatari, 190
monsters and monstrosity, 75–76, *75*, 84–85, *84, 85*
montage. *See* collage and montage

Moorcock, Michael, 31–32
Moore, Alan: background, 48; on character development, 63; on making judgments, 71; other works by, 48, 55; on politics, 50; publisher constraints and, 55; on superheroes, 53; *Watchmen* (see *Watchmen*)
Moore, Lee, 21
Morgan, Harry, 52
Morocco, 151
mother-daughter relationship: in *Building Stories*, 168–69, 179; in *Fun Home*, 110; in *Pretending Is Lying*, 112, 113
movies. *See* film
Munch, Edvard, 114
Museum of the History of Immigration, 128, 136
music: in *The Arrival*, 142–43; in *Building Stories*, 165, *166*; in *The Grand Narrative*, 200, *201*; in *Habibi*, 149; in *Pretending Is Lying*, 112, 117
Mussat, Xavier, 90
Mutiny on the Bounty (Lloyd), 12
Mysterious Island, The (Verne), 12–13
mystery (genre), 58
myths: in *Airtight Garage*, 39, 40; in *Ballad of the Salt Sea*, 12–13, 24; in *Epileptic*, 92; in *Habibi*, x, 150–51, 152; in *Watchmen*, 50, 52–53. *See also* Egyptian mythology

names: in *Airtight Garage*, 38–39; in *The Arrival*, 127; in *Pretending Is Lying*, 114
narration, form and. *See under* individual comic books
Native Americans, 136, 195
Neaud, Fabrice, 90
New City, 163
New Frontiersman, 66, 69
New Guinea, 8
New York: in *The Arrival*, 134–35, *140*, *141*; in *Habibi*, 152
New Yorker, 164
nightmares. *See* dreams
Nightshade, 55
Nite Owl (Daniel Dreiburg), 49, 62, 66
Nixon, Richard, 52
Noah, 152, 155, 157
nuclear war, 61, 71
Nude, The (Clark), *100*, 101

nudity: in *Building Stories*, 171–72, *172*, 173, *174*, 175–78; in *Fun Home*, *100*, 101; in *Habibi*, 152, *153*, 154; in *Watchmen*, 60, 214n23
numbers, 47

objectivism, 55, 214n16
objects. *See* decorations and paraphernalia
ocean, 11–13
Odyssey, 103
Oesterheld, Hector, 7
oil, 52
Omaha World-Herald, 163
oneiric imagination, 24, 74, 88, 95
On Growth and Form (Thompson), 195
Opéra Garnier, 33
Orientalism, 151–52
origami, 130, 133
ornament. *See* decorations and paraphernalia
Osterman, Jon, 63, 64. *See also* Manhattan, Dr.
Ouija boards, 81
Ozymandias (Adrian Veidt): Antarctic retreat of, 58, 61, 66; circles and, *67*, 69; on cover, *68*; at end, 58; faults of, 52; individualism vs. altruism in, 55, 56; plot and, 49; on responsibility, 71; Rorschach's journal and, 69; self-effacement and flamboyance of, 56–57; sources of, 214n21; violence and, 50, 64, 72

Pacific Ocean, 11–13
page design. *See* layout
painting, 111, 178, 205
Pale Horse, The (David B.), 73, 91
palindromes, 64
Pandora (Greek mythology), 210n6
Pandora (Hugo Pratt character): Corto Maltese and, *16*, 17; Escondida and, 10, 13; as main character, 10; the Monk and, 18; plot and, 8–9; themes of, 15
panels. *See* layout
Pantheon Books, 164, 166, 196
Papua New Guinea, 8
paradox, 128–29, 138
paraliterature, 21
paraphernalia. *See* decorations and paraphernalia
Paris metro, 28, 33, 40–41, *46*
parody, 37, 38, 46
Pasquier, Renaud, 86

patriarchy, 155
Pauwels, Louis, 80
Pazienza, Andrea, 44
Peeters, Benoît, 138, 162, 183
Peeters, Frederik, 222n9
Peplum (Blutch), 5
Perec, Georges, 165, 173
Perramus (Breccia and Sasturain), 217n9
perspective: in *Ballad of the Salt Sea*, 22–23; in *Building Stories*, 175–76, 178; in *Epileptic*, 86–87, *86*, *87*, 94; in *Fun Home*, 109, *109*; in *The Grand Narrative*, 194; in *Habibi*, 159–60; in *Pretending Is Lying*, 119; in *Watchmen*, 70, 214n31
Petitfaux, Dominique, 21, 23
Phantom, 21
Phantom Lady, 55
Phantom of the Opera, 21
Phénix, 7
Phil, 168, 171, 184
Philosophie magazine, 192–93
photographic images: in *The Arrival*, x, 130, 136, *137*, 138–39; in *Building Stories*, x, 176, 178–82, *180*; in *Epileptic*, 74; in *Fun Home*, 107, 108, 217n14, 217n15; in *The Grand Narrative*, 192–93
Pichard, Georges, 73
Piero (Baudoin), 145
Pierre, Michel, 14, 17
Pif Gadget, 10
Pignon-Ernest, Ernest, 214n29
Pillow Book, The (Greenaway), 155
piracy, 14
Pixar, 126
place. *See* background and foreground; space
Planète (Pauwels and Bergier), 80
Platteau, Didier, 25
plays on words, 33, 72
plot: of *Airtight Garage*, 27–28; of *The Arrival*, 126–27, 136; of *Ballad of the Salt Sea*, 8–9, 15–17, 19, 21; of *Building Stories*, 164, 167; of *Epileptic*, 74; of *Fun Home*, 98; of *The Grand Narrative*, 191; of *Habibi*, 146; of *Pretending Is Lying*, 120; of *Watchmen*, 49, 61, 63–64, 70
point of view. *See* perspective
politics: in *Building Stories*, 189; in *The Grand Narrative*, 196, 197; in *Habibi*, 150–51, 155, 157; in *Watchmen*, 49, 50, 52, 53, 58

pollution, environmental, 155
popular literature, 21, 22
pornography, 175
Portrait of the Artist as a Young Man (Joyce), 122
portraits: in *The Arrival*, 136, 138; in *Building Stories*, 176, *177*, 178–79; in *Epileptic*, 74–75, *75*, 215n7; in *Pretending Is Lying*, 114, *118*
postmodernism, 121–22
Potet, Frédéric, 170
Pratt, Hugo: adolescence, 13; background, 7–8; *Ballad of the Salt Sea* (see *Ballad of the Salt Sea*); creation of Corto Maltese, 13–14; David B. and, 94; on drawing and writing, 119; on himself, 12; other works, 7, 10, *11*, 14, 17, 22
Presley, Elvis, 202, *204*
Pretending Is Lying (Goblet), 4, 111–25; abstraction in, 120, 121–22, *123*; autobiography in, ix, 114, 124–25; background in, *116*, 117, 121; characters in (*see individual character names*); childhood in, 114, *115*, *116*, 117; covers and title pages, 122, *124*; drawing style in, 112, *115*, 118–19, 120–21; faces in, 113–14, *118*, 120, 217n9; father relationship in, 114, *116*, 117, *118*, 121, *123*; ghosts and specters in, 113–14, 122, *124*; love affairs in, 119, 122, *124*, 125; readers of, 112, 120–21, 122; sound in, ix, 117, *118*
Pretending Is Lying, form and narration in: absence of reciter, 119–20; drawing style and, 118–19, 120–22; ghosts and, 122; irony and, *116*, 117; structure of, ix, 112, 113; time and, 120
print, 163, 188
Prix de l'Audace, 190
process, creative. *See* working methods
prolepses: in *Building Stories*, 164, 187; in *Epileptic*, 82, 83–84; in *The Grand Narrative*, 197, *198*, 199, *200*, *204*
Prophet, 152
proportion. *See* perspective; size and proportion
Proust, Marcel, 106, 110, 179
psychoanalysis: of *Airtight Garage*, 30, 41–42; in *Are You My Mother?*, 97–98; of *Epileptic*, 77–79; of *Pretending Is Lying*, 122
puberty, 102, *102*
Public Theatre, 97

publishing: of *Airtight Garage*, 26, 37, 211n (chap. 2); of *The Arrival*, 126; of *Ballad of the Salt Sea*, 7–8, 209n (chap. 1), 210n5; of *Building Stories*, 166, 167; of Chris Ware's works, 163, 164; of Craig Thompson's works, 145; of *Epileptic*, 73, 215n (chap. 4); of *Fun Home*, 97; of Jens Harder's works, 190, 196, 221n (chap. 10); of *Pretending Is Lying*, 111, 125, 217n (chap. 6); of *Watchmen*, 48–49, 55, 213n2
Pure and the Impure, The (Colette), 106
Pustz, Matthew J., 71

Quality Comics, 55
Queequeg, 21
Question (character), 55
Quick, Shoot! (Harder), 190
Quimby the Mouse (Ware), 167
quotations. *See* sources and allusions

race and ethnicity, 126, 127
Rasputin (Pratt character): Corto Maltese and, 15, *15*, 17; malevolent ambiguity of, 9–10, 15, 17, 210n22; plot and, 8–9
Rasputin, Grigory (Yefimovich), 9
RAW, 163, 187
Ray, Jean, 81, 87
readers: of *Airtight Garage*, 28, 29, 31, 40–41, 44; of *The Arrival*, 128–29; of *Ballad of the Salt Sea*, 19, 22, 23; of *Building Stories* (see under *Building Stories*); of *Epileptic*, 77, 88, 91; evolution of comics and, 4–5; of *The Grand Narrative*, xi, 194, 205, 206; of *Habibi*, 162; of *Pretending Is Lying*, 112, 120–21, 122; of *Watchmen*, 50, 53, 58, 69, 70, 214n33
Reagan, Ronald, 50, 213n8
realism and documentarism: in *Airtight Garage*, 47; in *The Arrival*, 128, 130, *137*, 138–39; in *Building Stories*, 170–71, 173, 175–76, 178; in *Epileptic*, 82–84; in *Fun Home*, 103, *107*, 108, 110; in *The Grand Narrative*, 192–93, 206–7; in *Habibi*, 150, *150*, 155; in *Leviathan*, 191–92; in *Pretending Is Lying*, 119; in *Watchmen*, 50, 52–53, 57, 60. *See also* photographic images
reception, 4; of *Airtight Garage*, 26, 44; of comics medium, 3, 5; of *Epileptic*, 90; of *Fun Home*, 97; of *The Grand Narrative*,

191, 192–93, 208; of *Habibi*, 151–52; of *Watchmen*, 50
Redford, Robert, 213n8
references. *See* sources and allusions
reflexivity. *See* metanarrative
refrains, 38, 66
religion: Craig Thompson and, 145; *The Grand Narrative* and, 196; in *Habibi*, 147, 148, 150, 151, 152. *See also* spiritualism
resurrection, 14
rhymes. *See* braiding effects; circularity
rhythm. *See* music; time
Ricœur, Paul, 170
Rilke, Rainer Maria, 22
Rime of the Ancient Mariner, The (Coleridge), 9
Rizla, 39
Robbe-Grillet, Alain, 36
Robinson Crusoe (Defoe), 12–13, 21
Rorschach (Walter Kovacs): biography of, 63; on cover, 59; faults of, 52; inhumanity of, 56, 214n20; journal of, 67, 69; law and, 56; with placard on street, 70; plot and, 49; silhouettes and, 64; sources of, 55; superhero myth and, 52; symmetry and, 64, 214n19; violence and, 50
Roussel, Raymond, 33
routines, daily. *See* everyday life

Saint-Ogan, Alain, 31
Sasturain, Juan, 217n9
science, 152, 196
science fiction: *Airtight Garage* as, 29, 41; *Watchmen* as, 58
Scorpions of the Desert, The (Pratt), 7
Scream, The (Munch), 114
seafaring novel, 11
Seeking LTR (Goblet and Pfeiffer), 125
seizures. *See* epilepsy
self-effacement, 56–57
self-sacrifice, 79–80, *79*
Sempé, Jean-Jacques, 189
September 11 attacks, 150, 213n5
Sergeant Kirk (Pratt), 7, 10, *11*, 17, 22
serialization: of *Airtight Garage*, viii, 26, 28, 30–31, 36–40; of *Building Stories*, 165–66
seriousness, 103, 150
Serres, Michel, 192
setting. *See* background and foreground

sexuality: in *Airtight Garage*, 41–42; in *Are You My Mother?*, 97–98; in *Building Stories*, 168, 172–73, 175, 176–77, 178; in *Fun Home*, 98, *100*, 101, 102, 109–10; in *Habibi*, 151–52, 154–55, 160–61; in *Watchmen*, 64
sexual violence, 152, 154
Seymour, 66, 69
shading. *See* colors and values
Shanower, Eric, 27
Shea, Max, 72
Shelley, Percy Bysshe, 22
Shiva, Vandana, 155
Short History of America, A (Crumb), 194–95
silence: in *The Arrival*, ix, 127, 128, 141; in *Ballad of the Salt Sea*, 22–23; in *Fun Home*, 103; in *Pretending Is Lying*, 122. *See also* sound
silhouettes: in *Epileptic*, 75–76, *75*, 81–82, 94; in *Watchmen*, 64
Silk Spectre (Laurel Jane Juspeczyk), 49, 52, 55. *See also* Juspeczyk, Laurel
Silk Tapestry (Atangan), 219n6
size and proportion, 86, *86*, *87*. *See also* perspective
skeletons: in *Building Stories*, 175; in *Epileptic*, 88, *89*
Sketches from a Nameless Land (Tan), 126, 141
slavery, 146, 151, *153*, 159
Slütter, Christian, 8–9, 17, 18
smiley face. *See* happy face
Smolderen, Thierry, 29–30, 42
Snowman, The (Briggs), 136
Snyder, Zack, 48, 57
Solomon, 159
sound: in *The Arrival*, 128; in *Pretending Is Lying*, ix, 117, 118. *See also* silence
sources and allusions: of *Airtight Garage*, 29–30, 31–32, 38; of *The Arrival* (see under *Arrival, The*); of *Ballad of the Salt Sea*, 9, 11–12, 21–22, 107; of *Building Stories*, 164–65, 170, 175, 182, 187–88; of *Epileptic*, 91, 92, 94; of *Fun Home*, 99, 101, 105–7; of *The Grand Narrative* (see under *Grand Narrative, The*); of *Habibi*, 148–49, 150, 151, 159, 219n12; of *Pretending Is Lying*, 121; of *Watchmen*, 71–72. *See also* autobiography
space: in *The Arrival*, 141–42; in *Building Stories*, 164, 165, 167, 182–84, *182–83*; in *The Grand Narrative*, 193, 194; in *Habibi*, 162;

in *Pretending Is Lying*, 121–22; in *Watchmen*, 61. *See also* topography
spectral images. *See* ghosts and spectral images
Spiegelman, Art, 84, 109, 114, 163
Spiegelman, Vladek, 114
Spirit (character), 56
Spirit (Eisner), 38
spiritualism, 80–81, 87–88. *See also* ghosts
Stacpoole, Henry de Vere, 11
Staros, Chris, 145
Steiner, Rudolf, 89, 90
Stephanie, 168, 171, 172
Sterckx, Pierre, 44
Stevenson, Robert Louis, 11, 12–13
still lifes, 178
Story of My Double (Mœbius), 42
Story without Heroes (Dany and Van Hamme), 10–11
STP, 39
streets: in *Building Stories*, 169, 185; in *Epileptic*, 79; in *Watchmen*, 56, 61, 64, 70
style. *See* drawing style
Sub Rosa, 112
Sufism, 150
suicide: in *Building Stories*, 168, 172; in *Fun Home*, 98; in *Habibi*, 146
Sultan (character), 146, 150, *150*, 152, 161
superheroes, 50, 52–53, 55–57, 58, 213n9
Superman, 52, 57, 202, 204
surrealism: in *Airtight Garage*, 45; in *The Arrival*, 128, 130; in *Epileptic*, 95, *95*
Swamp Thing (Moore), 48
symbolism: in *Airtight Garage*, 36; in *The Arrival*, 128; in *Ballad of the Salt Sea*, 18, 23, 24; in *Building Stories*, 175, 178; in *Epileptic*, 84–88, 89, 90–92, 94; in *The Grand Narrative*, 192–93, 199, 200, *201*; in *Habibi*, 159–60; in *Pretending Is Lying*, 121–22; in *Watchmen*, 61, 66–67, 69–70, 71
symmetry: in *The Arrival*, 142, 143–44, *143*; in *Building Stories*, 182, *183*; in *Watchmen*, viii, 64, 66, 214n28
syncretism: in *Habibi*, 147, 160; in *Pretending Is Lying*, 121–22, 123
System of Comics, The (Groensteen), vii

Tan, Shaun: on animals, 131–32; *The Arrival* (see *Arrival, The*); background, 126; other works by, 126, 141; on silent narration, 128; working methods of, 139, 141
Tardi, Jacques, 88, 92, 94
Télérama magazine, 145
temporality. *See* time
Teulé, Jean, 139
theater, 111
Thompson, Craig (artist): background, 145; on ecology, 155; *Habibi* (see *Habibi*); other works by, 145, 146–47; working methods of, 148–49, 150
Thompson, Craig (character), 152
Thompson, D'Arcy, 195
Thousand and One Nights, The, 147
time: in *The Arrival*, 130; in *Building Stories*, 164, 167–68, 184–85, *186*, 188; comics medium and, 3; in *Epileptic*, 75, *75*, 82–83; in *The Grand Narrative* (see *Grand Narrative, The*: history and time in); in *Habibi*, 151–52, 154, 160, 162; in *Here*, 194–95; in *Pretending Is Lying*, 120, 125; in *A Short History of America*, 195; in *Watchmen*, viii, 58, 60–61, 63, 214n22, 214n24
Time magazine, 97
Tintin, 10
titles: *Airtight Garage*, 26, 31, 38, 39, 211n (chap. 2); *The Arrival*, 128; *Building Stories*, 164, 220n5; *Epileptic*, 74; *Fun Home*, 103; *The Grand Narrative*, 192, 207–8; *Pretending Is Lying*, 114, 124–25. *See also* covers and title pages
Tolstoy, Leo, 99, 101, 170
Töpffer, Rodolphe, 22
Töpffer Prize, 111
topography, 30, 32. *See also* background and foreground; space
Top Shelf Productions, 145
translation: of *Airtight Garage*, 210n (chap. 2), 211n6; of *Ballad of the Salt Sea*, 209n; of Chris Ware's works, 163, 164; of Craig Thompson's works, 145; of *Epileptic*, 73, 215n (chap. 4); of *The Grand Narrative*, 190; of Shaun Tan's works, 126; of *Watchmen*, 49, 213n3
Treasure Island (Stevenson), 11, 12–13

ultraviolence, 50
Ulysses (Joyce), 103, 105, *105*, 106, 122
Unforgettable (Gordon), 58

United States, 50
universality: in *The Arrival*, 129, 129, 130, 136–38; in *Fun Home*, 103; in *The Grand Narrative*, 197; in *Habibi*, 152

Vallotton, Félix, 95
values and colors. *See* colors and values
Van der Linden, Sophie, 141
Van Hamme, Jean, 10–11
Van Lier, Henri, 195, 207
"Vaudeville between Zuydcoote and Bray-Dunes" (Pratt), 17
Vaughn-James, Martin, 70
Veidt, Adrian. *See* Ozymandias
Verne, Jules, 12–13
V for Vendetta (Moore and Lloyd), 48, 66
Vietnam War, 52
viewing position. *See* perspective
vigilantism, 52, 55–56, 57–58
violence, 154; in *The Arrival*, 136–37; in *Ballad of the Salt Sea*, 19; in *Epileptic*, 77–80, 78; in David B.'s other works, 79; in *Habibi*, 146, 152, 154, 160, 219n18; in *Pretending Is Lying*, 112, 113; in *Watchmen*, 50, 55, 67, 71, 213n7. *See also* death
Voyage around the World, A (Bougainville), 21

waffle iron layout: in *The Arrival*, 141–42; in *Building Stories*, 182; in *Habibi*, 162; in *Watchmen*, 61, 63
Wake of the Red Witch (Ludwig), 12
Wanatolia, 146, 219n10
Warburg, Aby, 205
Ward, Lynd, 127
Ware, Chris: background, 163–64; *Building Stories* (see *Building Stories*); florist (character) and, 170–71; goal of, 181–82; other works by, 114, 163–64; self-deprecation of, 170–71, 220n12
Warnock, Brett, 145
Watchmen (Moore and Gibbons), 3, 48–72; adventure comics and, 50, 52–53, 58; apocalypse in, 49, 61, 67; circularity in, viii, 61, 66–67, 69–70, 214n24, 214n33; clothing in, 52, 56–57, 60, 66, 69; covers and title pages, 51, 54, 59, 62, 65, 68; decorations and paraphernalia in, 61, 64, 66–67, 69–70, 72; ending of, 61, 67, 69, 70; gender in, 53, 55, 57; genre and, viii, 50, 53, 58; good and evil in, 53, 66, 67, 213n13; innovations of, 50, 52, 53, 58, 60; maturity in, 47, 53, 57; plot of, 49, 61, 63–64, 70; politics in, 49, 50, 52, 53, 58; readers of, 50, 53, 58, 69, 70, 214n33; streets in, 56, 61, 64, 70; superhero conventions and, 50, 52–53, 55–57, 58, 213n9; symbolism in, 61, 66–67, 69–70, 71; symmetry in, viii, 64, 66, 214n28; violence in, 50, 55, 67, 71, 213n7
Watchmen, characters in: development of, 63; internal tensions in, viii, 55–56; mortality of, 50, 52–53
Watchmen, form and narration in: braiding effects, 70, 214n33; chapter division, 63–64, 70, 213n1; circularity, 67, 69–70, 214n33; genre and, 58; layout, 61, 63; metanarrative, 69, 72; perspective and, 70; realism and documentarism, 50, 52–53, 57, 60; symmetry, 64, 66; time and, viii, 58, 60–61, 63–64, 214n22, 214n24
water, 11–13, 157, 157, 158, 159–60
Wayne, Bruce, 57
West and East, 151–52
Western (genre), 37, 41
Wheeling (Pratt), 7
wide angle. *See* perspective
Wilde, Oscar, 102, 106, 216n7
Winnicott, Donald, 97–98
Womanews, 97
women. *See* femininity; gender
wordplay, 33, 72
working methods: of Alison Bechdel, 108, 217n14, 217n15; of Craig Thompson, 148–49, 150; of Dominique Goblet, 120–21, 125; of Jens Harder, 192–93, 206–7; of Mœbius (Jean Giraud), 30–31, 36–37, 44–46; of Shaun Tan, 139, 141
World War I: in *Ballad of the Salt Sea*, 8–9, 11, 15, 17, 18; in *Epileptic*, 80, 94
World War II, 80, 88
Wrestling Match in Vielsalm (Goblet and Théâte), 125
writing: in *The Arrival*, 129, 129, 133; in *Ballad of the Salt Sea*, 23; in *Epileptic*, 92, 93, 94; in *Fun Home*, 102–3, 102; in *The Grand Narrative*, 202; in *Habibi*, 147–49, 148, 149, 150, 155, 160; in *Pretending Is Lying*, 118–19, 118; in *Watchmen*, 69, 72

Yellow Dwarf, The (David B.), 73
Yellow Jar, The (Atangan), 219n6
You Are There (Tardi and Forest), 88, 92
Youth of Corto Maltese, The (Pratt), 14

Zam: Dodola and, 155, *156*, 159, 160–61, 219n18; education of, 147, 159; growth of, 154; plot and, 146; pollution and, 155; prayer by, 161; water and, 157
Zenda, 49
zooming in and out. *See* perspective

www.ingramcontent.com/pod-product-compliance
Lightning Source LLC
Chambersburg PA
CBHW030618230426
43661CB00053B/2055